HEED THE CALL

Psychological Perspectives on

Child Abuse

Barbara Lipinski, Ph.D.

Sojourner Press • *Los Angeles, California*

First printing, June 2001

Published by Sojourner Press
Los Angeles, California
United States of America

Copies may be ordered directly from
Pacific Meridian Center
Post Office Box 2808
San Buenaventura, CA 93002-2808
 (805) 641-1368

Library of Congress
Card Catalog Number 2001116354

Heed the call: Psychological perspectives on child abuse / Barbara Lipinski.
Includes bibliographic references and index.

1. Child abuse.   2. Child abuse-Psychological aspects.   3. Trauma-Childhood.
4. Psychotherapy.
I. Title. II. Lipinski, Barbara

ISBN 1-928702-05-8

Printed in the United States of America

Dedicated to
Sophia and Pythea

For Those Who Share a Concern With
Our Collective Destiny

ACKNOWLEDGMENTS

I am deeply grateful to those who have come before me, providing vision, clarification, and direction. Throughout my years of practice, research, and teaching I have been gifted with the voices of patients, students, and colleagues who have shared their stories of abuse, suffering, healing, and resilience.

I also wish to acknowledge my early mentors in this field: Susan Schechter, MSW, for showing the way of compassion and deep commitment to this work during my fieldwork assignment at the Chicago Loop YWCA-Women's Services; and Dr. Pauline Bart for her writings on the myths of a value free psychotherapy, her uncompromising focus on violence against women, the merits of empirical research, and feminist therapy during my studies at the University of Illinois.

I thank Keith Mar, MFT, of Santa Barbara for his supervisory acumen and discernment of the psychotherapist's role in treating child victims and adult survivors of sexual abuse; and Kathleen Baggarley, MFT, of Santa Barbara for modeling a deeply felt sense of tenderness, dedication, and passion in her work. I value our continued friendship now, twenty years later.

My gratitude is also given to Peggy Zorn, MFT. I have appreciated sharing the path of personal growth, recovery, and development with you and have been inspired by your courage. Your insights continue to permeate my work today.

I thank Dr. John Briere for his questions, challenges, and feedback while conducting my dissertation research at the University of Southern California; Dr. Frank Fox for his unwavering confidence, feminist guidance, and joyful mentoring during my years as a doctoral student and graduate teaching assistant at USC; and the California District Attorney's Victim-Witness Services Office in Los Angeles and Orange Counties for welcoming my research with adult survivors of childhood violence.

I have deeply appreciated the multicultural sensitivity and warm collegiality offered by Dr. Azadeh Familii, who has reminded me of the benefits in seeing the glass as half full. Your genuine perspective is invigorating, revitalizing, and hosts a perpetual renewal of life.

I gratefully acknowledge Dr. Regina Chace, who consistently models professional integrity, moral commitment, and intellectual honesty in the perseverance against waves of adversity. I am moved by your dedication to the field of police psychology and belief in the sustaining concept of hope and the mysteries of healing.

My work at Pacifica Graduate Institute was immeasurably sustained by my circle of friends, including Kathryn Brown, MFT, who has been a beacon of light, humility, and loving support through the years, Dr. Mary Watkins, whose wisdom and devotion to liberation psychology facilitated a return to my heartfelt political commitments, and Dr. Helene Shulman Lorenz who helped me touch the fertile ground at the edge of chaos and modeled passionate dedication to *la mestiza* consciousness. I am also grateful to Dr. Jim Hillman for assistance in seeing through and deconstructing ideas and for intellectually stimulating conversation and cherished personal reflections.

The re-enchantment of my life has been deepened by Mike, Krissy, and Ashton Arocho. I treasure our meaningful connections, uplifting moments of laughter, and multiple simultaneous conversations. I look forward to many more of these wondrous and refreshing experiences.

I acknowledge Nancy Filkins-Russo, MFT, for having faith in my life's work, providing an alchemical vessel of love, and demonstrating a gentle nurturing presence throughout the transformations of our relationship. Thank you.

As the final draft comes into focus my awareness is drawn to those who have been with me during this arduous journey, the readers of this work. Your presence has been sensed during the many months of writing and I thank you for the privilege of sharing this vision with you.

Permissions

Cover Photo: *Libyan Sibyl*, Fresco by Michelangelo, 1511-1512, Sistine Chapel, Vatican. Reprinted by permission of Christux Rex, Inc. <www.christusrex.org>

Please Call Me By My True Names, by Thich Nhat Hanh. Reprinted from *Call Me By My True Names: The Collected Poems of Thich Nhat Hanh* (1999) by Thich Nhat Hanh with permission of Parallax Press, Berkeley, California. <www.parallax.org>

Children of Alcoholics, Important Facts. Reprinted by permission of the National Association for Children of Alcoholics, 11426 Rockville Pike, #100, Rockville, MD, 20852. <www.nacoa.org>

Figure 1: *Delphic Sibyl*, p. 10: Fresco by Michelangelo, 1511-1512, Sistine Chapel, Vatican. Reprinted by permission of Christux Rex, Inc. <www.christuxrex.org>

Figure 2: *Asklepios*, p. 26: Grave Naiskos of a Seated Man. 75 BC. Reprinted by permission of The J. Paul Getty Museum, Malibu, California.

Figure 3: *Statuette of Aphrodite-Hygieia with Eros*, p. 146: Marble, AD 100-200. Reprinted by permission of The J. Paul Getty Museum, Malibu, California.

Figure 4: *Chartres Labyrinth Mandala*, p. 172: Courtesy Pacific Meridian.

TABLE OF CONTENTS

PART I

Heed The Call

Figure 1: The Delphic Sibyl. Fresco by Michelangelo, 1511-1512,
Sistine Chapel, Vatican. Reprinted by permission of Christux Rex, Inc.

◈ Chapter 1

Echoes

While traveling in Greece with an overseas psychology program, I experienced a profound response to a simple question posed to the Delphic Oracle. As many before me prepared for such an event, I engaged in a purification ritual, entered into initiation at the Eleusynian temple, participated in dream incubation at the abatons in Epidauros, and practiced an emptying of mind or surrender. Walking past the scattered stones and omphalos I stopped at the sacred site of the ancient pythoness priestess known as the sibyl. Naively I asked "What do I need to know at this time?" After several still moments the reply came: "Stop The Bloodshed" physically rocking me off balance as I stood on this mountaintop.

At once I knew there was a reservoir of meaning within this statement and felt a flood of impressions, literal connections such as deforestation in the name of development, the intentional killing of non-human animals for sport or human consumption, ongoing human religious battles, genocide, hate crimes, heroic bloodsheds of colonialism, memory fragments of recent wars, countless images, imaginal associations, and recollections of personal experiences. I was summoned to Heed the Call during that specific moment in time, by a source beyond my personal self. I felt affected by the soul of the world, Plato's familiar concept of the anima mundi.

I listened mindfully to the voice of the earth not knowing what to expect. Willingly, I accepted the message engulfing me. I was immersed in extraordinary images, confused as to direction, saturated with thoughts, awestruck by the embodied power of the message, and inspired in a penetrating manner. The multiple levels of meaning continue to unfold as I envision my life's work with greater clarity. Inspiration has embraced me to the way of compassion and peace in this work. Peace "demands greater fidelity to the truth" (Merton, 1961, p.125).

To Heed the Call is to receive openly, listen freely, deeply, with no preconception, and to allow for an incubation period to attend to the message. This contemplative practice lends itself to regenerative perspectives, liberating visions, and distinct clarity. In this grateful spirit I wish to propose that we, as professionals in the practice of psychology, Heed the Call of Abused Children.

Heed The Call

To give heed is to search out and hear attentively, to inquire and seek information. Synonyms for *heed* are hearken, to attend, listen, hear. *The Oxford Dictionary of English Etymology* indicates that *heed* is based on the development of an Old English term relating to "have a care, take notice" (1966, p.434). And the term *call* is derived from the Old English term for "cry out, summon with a shout" (p.136). Thus in one sense *Heed the Call* refers to the act of being summoned to take notice and have a care. This text may be seen as an invitation to take notice of the issue of child abuse, have a care about the plight of children in our world today, and in the spirit of psychological inquiry, seek and attend to the valuable information you gather.

The Children's Voice

During the past 40 years children have collectively cried out in alarming numbers. The great number of children who are physically and sexually abused in our world, along with the abandoned, neglected, abducted, and emotionally abused, have to a large extent been disregarded by society.

This societal disregard is evidenced by an ongoing collective denial of the inhumane treatment children are subjected to. The disregard is apparent in view of the following: national funding is regularly cut to social service programs for children and families, children have been behaviorally or characterologically blamed for their own abuse or accused of fabrication, the increase in child abuse reports across the country has been painted as a witch-hunt of falsely accused parents and responsible caretakers or a wave of hysteria, professionals have been repeatedly accused of implanting traumatic memories, and therapists have been sued for unprofessional conduct stemming from the use of hypnosis in the recovery of childhood memories. While each of these issues alone has investigative merit, taken together they reflect a disturbing societal statement. An active percepticide (Taylor, 1997) is occurring where the realities of damaging and dehumanizing acts are renounced or negated. Has the repression that began at the early part of the twentieth century been revived?

Dedicated researchers, scholars, child advocates, mental health practitioners, and social workers know the reality of child abuse and do their best in addressing the needs of these children and their families. Even with these exemplary individual and group efforts the backlash against the reality of child abuse has continued. To a degree society has neglected these abused children, almost to the point of tolerating this abuse. Has the collective voice for help fallen upon a society unable to hear? In light of contemporary events, such as the multiple incidents of school shootings, children killing other children, and children engaging in sexual violence toward each other, this deafness is extremely disquieting.

The Convention on the Rights of the Child

As we move into this millennium, it appears that many individuals are beginning to listen. For example, aspirational statements were adopted in 1924 when the League of Nations proposed the first Declaration of the Rights of the Child, followed by the 1945 United Nations Charter that included a declaration on the rights of children. These ethical and moral intentions were followed by two legally binding International Covenants subsumed within the International Bill of Human Rights.

In 1978 Poland proposed a draft of a legally binding international law on child rights: The Convention on the Rights of the Child. The Convention has become a very exciting development across the globe. It was further developed by the United Nations Commission on Human Rights with input from all societies, cultures, and religions over a ten year span, 1979-1989.

The Convention on the Rights of the Child is the first legally binding international instrument that addresses a full range of human rights: a set of non-negotiable standards agreed to and ratified by 191 countries. This number encompasses all countries except two, one being the United States of America, the other Somalia (lacking a recognized government). The US stipulates an intention to ratify but is presently the only industrialized country in the world yet to formally sign the agreement.

The Convention on the Rights of the Child initiates a new vision of the child, incorporating the concepts of human dignity, the best interests of the child, non-discrimination, maximum survival and development, and respect for children as human beings who are the subject of their own rights. This human rights treaty contains 41 articles delineating the required human rights that are to be protected for children. This is truly the inauguration of the process of change in the treatment of children.

Phenomenal achievements have been made in the advancement of children's rights during the past 10 years. Five countries in Sub-Saharan Africa have instituted laws prohibiting female genital mutilation, Sri Lanka developed a child protection authority, Pakistan initiated efforts to address child labor, and child rights sensitivity training was given to police in the Philippines, Cambodia, and Malaysia (United Nations Children's Fund, 2000). Agencies, governmental departments, and non-governmental agencies have been created all across the globe to respond to the protection and promotion of child rights. Although progress has been sporadic and uneven, countries that had no policies or few programs for children have initiated structures to respond to sexual exploitation, extreme violence and torture, and neglect of children. Children who are bought and sold or living on the streets are no longer relegated to the invisible darkness. Many countries are beginning to take notice of children's rights.

The Archetypal Child's Abuse

As the world consciously stirs to the call for action on the behalf of children, outworn philosophies, practices, and procedures will eventually be replaced or supplanted. The movement to protect children is in its infancy and improvement is incremental. Unfortunately, the number of children each year who are severely malnourished, physically neglected, sexually abused, sexually exploited for commercial purposes, tortured, abandoned to live on the streets, murdered, or forced into labor is staggering. In fact, the United Nations Children's Fund (2000) estimates that 250 million children across the world are forced into labor, although exact numbers are difficult to assess.

One might think that the United States of America is far ahead many countries in terms of children's rights. To a great degree we are, but there is still so much to improve and address. The number of children who receive services, safety, or treatment after abuse has grown each year. Welfare agencies and child protection agencies across the country regularly experience saturation and funding cutbacks.

From another perspective, the fact of continued and oftentimes unacknowledged child abuse in our culture may be drawing our attention to a collective problem within psyche. If seen as a symptom it points us "toward the pathology of the world" (Watkins, 2000, p.210). Analytically, if we look at the incidents of child abuse as a type of societal repetition compulsion, what is society attempting to overcome, gain mastery over, defend against, or compensate for?

From an archetypal perspective, the reality of child abuse may hold a symbolic significance within our culture: symbolic of the archetypal child's abuse or the divine child's abandonment or neglect. If we view *child* as a metaphor for the "childhood aspect of the collective psyche" (Jung, 1969, p.161), this message may reveal important aspects to us about postmodern society.

Jung viewed the child archetype as holding the potential of the future, holding both "conscious and unconscious aspects of the personality" (Jung, 1969, p.164). The divine child is viewed as a symbol for the Self. "It is therefore a symbol which unites the opposites; a mediator, bringer of healing, that is, one who makes whole" (p.164).

Imaginally, if the divine child is appearing to us from the past, the communication about our current state of affairs, as well as the future or potential is disconcerting. The divine child not heard, unheeded, and abandoned. If we choose to look away, not listen, and do nothing, do we participate in the destruction of divinity? One association I hold with the destruction of divinity is eventual catastrophe. A very dangerous proposition. The disconnected nature of the increasingly technological, progressively frenzied, and ambitious world that we reside in is likely a contributing factor. This neglect may be a type of cumulative debt that society has created. It may function as a collective compensation for the unchecked forward movement of society or serve as repression of the collective psyche's forgotten childhood state of being.

Tending Soul Through the Lens of Depth Psychology

Depth psychology as a discipline finds itself situated on a seminal precipice in our culture, able to contribute and illuminate this cultural phenomenon. Concerns with world soul, archetypal aspects of pathology, the numinous, deepening of soul within the psychotherapeutic process, the respect of images, dreamtending, and mythological insights all provide a way to see through and into this unlearning and relearning that must occur. The core of the spirit of the age (Woodman, 1982) is often reflected within psyche or more accurately within the manifestations of the collective psyche. Depth psychology brings reflection to these psychic processes (Aizenstat, 1995).

Psychology needs to reflect on itself. It may be time to once again move beyond any restricted views of the psyche that modern day psychology holds, liberating ourselves from outworn ideas (Jung, 1964) and liberating psychology from itself (Martin-Baro, 1994). A mythology of psychology that continues the movement of soul beyond the therapy room dynamically integrating a relational connection with our environment (Mack, 1995), imagining the interdependence of self-and-other-in-community (Watkins, 2000), and treasuring "contradictory perspectives" (Lorenz, 2000, p.227) within ourselves and the world.

Eastern perspectives serve to broaden our understanding of soul in terms of the balance within nature. Two Chinese characters for soul integrate both a spiritual and earthly perspective, *chien* which is heavenly and *ken* relating to the earth (Lipinski, 2001), thus integrating a heavenly and earthly nature in the perspective on psyche or soul. The panentheistic view provides another enlarging perspective of the soul where the body is located in the soul. This unfolds to *the body is also the soul*. The thirteenth century Sufi mystic Jelalludin Rumi wrote about a keen way of sensing "There is another way of seeing that sees through" (1995, p.271). Discovering and witnessing becomes a way of seeing or seeing-through (Hillman, 1975) which leads to a liberation of ideas and revelations.

I'm reminded of the experience of seeing the world through traveler's eyes when I travel within other countries. The concept of *jamais vu* illustrates the importance of this way of seeing. Jamais vu, unlike deja vu is the experience of feeling as though you were experiencing something for the very first time. I believe it is this precise attitude and openness to experience that is needed, opening the way to a new and more responsive psychology. This is a way of perceiving, seeking to understand, seeing, and knowing that Lugones (1990) termed "world" traveling, seeing other worlds fully, completely, and respectfully. World traveling is familiar to members of oppressed and marginalized groups who find themselves outside the mainstream construction of life (Gilfus, 1999). These valuable methods become necessary in order to survive amidst disempowering worldviews.

Let us hear the voices of the children so they do not become invisible and fall back into silence or secrecy. Let us hear in order to affirm their right to speak, acknowledge their suffering, assist in their healing efforts, and join in work toward prevention of abuse.

Paradoxically, the disempowered *child*, as archetype, can provide us with the all important thread out of this dark labyrinth, as Ariadne provided to Theseus in the classical myth of the Minoan labyrinth. This archetypal child can once again become a uniting symbol providing a way toward wholeness.

The disempowerment of the *child* and of children begins to change when each one of us becomes willing to witness, hear, and tend the message. This can be seen as the redemptive significance of the *child*. The child is providing us with the light needed to enlarge our consciousness on a collective and personal level. Psychologically this is the movement of individuation, and the child becomes the symbol of the self, beginning and end, pre-conscious and post-conscious. Alchemically, the imaginal child can be viewed as the bringer of healing or "panacea" (Jung, 1968, p.482), producing a transformation in the slumbering anima mundi.

My hope is to affect attitudes of consciousness around this issue and broaden and expand our view as psychologists. Each one of us can contribute to the decrease and elimination of child neglect, abuse, and exploitation through our actions and professional work. My desire is that the enclosed information on laws, psychological perspectives, procedures, assessment methods, interventions, and prevention efforts will assist you to this end. At the very least you will enhance your awareness of this issue, possibly be stirred or disturbed internally, and move toward change within your own personal life.

Resources

Child abuse and trauma resources are included in the appendix to assist professionals who seek more information on child abuse, domestic violence, adult survivors, sexual assault, trauma, child custody, cultural competence, prevention, and self-care. Ancillary information on professional associations and national clearinghouses for clinical and research information are listed in addition to 24 hour hotlines or information lines for referrals.

For those inspired by the crossroads of law and mental health, information on legal issues is integrated in sections on legal standards, family law, and evaluation. Crucial differences exist between therapeutic and forensic relationships (Greenberg & Shuman, 1997). Psychologists wishing to expand their practice should obtain training in these new areas of practice. Independent practitioners may utilize their professional skills in these forensic areas, which require a solid foundation in listening skills, an understanding of developmental issues and family dynamics, the ability to engage in critical analyses and assessments of complex situations, and a proficient grasp of ethical and legal standards. These specialties welcome skilled psychotherapists.

Format

The text integrates a traditional linear component focusing on empirical findings in the scientific literature with sections offering alternate *ways of knowing*. Part One has focused on the development and meaning of the title Heed the Call and continues in the next chapter with a brief overview on the prevalence and incidence of child maltreatment.

Part Two highlights legal standards and a number of ethical issues and practice concerns related to child maltreatment. Contributions from the legal field, ethical codes, and standards of practice are integrated. Definitions, the complex factors involved in disclosure, mandated reporting, and the assessment process used in developing reasonable suspicion based on indicators of maltreatment are presented. Indices of emotional maltreatment, physical abuse, Munchausen syndrome by proxy, child neglect, and sexual abuse are discussed.

Part Three begins with clinical and empirical research on the psychological impact of child maltreatment, covering traumatic reactions, symptomatology, disempowerment, prior victimization variables, coping processes, causal attributions, postraumatic stress disorder, and the construct of resilience. This section continues with critical perspectives on violence and abuse including family violence and intimate partner violence. Additionally the highly significant link between animal cruelty and violent behavior is discussed.

Part Four begins with Ariadne's thread providing a clue out of the current darkness with the assistance of the compassionate therapist. Diverse intervention methods are conceptualized ranging from initial crisis interventions to treatment models. Relevant approaches to crisis intervention, defusing, and critical incident stress debriefing are summarized in chapter ten. Depth psychological perspectives are interwoven throughout the sections on clinical treatment in chapter eleven and twelve. Selected treatment approaches and empirically validated methods with children and adults are emphasized within chapter twelve. The Meridian Assessment Paradigm is offered as an innovative depth psychological assessment model in chapter thirteen.

Part Five considers the poetics of tending soul through collaborative community efforts and self-care endeavors. Prevention efforts are proposed with suggestions for strategies incorporating dialogue and the council process. A commentary on spiritual and religious inspirations derived from the practices of Ahimsa and Tikkum Olam concludes chapter fourteen on prevention. The complex challenges facing therapists involved in this relational work with survivors of child abuse are covered in the next chapter. Topics include Eros and countertransference, gifts from the wounded healer archetype, vicarious traumatization, compassion fatigue, and the importance of self-care. The function of self-care is contextualized as an activity directly related to community that leads to a celebration of life within our professional lives, re-animation of eros, and restoration.

Suggested Activity

At the conclusion of select chapters a suggested activity, exploration, guided imagery, assessment, or reflection is posed in order to strengthen one's learning process through an experiential understanding. Taking a few moments to reflect and integrate this activity will enhance awareness of thoughts, feelings, and overall responses to the material presented.

At this point, I would like to encourage you to initiate a journal or create a distinct section in your current journal for written commentary on any thoughts, images, or feelings pertaining to heeding the call of children. How do you perceive the call? What do you see as your call in life? How could you begin to heed the call and engage in meaningful action? Please reflect on accomplishments you have made in this area and assess the level of satisfaction you have with your social response. A number of ways to contribute your unique gifts will be addressed in chapter fourteen.

Chapter 2

Prevalence of Child Maltreatment

Extreme stressors are encountered in our modern day society including events ranging from natural disasters to interpersonal victimization. One form of interpersonal victimization is child abuse and neglect, a pervasive social problem that intimately impacts the individual, family, and community.

Annual reports by the National Committee to Prevent Child Abuse and Neglect indicate that more than 3 million American children suffer from child maltreatment. Yet these numbers may reflect a very small fraction of the children who are actually victimized. The very nature of child abuse often prevents abuse victims from disclosing the abuse or seeking help. Empirical studies often result in much higher estimates than federal estimates (Ageton, 1983; National Child Abuse and Neglect Data Systems, 1998; Russell, 1983), although these numbers may underrepresent the actual number.

In 1997 alone, the National Child Abuse and Neglect Data Systems reported 1,196 child fatalities related to child abuse and neglect. However, the United States Advisory Board on Child Abuse and Neglect indicates the estimated number more likely approaches 2,000 deaths annually (NCANDS, 1998). The reason for this discrepancy is that a child's death may be classified as a specific medical cause rather than abuse or neglect.

Kempe, Silverman, Steele, Droegemueller, and Silver (1962) were among the first to study child physical abuse and report their findings in a major professional journal. The concept of the battered-child syndrome evolved from the unrecognized trauma that was familiar to pediatricians, social service workers, and radiologists. Kempe and his colleagues surveyed hospitals nationwide and discovered a high incidence of physical abuse where over 10% of the children died from their injuries and over 25% suffered permanent brain damage. These reports stimulated a major change in public policy including the development of reporting laws for child abuse in every state. Their findings are often considered the catalyst for the research in the latter part of the twentieth century.

Incidence and Victimization Rate

First, in order to clarify the basis for the statistics related to child maltreatment, the concepts of incidence or victimization rates and prevalence rates are presented. The concept of incidence comes from the field of epidemiology. Incidence refers to the number of new cases (originally of disease) that appear within a specified time frame (Kleinbaum, Kupper, & Morgenstern, 1982). Prevalence studies produce figures that attempt to estimate the number of individuals who have ever been victimized in their lives.

When applied to data, incidence refers to the number of separate incidents that occurred during a one year period. Another term often used to reflect incidence is victimization rate, which can be obtained through the division of the number of incidents within the set time frame, by the number of persons in the population. The rate is reported per 1,000 or 100,000 people. For example, yearly estimates of incidence in terms of type of child abuse report that the majority of reported cases are physical abuse, or approximately 5 per 1000 children, with emotional abuse as the next most frequently occurring type of abuse, approximately 3 per 1000 children, and sexual abuse as the least frequent type of abuse, approximately 2.1 per 1000 children. In terms of child neglect, physical neglect is the most frequently occurring type of neglect, involving approximately 8 per 1000 children, educational neglect is the second most frequently occurring, approximately 4.5 per 1000 children, and emotional neglect is the least frequent type, approximately 3 per 1000.

Varying Prevalence Rates

Varying prevalence rates of abuse have been attained in samples of clinical populations, college students, individuals living in specific geographic locations, and in community populations. Often the samples of adults receiving some form of psychological or psychiatric treatment yield higher prevalence rates than the broader community samples. The varying rates are also a product of the methodological differences in the studies, for example the specific manner in which questions are worded, the definition of terms, the number of questions, whether a survey is anonymous, use of written instruments or in person interview, in addition to the gender of the researcher. It may also be more difficult for some individuals to acknowledge childhood abuse, specifically sexual abuse, in the presence of another person.

In the first national prevalence study of adults regarding a history of childhood abuse, sexual abuse by an adult was reported by 27% of the 1,481 women surveyed and 16% of the 2,626 men. The sample conformed to census demographics for the United States and included the states of Alaska and Hawaii. Additionally, the researchers discovered that most of the childhood sexual abuse experiences were initiated by a person known to the victim (Finkelhor, Hotaling, Lewis, & Smith, 1990).

In a study focusing on male gender socialization (Lisak, Hopper, & Song, 1996), the sample of 595 men revealed that 17% of the men experienced physical and sexual abuse as children, 11% experienced sexual abuse alone, and 17% experienced physical abuse alone. The study disclosed that of those men who reported childhood abuse, 38% indicated they had perpetrated others, either physically or sexually. Of these 126 men, 70% reported having experienced childhood abuse. The study showed most perpetrators had been abused as children, but that most abused men did not perpetrate others.

When research focuses specifically on childhood sexual abuse among adult women, prevalence rates are in the range of 10% to 25%. Brickman & Briere (1984) conducted a random survey and found that nearly half of the 21% of women who had been sexually assaulted had been assaulted prior to the age of 17. Briere and Runtz (1985) report just under 20% of university women report sexual assault by an adult male. In her studies of adult women, Russell (1982) discovered that 25% of the total number of incidents of sexual assaults occurred to females who were 16 years or younger. In another study Russell (1983) discovered a prevalence rate of 28% to 38% of sexual assault among females before the ages of 14 and 18, respectively.

Although the prevalence rates that have been reported in the research above vary greatly, a figure of 20% has been noted by three different groups of researchers (Kilpatrick, Saunders, Veronen, Best, & Von, 1987; Russell, 1982, 1984; & Wyatt, 1990, as cited in Koss & Harvey, 1991), who used the same definition of sexual assault, and studied different geographical samples. The findings from these studies suggest that at least 20% (1 in 5) adult women have experienced sexual assault prior to the time of the relevant studies. However, it may be more accurate that 44% of adult women have experienced sexual assault (Russell, 1982) and that as many as 38% have been sexually abused as children (Russell, 1983).

Russell (1982) conducted a study under a federal contract to assess the lifetime incidence of sexual assault among adult women. She interviewed a random sample of 930 women in San Francisco and found that 44% of the women over the age of 17 had experienced sexual assault in their lifetime. This number was seven times larger than the calculated incidence rate based on reported sexual assaults. These figures were also higher than reported by previous studies. She discovered that 16% of the entire sample reported at least one experience of intrafamilial sexual abuse before the age of 18. Twelve percent of this group had been sexually abused by a relative prior to the age of 14. Forty percent of the intrafamilial sexual abuse was within the family of origin, with father-daughter and step-father daughter incestuous abuse the most common. Russell has cautioned that her numbers were likely underestimates of the true prevalence of child sexual abuse.

In a nationwide sample of 3,187 university women (Koss, Gidycz, & Wisniewski, 1987) a high victimization rate of 166 per 1,000 women was also found. The questionnaire used in the study contained 10 sexual victimization screening questions without using the term rape. Koss, Koss, and Woodruff (1990) reported another study they conducted in 1986 which focused on 2,291 adult women in Cleveland, Ohio. Their research was composed of a survey that utilized a questionnaire that included items on sexual assault. Again, the victimization rate was found to be very high consisting of 62 per 1,000 women. This was 15 times larger than the calculated incidence rate based on reported sexual assaults.

In studies of male college students, prevalence rates of childhood sexual abuse ranged from approximately 5% to 28%. Fromuth and Burkhart (1987) found rates of 20% and 25% in their study of male students, using extensive criteria including forced or threatened sexual abuse by peers, while Finkelhor (1979) found an 8% prevalence rate in his study of 266 male college students. Fritz, Stoll, and Wagner (1981) reported a 4.8% prevalence rate in their survey using a self-report questionnaire, and Risin and Koss (1987) found a 7.3% rate in a national sample of 2,972 male college students. Lisak and Luster (1994) reported a childhood sexual abuse prevalence rate of 17% for male college students (this included the criteria of physical contact) and a prevalence rate of over 25% when non-contact types of abuse were included. Collings (1995) found a child sexual abuse prevalence rate of 29% among college males in his study of 284 students.

Hall and Flannery (1984) conducted a telephone survey of 508 female adolescents in Milwaukee and found a 12% prevalence rate of sexual assault (rape and attempted rape). In empirical research with college students, Koss and Oros (1982) studied over 2,000 university students and reported finding that 37% of these women had been victims of sexual assault at some point in their lives, ranging from childhood to adulthood. This is a very significant number, for it means that 1 in 3.6 college women have been victims of sexual assault or attempted sexual assault in their lifetimes.

In a national sample of 1,725 adolescents from a study conducted over a five year period, Ageton (1983) conservatively reported rates of victimization that were from one and a half to seven times greater than the total number of sexual assaults recorded for all women in the Uniform Crime Reports for each year studied. Of interest is that Ageton had discounted responses to one item that had measured acquaintance rape, which accounted for 75% of the girls in her study. This would have increased her findings considerably.

In a study by Koss (1985) the Sexual Experiences Survey was administered to a national sample of 6,159 women and men enrolled in 32 institutions representative of the diversity of higher-education settings across America. Women's reports of experience and men's reports of perpetrating rape, attempted rape, sexual coercion, and sexual contact were obtained, including both the rates of prevalence since age 14 and rates of incidence during the previous year. Her findings support the high rate of undisclosed abuse and hidden rape among populations of college students, the age group with the highest risk of sexual assault.

In an epidemiological study of sexual assault in the Los Angeles area Sorensen, Stein, Siegel, Golding, and Burnam (1987) surveyed 3,172 participants, and found an overall prevalence rate of 14% for women since the age of 16. They discovered various prevalence rates ranging from 7% for Hispanic women to 28% for white women. Wyatt (1985) studied the prevalence of childhood sexual abuse among a stratified random sample of 126 African-American and 122 white women residents of Los Angeles County. She found that over half of all women experienced at least one incident of sexual abuse prior to the age of 18. Over 57% of African-American and over 67% of white women had reported one or more incidents.

A community study was conducted by Bagley, Wood, and Young (1994) of men aged 18 to 27 in Canada. In this study a prevalence rate of 15.5% was found, with almost 7% of the men reporting multiple incidents of abuse. In retrospective studies reporting face to face interviews with men, lower prevalence rates were reported, such as 6% in Finkelhor's study (1984) of Boston area fathers. When clinical samples are studied, the prevalence rates are often higher. In a survey of 100 male psychiatric patients Metcalfe and colleagues (1990) found a prevalence rate of 23%, while in DeJong, Emmett, and Hervada's (1982) review of studies they reported the prevalence rates as ranging from 11% to 17%.

Chapter Closing

As previously stated prevalence studies produce figures that attempt to estimate the number of persons who have been victimized. The range of figures highlight the difficulty in ascertaining precise child abuse prevalence rates. Although these rates fail to reflect the true scope of child abuse and child sexual abuse in particular, the magnitude of this problem in the lives of Americans is profound.

During this last century the abuse of children was studied empirically and clinically, resulting in statistical analyses, professional reports, and anecdotal case reports. Freud's well known and reverberating statement is one example: "Almost all my women patients told me that they had been seduced by their fathers. I was driven to recognize in the end that these reports were untrue and so came to understand that the hysterical symptoms are derived from phantasies and not from real occurrences" (1966, p.584). Late in life Jung commented on Freud's repudiation of his original discoveries of incest "we are dealing with an empirically demonstrable fact which meets with such universal confirmation that only the ignorant still try to oppose it" (Jung, 1954, p.178). Further clinical, empirical, and national studies with specific and universal definitions of physical abuse, emotional maltreatment, neglect, and sexual abuse should dispel any deficits in knowledge about the realities of child abuse.

23

PART II

Legal Standards,
Ethical Issues, and Practice
Concerns

Figure 2   Asklepios.   Grave Naiskos of a Seated Man. 75 BC. Reprinted by permission of The J. Paul Getty Museum, Malibu, California.

Chapter 3

Legal Standards and Definitions

It is our sacred duty to investigate continually how a patient can be helped and how harm can be avoided.

Adolf Guggenbuhl-Craig, 1995

K nowledge of legal standards, ethical issues, and family law is essential for psychotherapists working in the area of child abuse. As the statistics on prevalence of childhood abuse have indicated, even professionals working in areas such as inpatient facilities or outpatient clinics will greatly benefit from the knowledge. A variety of professional responsibilities and liabilities are associated with protecting children from abuse and neglect. Psychotherapists have an ethical and legal obligation to report suspected child maltreatment, generally referred to as child abuse. In California, when a practitioner has a reasonable suspicion of child abuse, a telephone report is made immediately or as soon as practically possible, followed by a written report within 36 hours. Every state has statutes categorizing child abuse as a crime, providing definitions for all terms, and establishing punishments.

There are three sources for laws relevant to child abuse and protection: statutes, regulations promulgated by the executive branch of government, and court decisions. For example, Congress passed the Child Abuse Prevention and Treatment Act in 1974. The National Center on Child Abuse and Neglect emerged from this Act. NCCAN publishes manuals to provide guidance to professionals involved in the child protection system and to nurture community collaboration and quality of service delivery. This agency also provides federal funding for research in child abuse including prevention and treatment.

Therapists are required to have a basic understanding of child abuse, including assessment and reporting, and how one develops a reasonable suspicion of child maltreatment. Reasonable suspicion is based on one's education, training, and experience. Once you have a reasonable suspicion you are expected to follow through with the procedure for making an appropriate report.

Given that each state has specific laws pertaining to the family, it is good practice to become informed about your state's laws and to seek advice from an attorney when faced with a legal question. Most professional associations such as the American Psychological Association and the American Association of Marriage and Family Therapists, provide legal consultation as membership benefits.

The following information paints a broad brush picture for nationwide practitioners in terms of potentially applicable laws, as these are applicable to practice within the state of California. The overview provides the legal standards and definitions you need to become familiar with, offers options for action, includes assessment guidelines, and concludes with immediate interventions. These elements will assist you in formulating your responses to a child abuse disclosure and the proximal events surrounding a child maltreatment report.

The Federal Definition of Child Maltreatment

Child maltreatment is defined as the physical or mental injury, sexual abuse or exploitation, negligent treatment, or maltreatment of a child by a person who is responsible for the child's welfare under circumstances which indicate harm or threatened harm to the child's health or welfare. This definition is drawn from the Federal Child Abuse Prevention and Treatment Act. 42 United States Code 5106g(4). See also, 45 C.F.R. 1340.2(d). By definition child maltreatment includes the acts of child abuse and child neglect. Definitions specific to a particular state will generally be found in one or more of its civil or criminal statutes.

Child Abuse and Neglect Reporting Act

Child abuse is defined as a physical injury that is inflicted by other than accidental means on a child by another person. A child is defined as an individual under the age of 18. Child abuse can result in physical injuries that may include bruises, abrasions, lacerations, cuts, scratches, scars, burns, fractures, bite marks, central nervous system injuries, or life-threatening injuries.

The term "child abuse or neglect" includes sexual abuse, willful cruelty or unjustifiable punishment, unlawful corporal punishment or injury, and abuse or neglect in out-of-home care. Child abuse or neglect does not include a mutual affray between minors, i.e., injuries caused by two children fighting by mutual consent (California Penal Code §11165.6, 2001). The elements of child abuse and neglect are further defined in specific sections of law.

Sexual Abuse

Sexual abuse refers to sexual assault and sexual exploitation. Sexual assault includes the following acts: rape, statutory rape, rape in concert, incest, sodomy, lewd or lascivious acts upon a child, i.e., adult exposing him or herself or masturbating in front of a child; oral copulation, sexual penetration, and child molestation, i.e., fondling sexually.

The specific conduct described as sexual assault includes the following: 1) any penetration, however slight, of the vagina or anal opening of one person by the penis of another person, whether or not there is the emission of semen; 2) any sexual contact between the genitals or anal opening of one and the mouth or tongue of another person; 3) any intrusion by one person into the genitals or anal opening of another person, including the use of any object for this purpose, except that, it does not include acts performed for a valid medical purpose; 4) the intentional touching of the genitals or intimate parts (including the breast, genital area, groin, inner thighs, and buttocks) or the clothing covering them, of a child, or of the perpetrator by a child, for purposes of sexual arousal or gratification, except that, it does not include acts which may reasonably be construed to be normal caretaker responsibilities; interactions with, or demonstrations of affection for, the child; or acts performed for a valid medical purpose; 5) the intentional masturbation of the perpetrator's genitals in the presence of a child.

Sexual exploitation refers to any conduct involving matter depicting a minor engaged in obscene acts, including preparing, selling, or distributing obscene matter, or employing a minor to perform obscene acts. Sexual exploitation also refers to promoting, aiding, assisting, employing, using, persuading, inducing or coercing a child to engage in prostitution, or a live performance involving obscene sexual conduct, or to either pose or model alone or with others for purposes of preparing a film, photograph, negative, slide, drawing, painting, or other pictorial depiction, involving obscene sexual conduct. Individuals who are responsible for the welfare of minors, such as parents, guardians, or foster parents are sexually exploiting children when they knowingly permit or encourage a child to engage in the above mentioned behaviors. Additionally, sexual exploitation refers to any person who depicts a child in, or knowingly develops, duplicates, prints, or exchanges, any film, photograph, videotape, negative, or slide in which a child is engaged in an act of obscene sexual conduct, California Penal Code §11165.1, 2001.

Adults Abused as Minors

In situations where an adult patient discloses sexual or physical abuse in childhood, a report of the abuse is not mandated. An Informal Opinion of the California Attorney General, published February 3, 1987, indicated the intention of the child abuse reporting law was to protect children. In light of this clarification, a therapist would read the reporting law literally, and report abuse in circumstances where a reasonable suspicion exists of *child* abuse. When therapists acquire reasonable suspicion that children are being victimized they are mandated to file a child abuse report.

Child Neglect

Child neglect is defined into severe neglect and general neglect. Overall child neglect refers to the negligent treatment or the maltreatment of a child by a person responsible for the child's welfare under circumstances indicating harm or threatened harm to the child's health or welfare. The term includes both acts and omissions on the part of the responsible party.

Severe neglect refers to the negligent failure of a person having the care or custody of a child to protect the child from severe malnutrition or medically diagnosed nonorganic failure to thrive. Severe neglect means those situations of neglect where any person having the care or custody of a child willfully causes or permits the person or health of the child to be placed in a situation such that his or her person or health is endangered, including the intentional failure to provide adequate food, clothing, shelter, or medical care.

General neglect means the negligent failure of a person having the care or custody of a child to provide adequate food, clothing, shelter, medical care, or supervision where no physical injury to the child has occurred. A child receiving treatment by spiritual means or not receiving specified medical treatment for religious reasons, shall not for that reason alone be considered a neglected child. An informed and appropriate medical decision made by parent or guardian after consultation with a physician or physicians who have examined the minor does not constitute neglect, California Penal Code §11165.2.

Willful Cruelty

Willful cruelty or unjustifiable punishment of a child refers to a situation where any person willfully causes or permits any child to suffer, or inflicts thereon, unjustifiable physical pain or mental suffering, or having the care or custody of any child, willfully causes or permits the person or health of the child to be placed in a situation such that his or her person or health is endangered, California Penal Code §11165.3.

Unlawful Corporal Punishment

Unlawful corporal punishment or injury refers to a situation where any person willfully inflicts upon any child any cruel or inhuman corporal punishment or injury resulting in a traumatic condition. It does not include an amount of force that is reasonable and necessary for a person employed by or engaged in a public school to quell a disturbance threatening physical injury to person or damage to property, for purposes of self-defense, or to obtain possession of weapons or other dangerous objects within the control of the pupil. It also does not include exercise of the degree of physical control authorized by the Education Code, and an injury caused by reasonable and necessary force used by a peace officer acting within the course and scope of his or her employment as a peace officer, California Penal Code §11165.4.

Abuse or Neglect in Out-of-Home Care

Abuse or neglect in out-of-home care includes sexual abuse, neglect, unlawful corporal punishment or injury, or the willful cruelty or unjustifiable punishment of a child, where the person responsible for the child's welfare is a licensee, administrator, or employee of any facility licensed to care for children, or an administrator or employee of a public or private school or other institution or agency. Abuse or neglect in out-of-home care does not include an injury caused by reasonable and necessary force used by a peace officer acting within the course and scope of his or her employment as a peace officer, California Penal Code §11165.5.

Minor Engaging in Sexual Relations

If the minor is engaging in a sexual relationship and is under the age of 14, a report is required unless the minor's partner is also under 14 and the partner is of similar age. An example here is two 13 year olds engaging sexually. With disparate age differences a report is required. If the minor is 14 or over, a report is not mandated, assuming no coercion is involved and the circumstances of the sexual involvement do not meet other reporting criteria. The following additional criteria require a report: 1) any person who is 21 years of age or older who engages in an act of sexual intercourse with a minor under the age of 16, and 2) any person who is at least 10 years older than the child who is 14 or 15 years old and commits lewd and lascivious acts. As previously mentioned lewd and lascivious is generally defined and interpreted by the courts as causing any touching of a child by the perpetrator or by the child at the direction of the perpetrator for the purpose of arousing, appealing to or gratifying the lust, passions, or the sexual desires of the person or the child. This conduct has been reportable for many years, but was expanded recently to include 14 and 15 year olds.

The following explanatory note refers to minors over 14 engaging in voluntary sexual relationships. This California Court of Appeals ruling held that "a fundamental part of the [child abuse] reporting law is to allow the trained professional to distinguish an abusive and non-abusive situation. Instead of a blanket reporting requirement of all activity of those under a certain age, the professional can make a judgment as to whether the minor is having voluntary relations or being abused" Planned Parenthood Affiliates v. Van de Kamp (181 Cal. App. 3d 245). Regarding minors under 14, the appellate court indicated their provisions contemplated criminal acts of child abuse causing trauma to the victim, and did not contemplate the voluntary sexual associations between young children under the age of 14 who are not victims of a child abuser and are not the subjects of sexual victimization.

31

Chapter 4

Reporting Child Abuse and Neglect

Therefore, the bias should be in favor of the child's safety;
everything should be done to prevent repeated trauma.

Kempe and Colleagues, 1962

Psychotherapists have ethical and legal obligations to report suspected child maltreatment, generally referred to as Child Abuse. In coursework required by professional licensing boards, one learns in depth how a reasonable suspicion of child maltreatment is developed. Reasonable suspicion is based on one's education, training and experience. Reasonable suspicion means that it is objectively reasonable for a person to entertain such a suspicion, based upon facts that could cause a reasonable person in a like position, drawing on his or her training and experience, to suspect child abuse or neglect. The pregnancy of a minor does not, in and of itself, constitute the basis of reasonable suspicion of sexual abuse. Once a professional has reasonable suspicion, it is important to know the procedure for making an appropriate report.

Mandated Reporters

Many professionals are legally mandated reporters of child abuse and neglect. The following list is a sampling of the individuals designated as mandated reporters: teachers, instructional aides, teacher's aides or assistants, classified employees of public schools, certificated pupil personnel employees of public and private schools, administrators and employees of youth centers or recreation programs, employees of child day care facilities, headstart teachers, public assistant workers, foster parents, group home personnel, personnel of residential care facilities, social workers, probation officers, parole officers, employees of school district police or security departments, administrators and counselors in child abuse prevention programs in public and private schools, coroners, medical examiners, investigators for the district attorney's office, family support officers, peace officers, commercial film and photographic print processors, firefighters, animal control officers, humane society officers, members of the clergy, psychologists, social workers, marriage and family therapists, licensed nurses, dentists, dental hygienists, paramedics, optometrists, physicians, child visitation monitors, and employees of police, sheriff's, probation, and welfare departments.

Members of the clergy, such as priests, ministers, rabbis, and other religious practitioners, are also mandated reporters. However, if knowledge or a reasonable suspicion of child abuse or neglect is acquired during a penitential communication such as confession, the clergy member is not subject to the mandating reporting requirement.

All mandated reporters are expected to undertake training in child abuse identification and reporting and the law does not excuse mandated reporters from their duty to report if they have not taken the training. Mandated reporters in California are required to make reports to agencies designated by each county. These agencies include police departments, sheriff's departments, county probation departments, and county welfare departments.

The following directive is integrated into California law: A mandated reporter shall make a report to an agency whenever the mandated reporter, in his or her professional capacity or within the scope of his or her employment, has knowledge of or observes a child whom the mandated reporter knows or reasonably suspects has been the victim of child abuse or neglect. The mandated reporter shall make a report to the agency immediately or as soon as is practically possible by telephone, and the mandated reporter shall prepare and send a written report thereof within 36 hours of receiving the information concerning the incident. Mandated reporters are required to follow through on the reporting requirement even if the child has expired, regardless of whether or not the possible abuse was a factor contributing to the death, and even if suspected child abuse was discovered during an autopsy, California Penal Code § 11166.

The reporting responsibility is considered an individual's duty and cannot be passed on to another colleague, supervisor, or administrator. The only circumstance permitting another individual to follow through on the reporting requirement centers around two or more persons jointly having knowledge of a known or suspected instance of child abuse or neglect. In this case a single report is made after a mutual agreement is reached as to who will make the telephone and written report.

Immunity

The mandated reporter is provided with absolute immunity from criminal and civil liability for reporting as required or authorized by the law and can receive monies for reimbursement of attorney's fees necessary to defend against a civil action brought on the basis of the report. The absolute immunity is provided to professionals for conduct giving rise to the obligation to report, including the collection of data, observation, examination, or treatment of the victim or perpetrator of child abuse. The immunity is applicable for the conduct performed in a professional capacity or within the scope of employment. In enacting the Child Abuse Reporting Act and the many associated amendments throughout the years, the legislature has prioritized the protection given to children by encouraging reports over the potential harm to innocent parties caused by child abuse investigations.

Mandated Reporting

It is essential to meet any reporting obligations-by phone immediately or as soon as practically possible and in writing within 36 hours-if a professional acquires a reasonable suspicion of child abuse in one's professional capacity. Therapists are not obligated to tell their patients of the report, but it is usually in the best interests of patients and the therapeutic relationship if this information is not withheld. In fact, informing the patient may be essential in order to preserve the therapeutic relationship. A therapist would use appropriate clinical judgment in discerning how to address this and may need to adjust the treatment plan to incorporate the issues that arise from the act of reporting of the abuse. In some instances, a referral to another therapist may be needed if the therapeutic relationship is irreparably damaged.

Child abuse and neglect reports are made to the agencies legally designated by the county to receive reports of child abuse and neglect: any police department, sheriff's department, county probation department if designated by the county, or the county welfare department. These agencies are required to accept reports from mandated reporters and other persons. At times the agency you make the report to lacks the jurisdiction to investigate, for example, in cases where you are practicing in one county and the reported abuse or neglect is occurring in another county or state. Due to 2001 amendments in the Child Abuse and Neglect Reporting Act in California, the agency is now required to immediately refer the case to the proper geographic jurisdiction for the investigation.

Most social service or welfare departments have specific child protective services units that employ trained professionals, often licensed social workers and family therapists, who take these initial reports. Typically, the report is assigned to another individual in order to conduct the investigation.

As stated earlier, a phone report is made immediately. The phone report of a known or suspected instance of child abuse includes your name, business location,

34

and telephone number; the child's name, address, and present location; child's school, grade, and class, if applicable; names, addresses, and telephone numbers of the child's parents or guardians; the nature and extent of the injury; any information that led you to suspect child abuse; and the name, address, telephone, and other relevant information about the person or persons suspected of abusing or neglecting the child. Even if all of this information is not known to the mandated reporter, making a report is still required.

The written reports are submitted on forms adopted by the Department of Justice, *Suspected Child Abuse Report*. In addition to the information indicated above, the written report includes a place for a narrative description, a summary of what the abused child or person accompanying the child said, and information on any known history of similar incidents for the child. The identity of the mandated reporter and the contents of the report are legally confidential, disclosable only to child protective agencies, designated counsel, by court order, or when the mandated reporter has waived confidentiality.

Disclosure of Abuse

A *disclosure* of abuse or neglect is generally defined as revelation of the abusive experience by a child, intentionally or accidentally. Some professionals define disclosure as a discrete event in which the child makes a clear and direct statement about the abuse (Bradley & Wood, 1996; Ceci & Bruck, 1995), while others see disclosure as a process that unfolds incrementally and may involve denial or recantation (Berliner & Conte, 1990; Sorenson & Snow, 1991; Summit, 1983). Disclosures of child abuse and neglect occur in many ways and may be direct, indirect, complete, or partial. Children may begin talking directly and specifically about what has occurred, although this is usually a function of their age, language ability, developmental level (Campis, Hebden-Curtis, & DeMaso, 1993), specific circumstances of the abuse (Faller, 1989), the level of posttraumatic stress, the severity of abuse (Elliott & Briere, 1994), their perceived safety, and the context of the therapeutic setting. Disclosures may be more difficult to make for child victims who are sexually abused within the family over long periods of time, do not perceive support from the nonoffending parent, and have experienced severe forms of abuse (Faller, 1989; Sauzier, 1989). Adolescent boys who are approaching puberty may be less willing to disclose sexual abuse due to the awareness of the stigma associated with homosexuality (Urquiza & Keating, 1990; Watkins & Bentovim, 1992). Maternal support has been found to be positively associated with disclosure (Everson, Hunter, Runyan, Edelsohn, & Coulter, 1989; Lawson & Chaffin, 1992) in child sexual abuse.

When disclosure is an incremental process unfolding over time, children may initiate revelations about the abuse by indirectly asking questions about the abusive behaviors in order to understand what has happened or to inquire into the therapist's response. Children may talk in terms that are vague or abstract, they may not have the vocabulary for communicating about the abuse specifically sexual abuse, may feel shame and embarrassment, have promised not to tell, or have been coerced or threatened with further harm, loss, or death if they disclosed the abuse.

Sorenson and Snow (1991) identified a four phase model of disclosure that seeks to explain this incremental disclosure process: denial, disclosure which may be tentative or active, recantation, and reaffirmation. A child victim's ability to verbally disclose experiences varied over time and was a function of external circumstances such as family pressure and coercion-which also contributed to recantation. Over 92% of the children eventually reaffirmed their allegations in this analysis of common elements of disclosure in 630 cases. Given the prevalent inappropriate reactions to a disclosure of child abuse such as disbelief, blaming, or minimizing, recantation has been considered a common phenomenon (Conte & Berliner, 1981; Rieser, 1991) and is also a risk factor for revictimization (Marx, 1996).

Responding to Disclosure

Asking open ended questions and avoiding suggestive, leading, or coercive type of inquiries has been endorsed as a standard of practice, e.g., "Tell me more about that, I'd like to know more about your experience." However, with extremely young children under the age of five, relying exclusively on open ended questions may be inadequate (Keary & Fitzpatrick, 1994). The use of pro-active focused questions may be more helpful in these circumstances, e.g., a child may say that he was touched in the wrong spot and a focused question might be "Do you have another name for this wrong spot?" (Austin, 2000). In a study of children 5-10 years of age, referred for child sexual abuse investigation, DeVoe and Faller (1999) found that most of the children did not disclose a spontaneous narrative about sexual abuse, suggesting that focused inquiry or a series of semi-structured interviews were necessary, a finding consistent with other studies (Wood, Orsak, Murphy, & Cross, 1996). Some children will disclose that a friend or sibling is being harmed, but they may be referring to themselves. Gently encouraging the child to be more specific or sharing what they know about the friend or sibling can lead to a more precise disclosure.

The ensuing impact of the abuse experience may be influenced by a therapist's manner in responding to these disclosures. Receiving a direct one-event disclosure or a process disclosure is an opportunity to provide support and impact the disclosing child's future psychological well-being. Being aware of the great courage or fear the child may be experiencing in making this disclosure will set the groundwork for an empathic and appropriate response. Fear of the consequences of disclosure has been identified as the strongest inhibitor of disclosure (Everson et al. 1989; Palmer, Brown, Rae-Grant, & Loughlin, 1999). Responding therapeutically, sensitively, and without blame may reduce feelings of embarrassment, shame, unworthiness, critical self-blame, and anger. Reactions that convey disapproval, horror, shock, or disbelief may prevent a full disclosure, contribute to the child's inner discomfort, and imply doubt or blame. Berliner re-affirmed this from another perspective by indicating "research and clinical experience do not support a general stance of skepticism toward reports from children, especially older children, or toward those in which the initial statement was spontaneous" (Berliner, Murphy, Hardoon, 1998, p.92). Creating a safe place for the disclosing child is an important element of this process, as is receiving the disclosure in a calm, interested, and caring manner, and using words the child understands. Inviting the child to share any feelings about the incident and accepting those feelings will also be helpful in the healing process. Acknowledging the abuse has been noted as an extremely important factor for the future psychological well-being of the child (Palmer et al. 1999).

Additionally, since self-blame is a remarkably damaging long-term consequence of abuse, in response to statements of self-blame many professionals assure the child that the perpetrator held the responsibility for the abuse and that he or she is not at fault for the abuse. Summit (1983) theorized children may take responsibility for the abuse in an attempt to achieve power or control over the abusive experiences as a way of cognitively surviving or coping with the tremendous helplessness. This perception was termed accommodation and has negative consequences including self-hate. Telling a child that he or she is not at fault does not discount the future differentiations of self-blame that can be highly empowering in psychotherapeutic treatment.

Significant research has focused on the impact of the subtleties and the psychological function of self-blame including characterological versus behavioral self-blame (Hobfoll et. al 1991; Janoff-Bulman, 1979, 1985; Meyer & Taylor, 1986), causal attributions of child sexual abuse (Dalenberg & Jacobs, 1994), attributions of negative events (Kaslow, Rehm, Pollack, and Siegel, 1988; Wyatt & Newcomb, 1990), and causal attributions of physical abuse (Brown & Kolko, 1999). Addressing and differentiating the causal attributions of abuse in psychotherapeutic treatment at a later date is an empowering process, allowing the patient an opportunity to intentionally change behaviors in order to protect him or herself from future abuse.

Becoming familiar with the process involved in making mandated reports and the subsequent response by social service agencies provides the therapist with a framework of the potential sequence of events. Assuring the child that efforts will be made to provide protection from the abuse can be made in this context.

Allegations of Abuse During Divorce Proceedings

At the close of this section, a comment about allegations of abuse made during divorce or custody proceedings is warranted. When children make disclosures of abuse, the veracity of their allegations may be challenged, specifically in the context of a divorce. Anecdotal reports (Gardner, 1987, 992) or studies involving small sample sizes (Green, 1986) cautioned about the potential of false accusations made by parents or children. A variety of correlational relationships between divorce and sexual abuse have been found (Faller & DeVoe, 1996). Feelings of devastation "seemed to cause some parents to use the child both as an object for need gratification and a vehicle for retaliation against the divorcing spouse, leading to sexual abuse" (p.16). In some instances a parent misinterprets a child's resistance to visit another parent, genuinely believing that abuse has occurred, misperceives a child's behavior, or in rare instances, may intentionally make false accusations. In Thoennes and Tjaden's (1990) study of over 9,000 custody visitation disputes and Faller and Devoe's (1995) study of 215 allegations of sexual abuse in cases of divorce the actual number of false allegations made by children was extremely small. Allegations were made in less than 2% of the cases and of those only 5% appeared to be false (Thoennes and Tjaden, 1990). These studies raised a number of issues: marital disruption may increase the risk of sexual abuse, precipitate the disclosure of sexual abuse by children, or result in the allegation of abuse by a parent. Ascertaining the veracity of the allegations fell on the discernment of evaluating professionals after consideration of the clinical interview, corroborating reports, medical findings or substantiation, police evidence, and context of the allegation. The results of these studies indicated that although certainty about trueness or falseness of parental allegations may be very difficult to attain in the context of divorce, the occurrence of these allegations was low.

Child Protective Services and the Courts

Child protective service departments within social service agencies protect children through the investigation of child maltreatment and the arrangement or provision of services such as education, treatment, and prevention. Many reports result in educational services arranged for parents in addition to supportive social services. In some instances, children who are found to be in danger are placed with responsible relatives or out-of-home foster care placements. Currently all states have enacted laws requiring that reasonable efforts be made for family reunification, i.e., returning children to their families in a timely manner.

Given the widespread discontent with social services across the nation, often attributed to the staffing cutbacks and extreme workloads, a national strategy for the protection of children was recently formulated by the United States Advisory Board on Child Abuse and Neglect. The role of government and delivery of services in child protection is now being reoriented toward prevention and treatment rather than investigation and moves to strengthen neighborhoods as environments for children and families have been proposed. This has resulted in the expansion of services such as home visitation, supportive services from local service organizations, in home parenting education or training, and family caseworkers working within a milieu environment providing comprehensive services to families.

Juvenile and family courts generally have the jurisdiction over civil child abuse and neglect cases. In severe cases where children are in clear danger of significant harm and providing assistance to the family within the home is insufficient, civil child protection petitions are filed. Civil child protection proceedings are initiated with petitions to the court filed by social service workers who have gathered evidence from the child abuse investigation detailing the specific type of abusive or neglectful situation the child is living in. All involved parties are notified of the hearing and a child may be appointed representation through a guardian ad litem or a court appointed special advocate.

At the hearing, a judge determines whether reasonable efforts have been made toward family reunification, such as efforts aimed at improving parental skills or ability to care for the child. The court addressing child maltreatment requires a *preponderance of evidence* as the standard of proof. Taking into account all of the evidence regarding the child's danger the judge may return the child home, enter a temporary protective or removal order, and/or mandate treatment for the parents and the family.

If a trial is initiated, pretrial conferences are often preferable in order to reach timely resolutions in the case. This prevents further trauma from occurring. If not resolution is reached the trial proceeds with the phase known as discovery where more information becomes available and confidential information unrelated to the child maltreatment case may be excluded. The trial or adjudicatory hearing begins shortly after this phase, where the judge renders a decision about the abuse or neglect. If child maltreatment is not proven based on the legal evidentiary requirements, the case may be dismissed. Otherwise the case moves to a disposition hearing where custody of the child is determined. For the benefit of the child, most states require the judge to render a decision within a timely manner, such as 30 days.

In extreme cases, children will likely remain in temporary foster placement and become involved in juvenile court proceedings for determination of future placement. In the most severe and hopeless situations such as murder or parental incapacity that cannot be remediated, parental rights may be terminated. The court requires a higher standard of evidence for termination of parental rights called *clear and convincing evidence*. Since this is a permanent act, with profound impact on all concerned, the decision must be in the best interest of the child or children. If the rights are terminated, hearings for permanency planning occur and the children become available for adoption. Alternatively, a relative can become a guardian or foster parents may agree to care for the children until they reach adulthood.

Child maltreatment cases may also be tried within the criminal courts. The criminal court process differs in many ways from the civil process and can be more traumatic for the children, particularly if they are required to testify directly in front of the defendant. Criminal courts also do not have the same kind of authority to mandate treatment for the family. The types of cases that often go to criminal court involve sexual assault, incest, sodomy, criminal neglect, and child molestation. Fortunately many states have special legislative provisions to protect the welfare of child witnesses who may experience distress when testifying in the defendant's presence in the courtroom. Some of these provisions include the use of closed circuit television, allowing videotaped depositions in lieu of testimony within the court, and arranging a meeting between the judge and the witness within chambers. Many of these legislative provisions have been challenged in court on the grounds that they are unconstitutional, unfair, or they violate a defendant's right to cross-examine witnesses.

Suggested Disclosure Experience

This activity consists of a brief guided imagery requesting that you think back in time. You may participate at your own pace. Please sit in a comfortable position and take several deep breaths. Begin to relax and feel the chair supporting your weight completely. As you take another deep breath notice your diaphragm as you slowly exhale all of the breath. Think back to a time in your life when you experienced neglect, an act of physical abuse, or witnessed violence by seeing or overhearing it. Note the images that arise. Explore the context, setting, the people present, and your age at the time. Get in touch with your thoughts or beliefs about what happened. Become aware of any feelings and somatic sensations that linger. Please look at the image once again. If you considered disclosing or followed through with a disclosure, recall the events that transpired. How was your disclosure received? Recall the comfort or discomfort you experienced.

As you think of this experience in the present, are there any lingering images, thoughts, or feelings you wish to avoid, minimize, or deny? Assess your comfort in sharing this experience with someone you trust and either choose to articulate your experience, write it down within a journal, or engage in a creative expression through drawing, sculpting, or painting. As you reflect on this exercise, how can this experience therapeutically inform your work with children and adults?

◈ Chapter 5

Assessment and Reasonable Suspicion

W hen it is objectively reasonable for an individual to entertain a suspicion of abuse based on one's education, training, and experience, *reasonable suspicion* is formed. The process involved in the development of reasonable suspicion is usually derived from the presence of multiple factors and the interpretation of these factors. The factors include observations of physical signs, behaviors, and emotional indicators. Physical marks on a child's body may be prominent, unusual behaviors may be present, explicit statements or disclosures may be made, emotional and psychological symptoms may appear, and parent-child interactions may yield information about familial interpersonal dynamics.

The following categories and indicators will assist in the process of formulating reasonable suspicion. Although the indicators are correlated with child maltreatment, they may or may not be indicative of child abuse or neglect in the specific instance you are assessing. At the absolute minimum, your professional curiosity will be engaged leading you to inquire and seek more information about the circumstances. However, mandated reporters do not engage in investigations of child maltreatment-they merely make the reports once reasonable suspicion is attained.

Becoming familiar with the literature on child maltreatment assists in the process of understanding the indicators of child abuse and neglect. Consultations with child protection service workers, attorneys, clinical supervisors, and professional associations are also good sources to rely on when experiencing confusion or difficulty when assessing potential indicators of child maltreatment.

Parental Clues to Assess for Child Maltreatment

A body of extensive literature exists on parental or perpetrator characteristics (Milner, 1991; Milner & Chilamkurti, 1991). One significant finding indicates that although a percentage of abused children become abusive parents, estimated at 30%, (Kaufman & Zigler, 1987), most of them do not become abusers (Widom, 1989). When an intergenerational history of child abuse or neglect exists, it functions as an important but not conclusive aspect in developing reasonable suspicion of child maltreatment.

Many of these parental and perpetrator characteristics reflect high levels of distress or dysfunction and inappropriate parenting strategies (Factor & Wolfe, 1990). Behaviorally parents have been found to exhibit inconsistent child-rearing practices that reflect critical, hostile, or aggressive styles (Trickett & Kuczynski, 1986). Cognitively abusive parents tend to hold negative attributions toward their children's behavior or tend to perceive their children in negative ways (Azar & Siegel, 1990). Abusive parents may exhibit little attention to their children or express limited positive affect and behavior toward them (Caliso & Milner, 1992; Kavanaugh, Youngblood, Reid, & Fagot, 1988).

Basic parental clues to assess for abuse: Parent may scapegoat the child; may be unable to describe positive characteristics of child; may have unrealistic expectations of the child, e.g., toilet-training a 6 month-old child; may be unduly harsh and rigid about child rearing practices; may turn to child to have his or her own needs met. If the parental explanation for the child abuse injury or symptom does not fit the injury, concern should be heightened.

Parental Clues to Assess for Child Maltreatment

Parent may be unable to describe positive characteristics of child; Perceives child in negative manner; Appears unconcerned about child's injuries or minimizes them; Limited attention expressed to the child; Inappropriate parenting strategies, e.g., rigid style or harsh discipline inappropriate to the child's age or misbehavior; Critical, hostile, or aggressive style of parenting; Unrealistic expectations of the child, e.g., toilet-training a six month-old child; May turn to child to have his or her own needs met; Parental explanation for the child abuse injury or symptom clearly does not fit the injury; Exhibits high level of psychological distress or behavioral dysfunction.

Indices of Emotional Maltreatment

Emotional maltreatment encompasses an injury to the intellectual or psychological capacity of the child. This is evidenced by observable and substantial impairment or deterioration in the child's ability to develop and function. Thus the socialization process is central in understanding emotional maltreatment and its impact. Emotional maltreatment exists in acts of commission and omission: when a parent or caregiver fails to provide for the appropriate emotional development of the child, intentionally inflicts mental suffering, or permits endangerment of the child. This type of maltreatment rarely constitutes one acute episode and is more often persistent, ongoing, and chronic within predictable and pervasive patterns (Hart & Brassard, 1994). It also co-exists with other forms of neglect or abuse.

Emotional maltreatment remains a unique child abuse category, in that it irregularly constitutes a mandated report. This is due to the variability between states: some jurisdictions permit reporting, other states mandate it, while others mandate specific subcategories such as willful cruelty. The infliction of willful cruelty is the only subcategory of emotional maltreatment that currently mandates a child abuse report in California. This constitutes behavior that willfully causes or permits any child to suffer, inflicts unjustifiable physical pain or mental suffering, or having the care or custody of any child, willfully causes or permits the person or health of the child to be placed in a situation such that his or her person or health is endangered. In attempts to clarify child abuse and neglect reporting requirements within California, the permissible section including the terms "may report" was inadvertently removed from the law. This allowed professionals to make reports when they had a reasonable suspicion of emotional maltreatment. Many anticipate the reintegration of this section into the Child Abuse and Neglect Reporting Act by 2002 or soon thereafter.

Emotional maltreatment has been the most controversial and at times ambiguous category of abuse. Advances have been made in understanding the developmental consequences of certain parental behaviors. An early framework proposed emotional maltreatment as an impairment to the child's competence in the world, i.e., ability to communicate, acquire patience, moderate goal setting, and ego development (McClelland, 1973). In light of this competence model four principles were developed to define the dangers to a child's developing competence. The first two were seen as threats to a child's infancy while the latter are threats to childhood and adolescence: 1) the punishment of a range of childhood positive behaviors including smiling, mobility, exploration, vocalization, and manipulation of objects in the environment; 2) discouraging caregiver-infant bonding; 3) punishment of self esteem; and 4) punishing interpersonal skills necessary for adequate performance in society (Garbarino, 1978).

Emotional maltreatment includes a range of parental or caregiver behaviors: verbal and emotional assault, isolation or close confinement of the child, extreme inattention to the child's needs for attention, affection, or emotional support, and the encouragement of severe maladaptive behaviors. Research-supported subtypes of psychological maltreatment were proposed in the last decade: spurn-

ing, terrorizing, isolating, exploiting, corrupting, and denying emotional responsiveness (Hart & Brassard, 1994). Emotional maltreatment may be revealed through
specific parental behaviors including: blaming, ridiculing, denigrating, publicly
humiliating, scapegoating the child, or other overtly hostile behaviors; demanding
excessive responsibility, demanding responsibility inappropriate for the child's
developmental level, or setting other rigid expectations; treating children in the
family unequally, singling out a child consistently to criticize or punish; and may
use fear-inducing, threatening, or violent behaviors toward the child or child's
loved objects or pets.

Cultural practices need to be taken into account when assessing emotional
maltreatment since several cultures use shame as a tool to shape behavior. Ho
(1989) reported the use of shaming as a traditionally employed reinforcer of "familial expectations and proper behavior within and outside the family" (p.528) in
Asian-American cultures. This example underscores the importance of looking at
the behavior within a cultural context as well as the impact of the given behavior
on the child.

Some behavioral indicators of child emotional maltreatment parallel other
categories of abuse. The child may not seek comfort when distressed (Crittenden
& Ainsworth, 1989); engages in frequent self-denigrating comments; behavioral
problems are noticed in school, such as aggression or disruptions (Hart & Brassard, 1991); evidence of social withdrawal, isolation, feelings of inadequacy and
unworthiness (Burnett, 1993; O'Hagan, 1993), reduced emotional responsiveness,
low self-esteem, and negative self-concept are evident (Rohner & Rohner, 1980;
Shengold, 1989).

The emotionally maltreated child may display similar signs of emotionally disturbed children, so it is essential to look to the parent's attitudes and behaviors, the societal and cultural context, and the child's developmental mastery of
tasks, including attachment during infancy (Bowlby, 1980), development of symbolic representation during toddler ages, development of self-control, gender identity
and social relationships during preschool, moral reasoning and peer relationships
during latency age, and renegotiation of family roles during adolescence (Hart &
Brassard, 1994). If developmental or other disorders are suspected, a referral for
psychological testing is pertinent.

Child behaviors are very important elements in assessing emotional maltreatment, but they should not be used as the sole basis for determining maltreatment. Neither does the absence of symptomatic behavior rule out abuse, since the
behavioral or psychological impact may be significantly delayed. The intensity,
frequency, chronicity, and pervasiveness of the acts along with the impact on the
child should all be considered when initially assessing emotional maltreatment.

> ### *Child's Behavioral Indicators of Emotional Abuse*
>
> The child may not seek comfort when distressed; Expresses self-denigrating comments; Exhibits behavioral problems (aggressive or disruptive); Demonstrates reduced emotional responsiveness; Displays extreme behaviors including aggression and hostility; Becomes self-destructive, withdrawn or suicidal; Somatic complaints including sleep disturbances; May exhibit low self-esteem or negative self-concept.

Physical Abuse

Physical abuse is generally used to describe any non-accidental (intentional) physical injury to a child caused by the child's parent or other caretaker. The range of physical indicators includes bruises, burns, bites, cuts, and fractures. These indicators may range from minor to severe manifestations and some may not definitively indicate physical abuse. For example, bite marks may indicate a deliberate form of physical abuse by a caretaker, an aggressive injury perpetrated by another child, a neglected or poorly supervised child bitten by an animal, or self-injurious behavior. Bruises may develop from play, but located on certain parts of the body may indicate abuse, such as the back of the legs or on the genitals. Other physical indicators are more likely manifestations of abuse including cigarette burns in unusual places, especially on the soles of the feet, palms of the hands, the abdomen, and the buttocks.

Burns resembling sock-like or glove-like markings on the hands or feet, or doughnut-like burns on the buttocks or genital area may be seen. These burns are caused by forced immersion in scalding liquids or extremely hot water. Appliance or tool burns such as fireplace pokers and irons, may leave an imprint on the child's body. A belt buckle print, palm print, or imprint around the torso would suggest the child had been hit with a rope, belt, or cord (Davis, 1982). Intentional infliction of abuse is often suspected in the presence of rope burns on the arms, legs, neck, or torso. Multiple fractures, spiral fractures, and dislocations may indicate repeated physical abuse (Faller, 1981). Severe shaking, or shaken baby syndrome, can lead to a myriad of neurological problems, acute symptoms consisting of vomiting, seizures, or brain swelling, retinal detachment, and hemorrhage (Crime and Violence Prevention Center, 2000). Abdominal injuries may occur from severe blows, kicks, or incidents of deceleration, where an individual is thrown against a wall. These injuries may involve the spleen, intestines, liver, kidney, bladder, or pancreas.

In all instances when physical indicators are unexplained or unreasonable explanations are given, preliminary suspicions about maltreatment should be developing. One begins to assess additional characteristics.

> **Child Physical Abuse Indicators**
> Bruises located on the face, lips, torso, back, or buttocks; Cigarette Burns, appliance burns, rope burns, scalding liquid burns;
> Fractures to the skull, nose, or facial structure; Several fractures in different stages of healing; Swollen or tender limbs; Lacerations and abrasions to the mouth, lips, gums, eyes, backs of arms, external genitalia, legs, or torso; Abdominal injuries including swelling and localized tenderness, constant vomiting; Bite marks, human adult or animal bite marks.

Behavioral Indices of Child Physical Abuse

The behavioral indices should serve as warning signs to look further. The information on child behavioral indicators and symptoms is derived in large part from literature involving clinical samples, unlike adult samples where studies were conducted with both clinical and nonclinical samples for comparison. Child behaviors are very important elements in assessing child abuse, however they should not be used as the sole basis for determining abuse. Conversely, the absence of symptomatic behavior would not rule out abuse, since developmental impacts on child behavior may be delayed or hidden. The behaviors may also represent responses to other traumas or mental disorders.

> **Physical Abuse Behavioral Indices**
> Child exhibits sudden changes in behavior or mood, e.g., extreme fear or withdrawn behavior around others, overly compliant, indiscriminate attachments, or changes in behavior with peers; Inability to establish good peer relations, aggressive behavior; Child may become hypervigilant, watchful, depressed, or underactive; May become accident prone or engage in self injurious behavior; Regressive behaviors; Child is unable to manage his or her behavior resulting in rages, panic, or agitation.

Munchausen Syndrome by Proxy Abuse

Munchausen syndrome by proxy is an insidious form of physical abuse that can result in severe physical and psychological impairment, disfigurement, unnecessary and painful medical procedures, and death: a healthy child is placed under repeated medical scrutiny by a caretaker, often the mother, who fabricates the signs and symptoms of illness. This fabrication is deliberate and involves covert or overt acts such as suffocation, administration of inappropriate or excessive medications such as insulin, ipecac syrup, or laxatives (Hughes & Corbo-Richert, 1999), arsenic poisoning, placing foreign fluids such as urine or blood into fluid samples, the use of bacteria or feces placed in feeding tubes, intravenous line contamination in hospital settings (Fulton, 2000), creating the appearance of an injury with menstrual or animal blood, or the actual cutting or injury of the child.

This disorder received its name from the wildly dramatic storytelling of Baron Hieronymus von Munchausen who had been known for his prevarication. He was a raconteur who shared world famous stories of his travels and over time has been remembered as an exquisitely convincing liar (Schreier & Libow, 1993). In 1951 an English physician described a factitious psychiatric disorder found in adults. The disorder became known as Munchausen syndrome, a factitious disorder that refers to the intentional production or feigning of physical or psychological symptoms in order to assume a sick role without any external incentives such as economic gain as in malingering (American Psychiatric Association, 1994).

In Munchausen syndrome individuals fabricate symptoms, submit to numerous medical procedures or invasive surgeries, and are usually characterized as openly hostile toward health care practitioners including the physician. This varies from Munchausen by proxy where the parent is using a child in service of gaining incentives and receives praise or admiration for the seemingly devotional parental behaviors. The child becomes a means to an end. Additionally, gender is a distinguishing variable: the literature disproportionately indicates an overwhelming number of females participating in munchausen by proxy, over 90%, with men perpetrating in approximately 5-9% of the cases studied (Hughes & Corbo-Richert, 1999; Raymond, 1987; Schreier & Libow, 1993).

This type of physical abuse is very difficult to assess for the caretaker's behaviors typically appear to be within a normal range of caring and the targeted child is often an infant or toddler. Parent child enmeshment often exists but may be perceived as warranted given the physical disorders. Cases become known when the medically knowledgeable perpetrator is discovered in the act of harming a child through closed circuit monitoring, the type used in intensive care units (Sabde & Craft, 1999), when the child habitually becomes well in the absence of the parent, through an older child's disclosures, or through interdisciplinary efforts resulting in confrontation of the suspected behavior. Although the prevalence of Munchausen syndrome by proxy is not known, it is considered to be a rare form of child physical abuse (Helfer, Kempe, & Krugman, 2000).

A parent may be highly attentive to the child, frequently at the child's bedside in the hospital or volunteering to assist other children in pain. In a review of the literature on Munchausen syndrome by proxy Hughes and Corbo-Richert (1999) indicated the marital relationship revealed instability and the non-offending parent was either physically or psychologically absent or unaware of the behaviors. A range of diagnoses were found among perpetrators who were assessed including personality disorder, depression, anxiety, and schizoaffective disorder. Many had histories of self-harm and somatoform or factitious disorders. In terms of the children, illness was found to be induced in half of the cases and simulated in the rest. Children suffered from developmental delays, conduct disorders, personality disorders, and Munchausen behavior.

Libow (2000) discovered independent illness falsification in an unrelated literature review of children from 8 through 18 years of age. She hypothesized that children initiated their fabricated illnesses as a result of earlier contacts with the medical field due to chronic illnesses. The role of parental coaching was not known in these cases. This review highlights the complexity of the development of factitious disorder and the importance of considering the continuum of medical health seeking behaviors that may contribute to a child's sense of competence and worth in the world. Children who are repeatedly exposed to medical procedures, examinations, or invasive surgeries experience a vastly different childhood than children who are not exposed. Thoroughly assessing and becoming aware of the impact of these experiences on the child's mental health will inform the therapist providing treatment.

Munchausen syndrome by proxy continues to remain relatively hidden and may be extremely difficult to detect given its bizarre manifestations. The *good mother* posturing is often ingenious and physicians or other health care providers may inadvertently collude in the harming behavior through an unconscious denial that any mother could hurt her child in this manner. This latter aspect is quite intriguing to assess from an archetypal perspective, given the profound symbolism of the mother archetype.

The mother archetype or Great Mother may be idealized within our society to such an extent that the devouring or brutal mother becomes obscured. The healer archetype is also operating in this scenario and tends to be in opposition to the mother-a tension between the two in a sense. Psychoanalytic theories posit that the mother may be seeking control over the physician for the purpose of inducing impotence in his (or her) role. The behavior is theorized to be fueled by internal conflicts and rage attributable to prior abandonment or abuse by parental figures, usually the father. Other theories focus on the fetishistic nature of the perversion in the mother's behavior, a *perversion of motherhood*.

Dawson (1994) suggested that Munchausen syndrome by proxy is a response to oppression, the devaluation of the feminine in our culture, and a response to various forms of persecution. He commented on this phenomenon in our heritage saying it "exists against a cultural macrocosm of revenge upon the patriarchal medical system that has a long bloody history of brutality against women" (p.69).

If viewed symbolically as a dynamic statement about living, this extreme form of physical abuse may be another tragic manifestation of inhumanity speaking out about the human condition in this age. A profound despair or murderous rage directed toward helpless children, in effect sacrificing their innocence through acts of mutilation, while attempting to find meaning or worth in existence. While frightening to imagine we are once again called to listen and heed the call.

Neglect

Neglect is defined as a parent's or other caregiver's inattention to the child's basic needs. Neglect includes: abandonment, lack of supervision, nutritional neglect, medical/dental neglect, inappropriate/insufficient clothing, hygiene neglect, shelter neglect, educational neglect, and the failure to thrive syndrome. A child who has been physically neglected may show observable signs of gross malnourishment, failure to thrive, or developmental delays (Crittenden & Ainsworth, 1989) but most types of neglect leave no physical marks. Behaviorally the child may engage in avoidant behavior, may isolate self, or interact less with peers than other non-neglected children (Hoffman-Plotkin & Twentyman, 1984). The child may be depressed, passive, or may seem uninterested in soliciting care and warmth from caretakers or teachers. However powerful these descriptors are, none of the examples convey the utter hopelessness of a neglected child's life.

Behavioral Indicators of Neglect
Gross malnourishment; Chronic hunger; Developmental delays; Avoidant behavior; isolates self; interacts less with peers; Depressed mood or passive behavior; Uninterested in soliciting care or warmth; Nonorganic failure to thrive.

Physical Indicators of Neglect
Child may exhibit poor hygiene evidenced by torn or dirty clothing, or inadequate garments for the weather conditions; Lack of supervision in especially dangerous situations or activities over long periods of time

Neglect is more frequently reported among younger children with reports declining as children get older, although neglect has also been found among adolescents. Furthermore, infants are more likely to be neglected. Neglect may exist when a caregiver fails to provide for adequate physical health care, mental health care, education, supervision, nutrition, household sanitation, or personal hygiene.

Various causes of neglect have been hypothesized including the economic, societal, and personalistic theories. While economic variables such as poverty do play a significant part in many cases of neglect, this does not account for most of the neglect. Weissbourd (1996) reported that African-American children were nearly three times more likely than white children to be poor. In that same year the Children's Defense Fund (1996) found 58% of abused and neglected children were white, 27% were African-American, and 10% were Hispanic. Societal theories of neglect attribute this form of maltreatment to the institutions and societal values that support it such as reductions in public assistance, welfare, and aid for dependent children. Personalistic theories attribute neglect to individual parental personalities and character structures (Polansky, Chalmers, Buttenwieser, & Williams, 1991). Cantwell (1980) attributed neglectful parenting to "lack of knowledge, lack of judgment, and lack of motivation" (p.184). Some parental indicators involve low motivation, feelings of apathy or futility, and chaos within the home. Neglect as a phenomenon may involve the interaction of all of these variables.

Nonorganic failure to thrive is a subcategory within neglect and refers to more than lack of nutrition. If understimulated, children experience impairments in psychomotor development and may not crawl, stand, or roll over at the developmentally appropriate times. For example, an eighteen month old child should know how to grasp and would request contact with the parents or caretakers. Children who are failing to thrive may be seriously ill and in danger of dying. Faller (1981) theorized infants sense the distancing feelings or disengaged attitudes of their parents and react negatively, showing little interest in food, and turning inward. Indicators of failure to thrive may present in a child who appears overly self-directed, does not look for adult contact, exhibits hoarding or gorging feeding behaviors, and engages in indiscriminate attachments.

Sexual Abuse

Sexual abuse includes any contacts or interactions between a child and an adult in which the child is being used for the sexual stimulation or gratification of the perpetrator or other person. Sexual abuse may also be committed by a person under the age of 18 when that person is either significantly older than the victim or when the perpetrator is in a position of power or control over another child. Examples include: genital fondling, molestation, exhibitionism, rape, pedophilia, incest, or other sexual exploitation such as child pornography or prostitution.

Sudden changes in behavior often serve as red flags that something of concern has occurred. Behavioral changes can function as indicators of distress at home, school, or among peers. The behavioral manifestations may also indicate the onset of a coercive relationship or the occurrence of a traumatic incident. Sudden change may manifest as a regressive behavior, a withdrawing or attention drawing behavior, or in physiological symptomatology.

A range of consequent behaviors may result from the sexual abuse. Children exhibit increased sexual behavior (Friedrich, Grambsch, Broughton, Kuiper, & Beilke, 1991; Gil & Johnson, 1993); may exhibit suicidal behavior (Lanktree, Briere, & Zaidi, 1991) may develop eating disorders; alcohol or other substance abuse problems (Singer, Petchers, & Hussey, 1989); may run away or be truant (Hibbard, Ingersoll, & Orr, 1990); may exhibit fear, anxiety, and concentration problems (Conte & Schuerman, 1987); engage in self injurious behaviors, such as cutting, burning, pulling out hair (van der Kolk, Perry, & Herman, 1991).

Sgroi (1982) described the progression in the sexual abuse of a child by perpetrators who have established a relationship with the child. The abuse may begin with nudity, disrobing, and genital exposure, and continue with observations of the child bathing, undressing, or excreting. Kissing, fondling, and masturbation may follow. Digital and penile penetration of the vagina and anus may occur after this.

Of course not all sexual abuse progresses in this manner, and children may be directly forced into sexual intercourse. Groth (1979) referred to the sexual abuse strategies used by perpetrators as grooming behaviors, where various coercive methods are used to elicit cooperation.

The severity of the following behavioral indicators may be directly effected by certain characteristics of the abuse experience such as the type of penetration, molestation by an immediate family member, abuse by more than one perpetrator (Friedrich, et. al, 2001), molestation before age 18, incest, longer duration over time, greater degree of trust in the abuser, degree of coercion, and greater age difference between abuser and victim (Finkelhor & Browne, 1985). Degree of trust in the relationship may be the key variable that combines with other intervening variables and results in noticeable changes in behavior and symptomatology.

Children's interests in sexuality should raise concerns in some situations and may be indicators of prior experiential knowledge gained from abusive or coercive relationships. When an interest in sexuality or compulsive sexual activities dominates other interests that are developmentally appropriate for the child's age, such as playing with schoolmates, concerns often arise about a child's behavior. The overt sexualized behavior described as sequela to sexual abuse is more characteristic with children from age two to six (Friedrich et al., 1992). Children are naturally curious about sexuality and these interests are usually balanced with other explorations within their lives.

Concerns may emerge when children exhibit more sophisticated sexual knowledge than peers coming from similar cultural or familial backgrounds. School aged children tend to engage in sexual explorations with other children their age, but concerns would arise when they engage in sexual behaviors with children much older or younger and when other children repeatedly raise concerns about another child's sexual behaviors, particularly situations where children utilize bribes, coercion, or physical force. Other causes of concerns are centered on children who exhibit disturbing toileting behaviors such as playing with or smearing feces, and any situations that involve oral or genital contact with animals.

Behavioral Indicators - Sexual Abuse

Sudden changes in behavior, clinging, regressive, withdrawal; Sleep disturbances; Increased sexual behavior; Alcohol or other substance abuse; Poor peer relationships; Truancy, delinquency, running away; Fear, Anxiety, Concentration problems; Expressions of discomfort, pain, or itching in the genital or rectal areas Unusual sexual knowledge for developmental level; Self injurious behaviors; Suicidal feelings or behavior

---

Suggested Activity

This chapter addressed the process of developing reasonable suspicion of child maltreatment based on a number of indices. Please take a few moments to reflect and integrate this activity in order to enhance your awareness of thoughts, feelings, and overall responses to the material presented. You are invited to note the stirrings, intrigues, discomforts, difficulties, and physical dis-ease you may experience from the material you have read thus far. Note your awareness of any bodily sensations indicating ease or discomfort. Reflect on whether you have reached a physical or psychological threshold of tolerance for the material. Notice your pace in reading, how other activities may divert your attention, how you may occasionally dissociate or daydream. In learning this material please allow ample time and kindness for your personal process. Reach out to a colleague and share some of the images in your awareness.

◈ Chapter 6

Ethical, Legal, & Practice Concerns

E thical, legal, and practice concerns emanate from psychological work with families, couples, and individuals seeking clinical assistance from therapists or formal evaluations from forensic practitioners. The following issues address the importance of developing competence in cross-cultural counseling, understanding standards of care, and becoming cognizant of the potential vulnerabilities that exist in multiple relationships. A brief review of the range of integral practice issues involving privilege, confidentiality, informed consent, and record keeping is presented with pertinent information on marriage, divorce, mediation, child custody evaluation, and testifying in court.

Cultural Competence

It is essential to understand the complex role that human diversity plays in our work. Clinicians cannot remain culturally encapsulated (Wren, 1962) defining reality according to one set of cultural assumptions and failing to consider or excluding other viewpoints. This is particularly true given the culturally pluralistic country that has developed over the past century. The US Bureau of the Census projects that culturally and linguistically diverse groups will represent a majority of the population by the year 2050 (Sue, Bingham, Porche-Burke, & Vasquez, 1999).

The practice of psychology is slowly evolving to incorporate diverse cultural perspectives (Abreu & Atkinson, 2000). The elimination of cultural bias within the field will likely demand more time and intentional scholarly and clinical efforts aimed at broadening the theoretical base of psychology and psychotherapy. A focus on multicultural counseling, strategies promoting greater cultural awareness, and the inclusion of minority perspectives in psychology have been embraced by many who have acknowledged the Western European foundation of traditional theories of psychology (Atkinson, Morten, & Sue, 1993; Pedersen, 1994).

In one sense, all therapeutic interventions are cross-cultural, given that we each one of us differs in our cultural specificity. However, I believe therapeutic work demands that we become more sensitive to variations in being and more inclusive of multicultural considerations. The phenomenon of acculturation points to the subtle variations that emerge when individuals uniquely integrate or synthesize the values, customs, beliefs, and ideology of a new or dominant culture for purposes of survival. Perspectives on the environment, relationships with nature, and the significance of animals are often determined by one's cultural background. These values may incorporate harmonious ways of being with nature, a respectfulness of creatures, or champion acts of dominion or control. Through the process of acculturation, the cultural values may be challenged, broadened, refined, or synthesized. We bring these attitudes, values, behaviors, and historical backgrounds to our relationships including the psychotherapeutic relationship.

Sue (1995) described the goals of an ethical multicultural practice: 1) becoming aware of our own values, biases, and assumptions; 2) increasing awareness of the cultural values, biases, and assumptions of the patients we work with; and 3) developing culturally appropriate and relevant interventions. Awareness of and sensitivity to individual and group differences and a willingness to examine underlying assumptions, ethnocentric attitudes, and personal limitations, assists us in working with other perspectives in a non-judgmental manner and enhances our continual development and practice of appropriate, relevant, and sensitive interventions in working with diverse patients. When differences of age, gender, race, ethnicity, national origin, geographic region, religion, sexual orientation, disability, language, or socioeconomic status significantly affect our work concerning particular individuals or groups, ethically informed behavior dictates that we obtain the training, experience, consultation, or supervision necessary to ensure the competence of our services, or make appropriate referrals.

The emic, or culturally specific perspective of groups, is a more congruent and appropriate way to work with diverse groups. *Emic* refers to culture-specific theories, concepts, and research methodologies, while *etic* refers to a culture-general or universal orientation. Emic approaches are helpful in understanding cultures through the eyes of the members of the culture. For example, several culturally specific interventions have been recommended to improve the relevancy and treatment outcome of programs for African American women (Roberts, Jackson, Carlton-Laney, 2000). These interventions include revising twelve step programs to incorporate positive and empowering statements for women, exposing women to historical and contemporary role models, utilizing affirming literature, and challenging counselors to shed the common stereotypes of African American women in order to break out of limiting thinking.

Newlon and Arciniega (1983) proposed a number of cultural factors to consider in the counseling or psychotherapeutic process: cultural identity, generational factors, cultural custom styles, language, geographical location and neighborhood, family constituency, religious traditions, and the manner in which individuality is viewed. This last aspect of individuality may be prioritized quite differently from the espoused American value of highly prizing one's individuality and freedom. It may reveal a more cooperative or collaborative sense of being within community, a responsibility to family over one's individual self, or a sense of personal value as measured by communal behavior, or personal behavior that serves or benefits the community or tribe. Individual values are often secondary to family in Native American, Asian American, African American, and Hispanic cultures (Gibbs & Huang, 1989; Sue, Ivey, & Pedersen, 1996).

Post modern thought lends insight to ways of thinking about and perceiving one's cultural biases and provides an interactive framework to understand projections. The process of reflexivity attempts "to locate the effects of the observer in the activity of observation" (Shulman, 1997, p.16). Cultural distinctions and differences are considered dialogical and socially constructed in this conscious, intentional, and evolving process. Dialogue allows for a critical analysis of the historical and social dimensions that contribute to the development of culture and provides a way to understand and negotiate differences. Multiple and contradictory realities can also exist within this framework revealing the true richness of this perspective.

Beyond a therapist's theoretical orientation within psychology, maintaining sensitivity to the variations of culture, race, and ethnicity is essential. Considering the patient's experience and felt impact of institutional racism, acts of oppression, and the influence of assumptions about social class may contribute another aspect of relevance to therapy. History of oppression (Locke, 1997), the importance of the kinship care network, historical trauma and sovereignty have been identified as important factors to consider when treating diverse groups (Korbin & Spilsbury, 1999). Although personal experiences of bias vary widely, the reality of racism persists in America. Failing to consider external factors when assessing and treating patients limits therapeutic effectiveness, impedes a positive outcome, and perpetuates oppression. Perspectives on relationships with nature and the value of animals, whether they be harmonious, control oriented, or of a conquering type of mentality are often determined by one's cultural background. Paniagua (1998) provides guidelines for the assessment and treatment of African Americans, Hispanics, Asian Americans, and Native Americans. Sections present considerations for each cultural group and provide the cross-cultural skills necessary for avoiding bias as a therapist. Sue and Sue (1999) also offer important parameters in *Counseling the Culturally Different.*

Guidelines for working with Hispanic families have been offered by Bean, Perry, and Bedell (2001). They recommend providing family therapy as the preferred modality and encourage separate interviews with family subsystems. They have also encouraged therapists to assess for beliefs in folk medicine, serve as advocates for the family with other social service agencies, and seek to understand the sociopolitical oppression the family may have experienced by gathering information about the immigration experience.

Therapists also attempt to identify situations in which particular interventions or assessment techniques or norms may not be applicable or may require adjustment in administration or interpretation because of factors such as gender, religion, age, culture, race, ethnicity, language, national origin, sexual orientation, disability, or socioeconomic status. When deciding to use tests, which tests to use, or how to interpret test results, caution is used when the patient is from a background significantly different from the normative samples. For example, the widely used MMPI, Minnesota Multiphasic Personality Inventory, did not include African Americans, Native Americans, Hispanics, or Asian Americans in the original normative sample. Fortunately it has been revised and the MMPI-2 incorporated a more representative sample. Many tests can yield misleading results if a person's group status is not considered. For instance, norm-referenced tests may lack validity when used with individuals from groups which were not adequately represented in the test's normative sample.

Standards of Care

Standards of care are duties imposed on psychotherapists. The acceptable standard of care is actually a minimum standard, not a best standard or standard of perfection. A standard of care is formulated on a number dimensions and not one is sufficiently comprehensive to solely guide professional responsibility. Although the standard of care assumes different forms based on changes in the law, regulations, ethics, and common practice, in the area of child abuse, a number of practice standards exist. The American Psychological Association and the American Professional Society on the Abuse of Children have promulgated a number of practice guidelines that inform the practicing psychotherapist. Becoming familiar with these practice guidelines and current research literature will provide the preliminary tools to frame the treatment. The following listing includes the various dimensions that define minimum standards.

Statutes, applicable state laws, and federal regulations, such as child abuse reporting laws; Regulations of the specific licensing boards, including advertising subtleties, supervision expectations, or training; Court cases, such as Tarasoff; Professional Association's Ethical Codes and Principles, (one should be aware of these for the respective profession one is associated with); Rules and regulations of the institution where one is employed (e.g., working within the armed forces would require knowledge of the different rules around confidentiality); and Consensus of the professional community.

The consensus of one's professional community is indispensable when contemplating an action that may be questionable. Framing a question such as "Is this act something I would willingly and openly share with my colleagues" or "How would my colleagues react to my decision to follow through with this course of action" or "Is this behavior endorsed within my community" could provide the necessary initial information for your decision making process, particularly if you believe your colleagues would disapprove or oppose your action. Naturally, the next step is to consult with other colleagues within your community, particularly those you believe would disagree with your course of action. Even in terms of ethics cases adjudicated in court, when there is no case law precedent, the standard of care applied to these legal matters is based on the behavior of what similar professionals would do in these instances (Hopkins & Anderson, 1985).

Multiple Relationships

During the latter part of the twentieth century, professionals, associations, and licensing boards became actively concerned about the moral, ethical, and therapeutic aspects of dual relationships, or multiple relationships. Entering into multiple relationships with clients is rarely advised. The ethical and legal prohibitions were created for very important reasons, including the recognition of the vulnerability that exists within a client-therapist relationship, where intimate feelings (Marmor, 1977), thoughts, images, and behaviors are revealed during times of distress, psychological pain, and at times overwhelming circumstances.

Complex problems emerge when therapists expand their professional relationship with a client into another kind of relationship. Disrespecting roles and boundaries or violating a client's trust can be extremely harmful, even lethal. Notwithstanding the prohibitions against sexual multiple relationships, three national studies of psychologists (Holroyd & Brodsky, 1977; Pope, Keith-Speigel, & Tabachnick, 1986; Pope, Levenson, & Schover, 1979) revealed that 9 to 12% of male psychotherapists had sexual contact with their clients and 2 to 3% of female therapists had done so. Anecdotal reports and clinical studies have indicated that a large percentage of the individuals who are victimized by their therapists have histories of childhood sexual abuse (Elliot & Guy, 1993; Pope & Bouhoutsos, 1986). Entering into any kind of multiple relationship should be evaluated thoughtfully and with great awareness when working with individuals who experienced betrayal within previous intimate relationships, including childhood relationships that resulted in sexual abuse and incest.

Of course, other types of multiple relationships may be inevitable when it is not feasible to avoid social and nonprofessional contact, such as in small communities. However, they are considered unacceptable if they impair the therapist's objectivity or they harm or exploit the patient. Violations expose the therapist to license suspension and or revocation actions, as well as potential civil liability. Multiple relationships are an ethical rather than a legal prohibition, with the exception of sexual relationships, which are legal prohibitions.

Multiple relationships with clients occur when a psychotherapist "engages in another, significantly different relationship with the patient" (Pope, 1991, p.21). Ethical problems often emerge when therapists expand their professional relationship with a client into another kind of relationship. Of course, multiple relationships may be inevitable where it is not feasible to avoid social and nonprofessional contact, such as in small communities (Biaggio & Greene, 1995). Small communities may be designated by geography such as rural communities (Gates & Speare, 1990), or affiliation, as in ethnic minority communities (Sears, 1990) and gay or lesbian communities (Smith, 1990). In fact, Berman (1990) developed the term overlapping relationships to describe the unavoidable types of multiple relationships that may occur for therapists and their clients. The American Psychological Association also acknowledged "In many communities and situations, it may not be feasible or reasonable for psychologists to avoid social or other nonprofessional contacts with persons such as patients, clients, students, supervisees, or research participants" (1992, p.1601).

These overlapping types of relationships are problematic if they impair objectivity or harm or exploit the client. Fortunately, the Feminist Therapy Code of Ethics (Feminist Therapy Institute, 1987) provides guidelines regarding the management of overlapping relationships. The guidelines encourage the self-monitoring of one's public and private statements and strictly prohibit any sexual intimacies or overtly or covertly sexualized behaviors with a client or former client (Section IIIa,b,c). Discussing the possibilities of running into patients within small communities provides information on how to best handle these situations. In most ethical codes, the therapist is responsible for maintaining professional boundaries, thus a therapist initiated discussion can provide an opportunity for the client to disclose thoughts and feelings about these potential encounters prior to their occurrence.

Arons and Siegel (1995) described the consequences of finding oneself in unexpected situations with patients, such as encountering patients while engaging in political or religious activities. They paralleled the therapist's experience to the exposure of the Wizard of Oz by Toto; being seen in one's full human vulnerability by a client, the way the wizard was seen once the cloth curtain was pulled aside. The feelings of shame or inadequacy that arise may affect the therapeutic relationship through the transference and countertransference. Preparing for these kinds of encounters through imaginal exercises or personal psychotherapy can provide "insight into which parts of our professional persona are there to support our work and which parts stem from our fears, self-criticism, and difficulty accepting unexamined aspects of ourselves" (p.134). Self-exploration around these issues can provide great benefits.

The legally prohibited acts that expand the therapeutic relationship include any kind of sexual contact or sexual misconduct by a psychotherapist with a patient that is categorized as illegal, unethical, and unprofessional. *Sexual contact* means touching an intimate part (sexual organ, anus, buttocks, groin, or breast) of another person. *Touching* means physical contact with another person either through the person's clothes or directly with the person's skin (e.g., intercourse, fondling, etc.). *Sexual misconduct* includes nudity, kissing, spanking, as well as sexual suggestions or innuendoes. These prohibitions are applicable both during the professional relationship, and for two years following termination of therapy. Most states have criminal penalties for these sexual offenses often resulting in jail or prison sentences, depending on whether the crime is charged as a misdemeanor or felony. Any proven offense also subjects the therapist to license suspension and/or revocation, and leaves the door open to civil liability.

Ethically committed psychotherapists remain cognizant of their potentially influential position with respect to clients and avoid exploiting their trust or dependency. This practice is essential when working with child abuse survivors.

Treating Minors

Each state promulgates laws related to the treatment of minors. This section presents ethical and legal aspects involved in the treatment of minors. First, no minor under the age of 12 can receive outpatient mental health counseling without parental consent. Second, all minors who are emancipated can receive outpatient counseling without parental consent.

Therapists may treat minors 12 years of age and over without parental consent if specific criteria are met: the minor, in the opinion of the attending professional person, is mature enough to participate intelligently in the outpatient services and if the minor would present a danger of serious physical or mental harm to self or to others without the mental health treatment or counseling or is the alleged victims of incest or child abuse (Family Code §6924). A minor who is 12 years of age or older may consent to medical care and counseling relating to the diagnosis and treatment of a drug or alcohol related problem also. Counseling means the provision of counseling services by a provider under contract with the state or a county to provide alcohol or drug abuse counseling services (Family Code §6929). To summarize, it is legally permissible to treat a minor twelve and over without parental consent when the minor consents *and* is either legally emancipated, or meets the criteria on an exception within specific preconditions and treatable clinical issues.

The consent of parent or legal guardian is not necessary to authorize the provision of services. It is advisable to involve the minor's parents, parent, or legal guardian in the mental health treatment, unless in the opinion of the professional person who is treating the minor, such involvement would be inappropriate. In these circumstances, the therapist would state in the record whether and when the contact with the parent, parents, or legal guardian were attempted, and whether the was successful or unsuccessful, or the reason why it would be inappropriate to contact the parent, parents, or legal guardian of the minor.

Confidentiality

Many are familiar with the Hippocratic oath, a modern pledge initiated around 400 BCE. Considered the father of medicine and medical ethics, Hippocrates offered two precepts which are foundational in psychotherapeutic practice today: confidentiality and the obligation to do no harm to patients. The standard of maintaining confidentiality and the attitude of nonmaleficence (do no harm) are well integrated into ethical codes of conduct in the healing arts professions.

Generally, minors are entitled to the protection of confidentiality unless there is an applicable legal or ethical exception. Exceptions are the same as with adult patients, e.g., threats of violence to another, reporting abuse, patient gravely disabled, etc. An additional exception is the right of parents to inspect the therapist's records concerning their child when the treatment is with parental consent. If full disclosure is not in the best interests of the minor patient, the therapist can provide a summary and use arbitration if necessary to determine minimum disclosure. If this is unsatisfactory the therapist would wait for a court order in order to disclose more.

Access to records and information pertaining to a minor, including but not limited to medical, dental, and school records, cannot be denied to a parent because the parent may not be the child's custodial parent. However, the parent is legally not entitled to inspect or obtain copies of the records if the therapist determines that access to the records would have a detrimental effect on the professional relationship with the child or the child's psychological well-being or physical safety.

The ethical and legal responsibility to maintain the confidentiality of patient-therapist communications, including the fact that a particular person is or is not a psychotherapist's patient, is essential both to the effectiveness of therapy and the patient's well-being. Everything disclosed by a patient to a therapist is considered confidential. Under most circumstances, such information is not released without the explicit written consent of the patient. However, in certain circumstances, confidentiality must be or may be breached. Child abuse is a situation in which confidentiality must be breached. When a therapist, in his or her professional capacity, knows or reasonably suspects that a child is being abused or neglected, he or she is legally obligated to make a report to the appropriate agency.

Before therapy begins, it is wise to provide an office policies form or therapeutic contract, including a brief outline of situations in which confidentiality must and may be breached. Such a form can help to reduce the problems associated with mandated or optional breaches of confidentiality. This can also help you meet the ethical obligation of informing patients of the legal limits of confidentiality.

Privilege of Confidentiality

Psychotherapist-patient communications are considered privileged communications. Patients can freely express themselves, describing the problems and issues they are facing in an honest and open manner, knowing the communications are protected by the psychotherapist-patient privilege. The privilege can benefit and protect the patient, however it does not offer protection in all instances, as there are limitations on the scope of privilege. A communication considered privileged is a "communication that the holder of the privilege must authorize disclosure of and testimony about" (Caudill & Pope, 1995, p. 171). The psychotherapist-patient privilege is codified by statute, which means it is defined by law. Since the focus is within the context of legal proceedings where attempts are made to have the content of confidential patient therapist communications revealed, no disclosure can properly be made by the therapist to anyone else unless there is an appropriate waiver of the privilege or the privilege is limited by an exception.

Privilege may only be asserted or waived by the holder of the privilege. This is usually the patient, however the psychotherapist is required to assert the privilege, to "claim" the privilege on the patient's behalf, when a party attempts to have a psychotherapist reveal the content of a patient's communication in a legal proceeding. Without an appropriate waiver, the information remains confidential, and is not subject to disclosure.

With respect to a situation in which a minor has requested and been given mental health treatment pursuant to an exception, the minor holds the privilege. This also applies if she or he is treated as an adult due to emancipation. Several years ago, Evidence Code 1014.5, which referred to the psychotherapist holding the privilege, was eliminated. The patient has the right to assert privilege as a means of blocking disclosure of confidential information during a court or other legal proceeding. The holder of the privilege maintains this right. If the minor has a court appointed legal guardian or conservator that individual becomes the holder of the privilege. The minor's parents are not the holders of the privilege unless they have been court appointed as such (Pelchat, 2001).

Waivers and Limitations of Privilege

The client may waive the privilege. There is no privilege if it has been waived by the client, the holder of the privilege. If a client wishes to have the patient-therapist communications disclosed in a legal proceeding, the therapist cannot prevent him or her from doing so. The client, even if a minor, is generally the holder of the privilege. The Evidence Code currently names only three holders of the privilege: the patient, legal guardian or conservator of the patient, or the personal representative of the patient if the patient is deceased.

There are a number of limitations to privilege that require or permit the disclosure of confidential communications. The legally mandated disclosures include reporting child, dependent adult, or elder abuse. There is no privilege if the patient is a child under the age of 16 and the psychotherapist has reasonable cause to believe that the patient has been the victim of a crime and that disclosure of the communication is in the best interest of the child. There is no privilege if the patient is dangerous to him or herself, others, or property of others, the therapist has reasonable cause to believe this is the case, and the disclosure is necessary to prevent the threatened danger. This law is broader than the other exceptions to privilege since it applies to clinical settings and legal proceedings.

There is no privilege if the patient sought therapy to aid in planning, committing, escaping punishment, detection, or apprehension regarding a crime or tort. There is no privilege when the patient's emotional condition is raised as an issue by the patient or his/her representative. Examples of this exception includes a worker's compensation suit regarding stress, a proceeding to determine sanity in a criminal action suit, or proceedings to establish competence.

There is no privilege when either a psychotherapist or patient alleges a breach of duty arising out of the psychotherapist-patient relationship (e.g., within a malpractice lawsuit). This law has limited applicability outside the context of legal proceedings, e.g., if a patient refuses to pay his or her bill for therapy, the therapist may reveal information relevant to collecting payment, such as the patient's name and address and the amount owed, but no other information may be revealed to collection agencies.

Informed Consent

In the times of Hippocrates health practitioners were advised to conceal procedures from the patient. "Perform all this calmly and adroitly, concealing most things from the patient while you are attending to him" (as cited in O'Neill, 1998, p.10). Fortunately, the times have changed in favor of patients' rights. The current standard of care emphasizes the affirmative duty of the psychotherapist to inform the patient about the treatment process including the possible shortcomings and risks. This is a very important concept in psychotherapy. The widely accepted procedure for informed consent generally contains three parts: 1) providing the patient with significant information concerning psychotherapy-when the patient has the capacity to consent, 2) obtaining the patient's freely expressed consent, and 3) documenting the consent in the patient record.

If the patient is not legally capable of giving informed consent, the practitioner should provide information about the "proposed interventions in a manner commensurate with the person's psychological capacities" (APA, 1992, standard 4.02c) and seek assent to the interventions. Consent should be obtained from a legally authorized person, as permitted by law.

In many professional association's codes, such as the American Counseling Association's Code of Ethics and Standards of Practice, practitioners are encouraged to make full disclosures to patients, both at the initiation of the work and during the work. This is a very realistic standard for the psychotherapy process since the issues of time and duration play a significant role. Pope and Vasquez (1991) state "As the treatment plan undergoes significant evolution, the patient must adequately understand these changes and voluntarily agree to them" (p.75).

What type of therapeutic information is disclosed with the intent of informed consent? "Counselors inform clients of the purposes, goals, techniques, procedures, limitations, potential risks, and benefits of services to be performed, and other pertinent information. Counselors take steps to ensure that clients understand the implications of diagnosis, the intended use of tests and reports, fees, and billing arrangements" (National Board of Certified Counselors, 1997, Section B8). Additionally, O'Neill (1998) believes that specific information about alternative treatments should be included even if they are out of the therapist's scope of training and experience, thus necessitating a referral.

Record Keeping Guidelines

Acting in a professional manner requires keeping some basic records and notes concerning patients' biographical, residential, occupational, and related basic information; as well as legally required entries such as reasons why a minors were treated without parental consent. When therapists know that records will be subject to legal scrutiny, they are ethically bound to create records in the quality and detail that would be useful to the proceedings: record keeping should be comprehensive, accurate, and document all professional activities with patients. Signed consent forms for unique or unusual clinical interventions are highly recommended. Records would also indicate how abuse memories were revealed, by whom, and in response to what type of therapeutic question. Additional reasons for keep records include: a) treatment continuity; b) helping transition to other therapists or when patient returns after time off; c) verification of mental status for disability or workers' compensation claims; d) a resource for future research, writing, or teaching; e) liability protection if the therapist is called upon to justify treatment, in a court case, lawsuit, or ethics committee investigation. However, it may be in the best interests of the patient to limit the content of the notes and records in some situations. Keep in mind that whatever data or information is put into the patient record is subject to full disclosure in some form of legal proceeding.

No clear legal or ethical standards of practice speak to the overall content and length of records or notes. For the most part, these are discretionary decisions for the psychotherapist. Some practitioners favor lengthy and detailed notes; while others prefer brief and sketchy ones. The basic rule is acting in the best interest of the patient, and reasonable minds may differ on what this requires. Content minimally includes identifying data, dates of services, types of services, fees, assessment, plan for intervention, consultation, summary reports, testing reports, and supporting data as may be appropriate, and any release of information.

These confidential documents belong to the therapist and are kept in a locked, safe, and secure place. The patient has the right to request copies, and the therapist, for good reasons, can provide only a summary. If a patient insists on full access, and the therapist objects, mediation is the next level of response. Ultimately, if records and/or notes are subpoenaed, it is best to refuse access until ordered by a court to comply.

Practice Issues Pertaining to Marriage and Divorce

Psychologists can provide services to individual minors, parents, couples, or the entire family after a disclosure of child abuse or neglect. The following information on the parameters of marriage and divorce will assist therapists who engage in mediation, child custody evaluation, or testify in court proceedings.

First, there is no minimum age for marriage. 18 year olds can consent to marriage, however minors under the age of 18 require written consent of at least one parent or guardian, and a court order granting permission. Premarital counseling may also be required. Emancipated minors are persons under the age of 18 years who come within the following description: (a) Entered into a valid marriage, whether or not such marriage was terminated by dissolution; or (b) On active duty with any of the Armed Forces of the United States of America; or (c) Has received a declaration of emancipation from the superior court of a county. A minor must also be at least 14 years old before he or she can receive such a declaration.

Since 1970, *dissolution of marriage* has replaced the term *divorce*. Dissolution is available to either spouse on a no fault basis, and the primary operable legal ground is a claim of *irreconcilable differences*. To file, either spouse must first reside in California for a minimum of 6 months, and 3 months in the specific county. Final judgment of dissolution of the marriage may be issued a minimum of 6 months after service of the summons and petition for dissolution.

Child custody is an important determination. The courts have jurisdiction to modify custody, visitation, and related legal rights of the parents at any time until the child is 18 years old. The basic rule is that custody and related rights are determined in accordance with *the best interests of the child* with a preference towards joint custody, followed by a consideration of either parent (leaning towards the one most willing to allow the other parent unrestricted contact with the child. If the child is old enough to state an *intelligent preference*, the court will consider it, but the child's wishes are not automatically granted. The decision concerning the amount paid by the parent, child support, is based upon the need of the child and ability of the parent(s) to pay. Either or both parents may be ordered to pay what is necessary for the support, maintenance and education of the child. The amount is always subject to later modification until the child is 18 years old.

Spousal support or alimony is the amount awarded either spouse based upon need and ability to pay. Consideration is given to the duration of the marriage and the employability of the spouse seeking support. The amount and terms may be modified by the Court at any time. Support is terminated upon death of the spouse, remarriage of the spouse receiving support, or other contingencies provided for in the settlement agreement or order.

Mediation

Mediation is a confidential process to assist divorcing or divorced parents work out an agreement about custody and visitation issues. A neutral setting is provided and the parents meet together and develop an agreement that is in the best interests of the child or children. A skilled and trained individual, often with a minimum of a Masters of Arts degree plus training and experience in conflict resolution, works as a mediator to assist the parents in this resolution process. The aim is to work out a parenting plan and set aside fault and blame. Many jurisdictions have mediation services connected to the Superior Court. California law requires that couples who disagree with the child custody or visitation orders must attend mediation before their court hearing on the matter.

When domestic violence is an issue or a restraining protective order is in effect, mediation can begin with separate interviews of the parents, and the parents can be escorted to and from their cars, or in and out of the court building by marshals. A parenting plan is created in these instances, in which the child's and victim's safety is assured.

Child Custody Evaluations

Child custody evaluations are conducted when a suitable child custody arrangement cannot be agreed to by divorcing parents or parents who wish to restructure parental rights and responsibilities. The courts may modify custody and visitation rights until the children are 18 years of age. If you provide or provided psychotherapeutic services to a member of a family contemplating a child custody evaluation, it is considered inappropriate to function as an expert witness i.e., the child custody evaluator, for this particular family. However, it is likely that you would be interviewed or called to testify as a fact witness within this case regarding information you became aware of during the psychotherapeutic relationship. Evidence code §730 states "When it appears to the court, at any time before or during the trial of an action, that expert evidence is or may be required by the court or a party to the action, the court on its own motion or on motion of any party may appoint one or more experts to investigate, to render a report as may be ordered by the court, and to testify as an expert at the trial of the action relative to the fact or matter as to which the expert evidence is or may be required."

Qualified persons who conduct child custody evaluations include licensed marriage and family therapists, licensed clinical social workers, and psychologists. Psychological testing is often conducted and if the child custody evaluator is not qualified to administer and interpret the results, a referral to a qualified individual is made. Usually a minimum of a master's degree in a mental health field is required, with the additional training and knowledge of issues such as child development, divorce, and the legal standards and process involved in these matters. Competence to conduct an evaluation involves one's professional education, training, experience, and/or supervision.

When conducting an evaluation, the child's or children's best psychological interests are paramount. The evaluator is functioning as an expert witness, not as a psychotherapist or mediator. An expert witness is required to be neutral and nondiscriminatory, focused on the parental capacity of each parent, and the psychological development and needs of the child. Data gathering techniques include history taking, clinical interviews with each parent and child separately and together, first hand observations in the office and home, psychological assessments, and ancillary information, such as pertinent knowledge from teachers, colleagues, relatives, and neighbors. If it is deemed appropriate and the child is mature enough, i.e., sufficient age and capacity to state a preference, the court will also consider the child's wishes.

An evaluation often results in a professional opinion containing a recommendation in the best interests of the child or children. Since the ultimate issue is actually decided by the judge, another way of understanding 730 evaluations, is that the expert witness assists the Superior Court Judge in making a decision as to the best custodial arrangement.

One last note regarding joint custody versus sole custody. In studies conducted by Ackerman and Ackerman (1997), experienced professionals indicated they preferred joint custody with primary placement with one parent or joint custody with shared placement. A less preferred child custody arrangement was reported to be sole custody with visitation privileges. Although a form of joint custody may be preferred, in high conflict or hostile and violent families, sole custody by one parent, with visitation privileges by the other may be the best possible arrangement. Many variables are weighed, including history of domestic violence, the amount of hostility, anger, and bitterness between the parents, willingness of the parents to enter into a joint custodial agreement, substance abuse, parenting skills and behaviors, move away issues, quality of the parent-child relationship, and psychological stability.

In terms of domestic violence during dissolution of marriage, Johnston and Campbell (1993) reported five basic types of interpersonal violence seen within custody disputes and the resulting impact on the children: ongoing or episodic male battering, female-initiated violence, male-controlling interactive violence, separation-engendered violence or postdivorce trauma, and psychotic and paranoid reactions. They recommended against sole or joint custody for a father who is involved in ongoing or episodic battering, and against sole or joint custody for a parent who is experiencing psychosis or has paranoid delusions. The safety of the children is the guiding rule. For more information on professional guidelines in conducting child custody evaluations, please refer to the American Psychological Association's Guidelines for Child Custody Evaluations in Divorce Proceedings (1994) and the Standards of Practice for Child Custody Evaluations promulgated by the Association of Family and Conciliation Courts (1995).

Testimony

Occasionally psychologists provide testimony within a court of law. The experience can be stressful or frightening for anyone unfamiliar with this process. Psychotherapists may be called as fact witnesses or expert witnesses: expert witnesses are directly hired as such in civil or criminal matters to provide specialized knowledge to the trier of fact, the judge, while a fact witness is subpoenaed to testify to the facts of a particular case. Myers (1992) addresses the process of testifying in child abuse and neglect litigation and offers legal parameters for interviewing children.

Without an applicable legal or ethical exception, therapists don't testify regarding a patient since everything disclosed by a patient to a therapist is considered confidential, including the therapist's thoughts based on such information, such as the diagnosis and assessment. This includes the fact that the patient is in therapy. Applicable legal exceptions include reporting child, dependent adult, or elder abuse and when functioning as a court appointed evaluating psychologist.

In cases where a subpoena is received, seek out consultation or legal counsel when confronted with a complex disclosable incident or situation. After doing so, learning that one will need to testify, and preparing thoroughly, following this advisement may prove extremely helpful before the testimony "explicitly relax or engage in productive work just before your court appearance" (Brodsky, 1998, p.112).

Suggested Activity-Reflections

Part II has focused on legal, ethical, and practice concerns, disclosure, mandated reporting, and cultural competence. Please take a few moments to reflect on your level of cross-cultural competence, become aware of your perspective on multiple relationships, and review the breadth of knowledge you possess on the ethical and legal aspects of providing psychological services. Would you feel comfortable providing services to members of any cultural group? Are you aware of holding a bias that would prevent your full participation in work with a particular family, couple, or individual? In your reflection on multiple relationships, identify a relationship you were involved in that fits this definition. As you recall the elements of the relationship, is there anything you would do differently today? Perhaps you have identified a lack of knowledge or bias that you can address through an academic course, consultation, or professional continuing education. Reflecting on growing edges, identifying cultural assumptions, and actively engaging in remedial measures will serve you well.

PART III

Clinical and Empirical
Research

Chapter 7

Psychological Impact of Child Maltreatment

Clinicians and researchers have studied the short and long term impact of abuse experienced in childhood. Child abuse is considered a risk factor for the development of a range of medical, cognitive, behavioral, and emotional issues. The medical impacts may consist of head injuries, physical impairments, malnutrition, and failure to thrive. The psychological issues include conduct disorder, eating disorder, attention deficit hyperactivity disorder, interpersonal difficulties, posttraumatic stress disorder, sexualized behavior, major depression, alcohol and drug disorders, and self-injurious behavior. There is also evidence of an association between the persistent, ongoing, and chronic adversity experienced in early childhood abuse and neglect with enduring neurobiological consequences (Surgeon General's Report on Mental Health, 2000; van der Kolk, 1996).

Attachment Theory

The child development theories provide insight into the lasting effects of one's early environment. Impasses or problems can occur at many stages within the developmental process. In terms of an infant's early development the psychologically dynamic state of nurturing an infant's growth and desires is referred to as the holding environment (Winnicott, 1965). The infant develops within this holding environment and atmosphere where good enough parenting is provided. Bowlby's (1980) internal working model of attachment is also central to understanding the impacts of caregiving environments. Children respond to the varying degrees of bonds with caregivers, experience themselves in critical ways in reference to the presence or absence of these bonds, and learn about roles in relationships.

Attachment is conceptualized as secure, resistant, avoidant, or disorganized (Alexander, 1992), reflecting an internalized working model developed in response to one's environment. Secure attachments develop from interactions with caretakers who are consistently responsive and supportive and attuned to the needs of the child. Caregivers who behave unpredictably and punitively contribute to the formation of insecure attachments. Children develop protective mechanisms evidenced by distancing behaviors, avoidance of intimacy with others, or combinations of approach and avoidance behaviors. A consequence of parental rejection and dismissiveness is subsequent insecure attachment (Alexander, 1992) observed in abusive and neglectful families.

When a parent is unavailable to provide the necessary mirroring and holding due to a self-focus, preoccupation, or narcissism (Covitz, 1986), the child learns not to experience his or her own emotions (Miller, 1981). Some children learn to adapt and become compliant, meeting the needs of the other. Children become self-alienated and rely on defense mechanisms such as splitting and denial in order to contain their true feelings. Depression soon follows as a consequence of being unable to experience true feelings and rage develops as a response to the parent's lack of recognition (Kernberg, 1975). These theories allow for an understanding of the distorted mechanisms leading to a child's rage turned inward and the formation of a false self, or persona. These early developmental elements speak to every child's vulnerability and dependence on caregivers for functioning, growing, and experiencing basic life. One can begin to see the damaging impact of child abuse and neglect.

Short and Long Term Effects

Clinical and empirical studies have documented a correlation between child abuse and long-term psychological problems, specifically forms of child abuse such as psychological maltreatment (Briere & Runtz, 1988a; Garbarino, Guttman, & Seeley, 1986; Hart & Brassard, 1987), sexual abuse (Briere & Runtz, 1991; Browne & Finkelhor, 1986), and incest (Finkelhor, 1990; Herman, 1981; Meiselman, 1990; Russell, 1986).

Childhood abuse has long-lasting effects such as depression, anxiety, and sleep disturbances. (Briere & Runtz, 1988b; Burgess & Holmstrom, 1974a, 1974b; Walker, 1983). Child abuse can result in a range of symptoms, including the following: anxiety, depression, dissociative disorders, sleep disturbances, fear or vulnerability, self-destructiveness, self-blame, humiliation, shame, lowered self-esteem, difficulty in concentration, amnesia, change in sexual behavior or satisfaction, and interpersonal difficulties.

Depression and Anxiety

As individuals have become empowered to discuss and shed light on the incidents of abuse in their lives, it has become evident that interpersonal victimization is a significant correlational factor in depression (Kaslow & Carter, 1991). Depression and anxiety are commonly associated with early childhood sexual abuse (Browne & Finkelhor, 1986). Research (Bagley & Ramsay, 1986; Peters, 1988) that investigated depressive symptoms in a random sample from the general population using standardized measurement instruments and self-report, found more depression in women who had experienced childhood sexual abuse than those who had not been abused. Similar outcomes were reported in samples of college women (Briere & Runtz, 1986; Sedney & Brooks, 1984).

Saunders, Villeponteaux, Lipovsky, Kilpatrick, and Veronen (1992) screened 391 adult women for a history of childhood sexual abuse and assessed them for past and current mental disorders. They found that one third of the women in their community sample had experienced sexual abuse in childhood. These women had significantly higher lifetime prevalence rates for depressive disorders, sexual disorders, and anxiety disorders. They were also more likely to have attempted suicide or experienced suicidal ideation.

Furthermore, the association of depression and suicidal ideation has been documented in the clinical studies of Herman (1981) and the general population studies of childhood sexual abuse conducted by Bagley and Ramsay (1986). The extensive research study by Briere and Runtz (1986) also found that of the women studied in the crisis intervention program of a community health center, those who had experienced childhood sexual abuse were more likely to have made at least one suicide attempt in the past than non-abused women. Their analysis discovered that childhood sexual abuse was associated with suicide attempts that had occurred in childhood or adolescence.

In a nonclinical sample of adult women, those who reported a history of childhood sexual abuse experienced higher levels of anxiety in addition to depression, dissociation, and somatization (Briere & Runtz, 1988b). These symptoms may represent a kind of conditioned response to sexual victimization that continues into adult life. This type of conditioned response has also been hypothesized by Burgess and Holmstrom (1974b) in their studies of chronic rape trauma.

Anxiety reactions have also been noted in long-term reactions to childhood abuse (Briere, 1984; Burgess & Holmstrom, 1974a, 1978; Sedney & Brooks, 1984). In the study by Briere (1984) 54% of the victims reported anxiety attacks versus 28% of the nonvictims. Bard and Sangrey (1985) also discovered that fear, anxiety, and shock reactions are frequently reported in all categories of crime victims.

Dissociative Disorders

Historically, dissociative disorders have consistently been linked to childhood sexual abuse, initially by Freud (1962/1896) and much later in the writings of more contemporary clinicians (Blake-White & Kline, 1985; Briere & Runtz, 1987; Coons & Milstein, 1984; Gelinas, 1983; Putnam, 1988; Summit, 1983). However, the relationship between childhood sexual abuse and the development of dissociative identity disorder is of a correlational nature. Dissociation has been considered to be an adaptive response to an overwhelming trauma that typically occurred in childhood (Putnam, Guroff, Silberman, Barban, & Post, 1986). A theory regarding the etiology of dissociative identity disorder is that it is a posttraumatic disorder of the dissociative type (Ross, 1990). In addition to early childhood physical, sexual, and emotional abuse, Ament (1987) has suggested that multiple personality disorder may originate during adulthood in response to some type of trauma such as sexual assault.

Dissociative symptoms were not systematically assessed in victims of childhood abuse until the empirical studies of Briere and Runtz (1988b). Prior to that time there was not a reliable measure of dissociation. Briere & Runtz (1988a) developed an initial dissociation scale consisting of the following five items: (a) feeling outside of your body; (b) not feeling like your real self; (c) spacing out; (d) losing touch with reality; and (e) watching yourself from far away. The symptoms of dissociation and somatization were most predictive of abuse history among their university sample of adult women (Briere & Runtz, 1988b).

Somatization

Somatization has been defined as "distress arising from perceptions of bodily dysfunction" and includes "somatic equivalents of anxiety" (Derogatis, Lipman, Rickels, Ulenhuth, & Covi, 1974, p. 4). Somatization involves a sensitivity or preoccupation with the body's functions and processes, including disease or impairment. This type of sensitivity may increase the acute awareness of physiological processes, thus increasing the subjective experience of the processes, as noted by Beck and Emery (1985) in their studies of the manifestation of anxiety. Briere and Runtz (1988b) found that the symptom of somatization covaried with a history of childhood sexual victimization. Greater somatic concerns have been reported in populations of adult women who have histories of childhood sexual abuse (Briere, 1984; Courtois, 1979; Sedney & Brooks, 1984).

Impaired Social Functioning

Impaired social functioning has been reported by victims of crime and has been noted in studies with sexual assault victims (Kilpatrick et al., 1981; Scheppele & Bart, 1983) and adults who have histories of childhood sexual abuse (Briere, 1984). Clinical reports by Herman (1981) have indicated the significant interpersonal problems experienced by individuals who were sexually victimized as children. Difficulties in longer term relationships and fear of intimacy have been reported by Meiselman (1978). Tsai and Wagner (1978) have also reported the experiences of isolation and alienation.

Chronic and persistent experiences of life events that are not controllable decrease a person's ability to perceive support or help in future interpersonal relationships. This decreased ability seriously undermines the establishment of trust in relationships and affects social functioning (McFarlane, Norman, Streiner, & Roy, 1983). Individuals who perceive an event as controllable engage more effective problem-focused coping responses and consequently experience less distressful psychological symptomatology.

Thus, when an individual holds a damaged self-image, a diminished sense of self-efficacy and worth, compounded with an absence of a sense of invulnerability or personal control in life, the ability to perceive oneself as an individual with power, strength, and capability may also be diminished. This in turn, may relate to deficits in coping. Disempowerment, discussed in the next chapter, is represented by these qualities.

The victimization literature documents associations between traumatic reactions and the degree of trust in a victimizing situation. There is some evidence that sexual abuse victims experience problems within intimate relationships. One study found sexual assault victims reported decreased trust in men and fears of getting close to either men or women (Ellis, Atkeson, & Calhoun, 1981). Courtois (1979) and Meiselman (1978) indicated that women with histories of childhood sexual abuse reported difficulties in close relationships with others.

Briere (1984) found that fear and distrust were both prominent in a clinical sample of women with histories of childhood sexual abuse. Many women also felt isolated from others, which may be related to fear and distrust. Briere and Runtz (1986) suggested the interpersonal difficulties of some childhood abuse survivors may contribute to suicidal ideation and behavior.

Sexual Problems

Several clinical studies (Becker, Skinner, Abel, & Treacy, 1982; Briere & Runtz, 1987; Elliott & Briere, 1990; Meiselman, 1978) have found sexual problems or sexual dysfunction reported more frequently in populations of individuals who had histories of childhood sexual abuse. Two nonclinical studies (Courtois, 1979; Finkelhor, 1979) have found the same results, while a study by Fromuth (1986) did not find this to be the case.

In clinical studies of incest survivors, Meiselman (1978), reported that the majority of sexual problems consisted of atypical patterns of sexual arousal and response, that may not emerge until involvement in an enduring sexual relationship. In a study exploring the types of sexual problems experienced by rape and incest victims, Becker et al. (1982) found that a complete lack of sexual desire is sometimes reported. McGuire and Wagner (1978) discussed a more frequent sexual problem seen in women who have histories of childhood sexual abuse, consisting of situational orgasmic dysfunction, where the situation is related to the original traumatic experience. Maltz and Holman (1987) believe that situational orgasmic dysfunction may take the form of avoidance of specific aspects or types of sexual intimacy that tend to trigger the range of traumatic effects of incestuous abuse. Additionally, they have stated that denial or suppression of sexual feelings may be present in those who have been incestuously abused.

In a nationally representative survey of 2,626 adult Americans, Finkelhor, Hotaling, Lewis, and Smith (1989) found a significant relationship between childhood sexual abuse and later sexual dissatisfaction. However, they have cautioned that a history of childhood sexual abuse is only a risk factor for the development of difficulties that may include sexual dissatisfaction, and not a causal factor.

A variety of assessments have been made regarding the experiences of children and adolescents who have been sexually abused. Summit (1983) proposed a child sexual abuse accommodation syndrome. The theory inherently provides a way for the child to cope with her or his inner pain and the societal system. Porter, Blick, and Sgroi (1982) proposed ten impact issues that affect sexually abused children in varying degrees. Finkelhor & Browne (1988) proposed an integrated conceptual model called the four traumagenic dynamics model. This model guides the understanding of the general effects of child sexual abuse, from the perspective of cognitive and affective distortions which lead to symptoms and dysfunctional behavior that characterize victims of abuse. The model emphasizes the trauma of sexual abuse as stemming from the conditioning process that precedes and follows the sexual abuse (Finkelhor, 1990).

Child Sexual Abuse Accommodation Syndrome

Summit (1983) proposed the child sexual abuse accommodation syndrome to reflect the most typical reactions noted in abuse victims. The five most common reactions that were conceptualized into a child sexual abuse accommodation syndrome are within the categories of secrecy, helplessness, entrapment and accommodation, delayed unconvincing disclosure, and retraction.

Secrecy and helplessness are seen as preconditions and results of the abuse. Summit has proposed that unless the victimized child "can find some permission and power" (1983, p.182) to disclose the abuse, and an empathic and non-punitive response to the sharing of the secret, the child may grow into adulthood with difficulties in intimacy, trust and self-validation. Helplessness is also viewed as a precondition and result of the abuse. Due to a dependent child's age and status, he or she is often helpless to resist the adult's coercion, or to complain. Summit (1983) has described a process where a child submits quietly and eventually experiences self-condemnation and self-hate for his or her participation.

The last three categories are the consequent results of victimization for the child who endures continuing helpless victimization. In an attempt at achieving some power and control over the continuing abuse, and as a way of surviving and coping with it, the child begins to accept the responsibility for the abuse (entrapment and accommodation). The consequence for this perception is often negative expectations and self-hate (Summit, 1983). Some children will continue with these accommodations, well into adulthood. However, if these coping mechanisms break-down, a delayed or unconvincing disclosure may occur, followed by a retraction. This is due to the child's ambivalence of guilt and feelings of obligation to preserve the family. Summit's accommodation syndrome has parallels with rape trauma syndrome (Burgess & Holmstrom, 1974b) where the victim often experiences shame, self-blame, and secrecy.

Functional Impact Issues

Ten functional (as opposed to diagnostic) impact issues from child sexual abuse have been defined: "damaged goods" syndrome; guilt; fear; depression; low self-esteem and poor social skills; repressed anger and hostility; impaired ability to trust; blurred role boundaries and role confusion; pseudomaturity coupled with failure to accomplish developmental tasks; and self-mastery and control (Porter, Blick, & Sgroi, 1984). Sexual abuse by anyone, whether a family member or not, is likely to produce the first five issues to some degree. The last five are postulated to affect intrafamily child sexual abuse victims.

Traumagenic Dynamics Model

The traumagenic dynamics model is an explanatory construct for understanding the general effects of child sexual abuse in a systematic manner (Finkelhor & Browne, 1985). The four dynamics in combination tend to distort the child's self-concept, world-view and affective capacities: traumatic sexualization consisting of flashbacks, negative distortions of body and sexuality; stigmatization, derived from the distortion of one's sense of value and worth; betrayal, encompassing grief reactions, depression, and anger; powerlessness or disempowerment contributing to a distortion of one's perceived ability to control life resulting in nightmares, anxiety and phobias. In this model, inferences can be made about the predominant concerns of the victim, based on the presence of these dynamics.

Sexual Behavior

The prominent symptom clusters of sexual behavior and symptoms related to post traumatic stress disorder were identified by researchers in a comprehensive review of the literature focused on consequences of child sexual abuse (Kendall-Tackett, Williams, & Finkelhor, 1993). These symptom clusters were the most reliably identified predictors. The findings supported both Finkelhor and Browne's traumatic sexualization component of the traumagenic model of abuse as well as Walker's postulations on post traumatic stress disorder.

A recent study examining child sexual behavior in 2,311 children from the ages of 2 through 12 (Friedrich et. al, 2001) found that sexual behavior was an abuse-specific variable and was significantly related to sexual abuse in children. Children were from a nonclinical sample, an outpatient psychiatric sample, and a sexual abuse comparison group. Although sexual behavior was not unique to those children who experienced sexual abuse, more sexual behavior was seen in the children who were penetrated orally, vaginally, or anally, were abused by family members, abused by more than one individual, and were abused frequently over a span of time. However this study did not find physical force as a significant predicting variable of child sexual abuse.

Post-Sexual Abuse Trauma

Briere and Runtz (1987) and Briere and Zaidi (1989) noted the problems resulting from severe childhood sexual abuse-chronic anger, substance abuse, self-destructiveness-may cause individuals to be labeled with personality disorders, especially borderline personality disorder. Westen, Ludolph, Misle, Ruffins, and Block (1990) raised the question about the extent to which chronic posttraumatic stress disorder becomes integrated into a victim's personality structure. As this occurs differentiating between the integrated structure and the presence of borderline personality disorder becomes more difficult. This aspect of the impact of chronic abuse on an evolving character structure needs to be further explored given that many abuse survivors are diagnosed with personality disorders. Briere (1984) found almost all of the symptoms traditionally listed for borderline personality disorder had been independently reported as victimization effects in the sexual abuse literature. It may be more appropriate to use the phenomenological term "abuse related borderline symptoms."

Instead of using these oftentimes stigmatizing and inaccurate labels, the more global notion of post sexual abuse trauma may describe these effects (Briere & Runtz, 1987). Post sexual abuse trauma refers to "symptomatic" behaviors that were initially adaptive responses, accurate perceptions, or conditioned reactions to abuse during childhood (Briere & Runtz, 1988a), but that became contextually inappropriate components of the victim's later personality. The developmental and adaptive aspects of such post sexual abuse trauma distinguish it, to some extent, from the more static aspects of delayed posttraumatic stress disorder. Posttraumatic stress disorder has been found to be too narrow, for it focuses on the affective realm and it does not include cognitive effects, suicide attempts, drug addiction, alcoholism, or having been revictimized. Additionally, each of the criteria for posttraumatic stress disorder has been described in the literature as a long-term effect of childhood sexual abuse including the presence of a psychologically distressing event, re-experiencing of the trauma, numbing of general responsiveness, sleep disturbance, concentration problems, and impaired memory.

The literature on childhood sexual abuse suggests that certain characteristics of the abuse experience produce more serious effects: penetration orally, vaginally, or anally, molestation by an immediate family member, abuse by more than one perpetrator (Friedrich, et. al, 2001), molestation before age 18, incest, longer duration over time, perhaps greater use of force/coercion by the abuser, greater degree of trust in the abuser, greater age difference between abuser and victim (Courtois, 1979; Finkelhor & Browne, 1985; Tsai, Feldman, Summers, & Edgar, 1979). Degree of trust in the relationship may be the key variable that combines with other intervening variables and results in greater long-term symptomatology. Further explorations are needed to understand these relationships.

Anecdotal reports associate damage from early childhood sexual abuse with resultant infertility, an inability, or a clear decision to remain childless (May, 2000). Emotional and physical abuse has been cited as a significant decision-making variable in choosing to bear or father children.

Trauma Theory

The word trauma evolved from the Greek term *wound*. Figley (1985) defined trauma as an "emotional state of discomfort and stress resulting from memories of an extraordinary, catastrophic experience which shattered the survivor's sense of invulnerability to harm" (p.xix). This type of wounding could dramatically alter a person's world view and beliefs, affecting cognitive, imaginal, behavioral, emotional, and spiritual components.

From the perspective of trauma theory, violence and victimization is not viewed as being symptomatic of underlying psychiatric or behavioral problems but is viewed as an event or events that are "sufficiently traumatic in themselves to evoke a predictable constellation of feelings and behaviors only minimally related to individual differences" (Stark & Flitcraft, 1988, p.126).

Posttraumatic Stress Disorder

A victim may indeed display the "classic triad of PTSD: haunting, intrusive recollection; numbing or constricted feeling and focus; and a lowered threshold for anxious arousal" (Ochberg, 1988, p.8), but is much more likely to experience symptoms that may not reach the threshold for PTSD such as shame, self-blame, subjugation, morbid hatred, paradoxical gratitude, defilement, sexual inhibition, resignation, second injury or second wound, and socioeconomic status downward drift. Until there is a diagnosis of victims stress disorder, Ochberg believes that clinicians will need to use the officially recognized diagnostic categories that best fit each individual victim.

Herman (1992) concurred with the premise that the diagnostic category of posttraumatic stress disorder does not accurately fit for many survivors of abuse and violent crime. She acknowledges the derivations for the disorder were based on prototypes of specific traumatic events such as combat, disaster, and rape. Victims and survivors of chronic and persistent trauma, such as childhood sexual abuse, often develop alterations within their personality, involving deficits in identity, and develop problems with relationships.

A new syndrome inclusive of prolonged, repetitive trauma was proposed: complex posttraumatic stress disorder (Herman, 1992). This syndrome is best understood as a spectrum of conditions as opposed to a single discrete disorder and is composed of seven diagnostic criteria including "a history of subjection to totalitarian control over a prolonged period" (p.121). Examples include experiences of spousal abuse, and childhood sexual and physical abuse. The other six criteria are: alterations in affect regulation, consciousness, self-perception, relations with others, perception of the perpetrator, and in systems of meaning (Herman, 1992). The specificity of this syndrome was not incorporated into the DSM-IV (American Psychiatric Association, 1994; 2000), although some aspects were integrated under the diagnostic category of post traumatic stress disorder.

More than a decade ago Walker (1990) postulated that posttraumatic stress corresponded to the pattern of psychological symptoms experienced by children, adolescents, and adults who had been sexually abused. The symptoms were categorized into three specific groups: a) symptoms of cognitive disturbance including flashbacks, dissociative states, and other recurrent, intrusive, or conditioned memories of the traumatic events; b) avoidance symptoms including depression, disturbances in interpersonal relationships and sexuality, loss of interest in activities, changes in habits, and sleep disorders; and c) heightened arousal symptoms such as anxiety, fearfulness, phobic responses, irritability, concentration problems, hypervigilance to cues of possible danger, and an exaggerated startle response. Post traumatic stress disorder as a diagnosis (APA, 1994; 2000) currently incorporates childhood sexual or physical abuse, violent personal assault, sexual assault, witnessed assaults, children's developmentally inappropriate sexual incidents, and domestic battering. As continued empirical studies are completed and work groups form to review the evidence for any new specifiers, posttraumatic stress disorder as a diagnostic category will likely expand its breadth and narrow definitions and subcategories.

◈ Chapter 8

Disempowerment, Coping, and Resilience

As the previous chapter on the psychological impact of child maltreatment has shown children and adults express a range of significant responses in light of their experiences. Short term reactions and long term consequences of abuse are equally important to consider given the context of the abuse or neglect-occurring during the vulnerable childhood developmental periods of life. Inevitably the abuse impacts a child's perception of self, others, community, and the outside world. The effect is felt within one's interior life, in the form of self perceptions, personal power, affect, and relationship to internal states of being. The intimate relationships with others contribute to developing perceptions in the realms of trust, intimacy, reliability, social competence, and dominance and promote a sense of the world as a place of safety or danger. A range of consequences, coping strategies, and strengths will be explored in this chapter including the psychological integrity of resilience.

Disempowerment and Cognitive Appraisals

Disempowerment refers to the process in which one's "will, desires, and sense of efficacy are continually contravened" (Finkelhor & Browne, 1985, p.532). Disempowerment is the dynamic of oppression and the act of rendering someone helpless or powerless, as is often the case in child abuse. Additionally, an expanded definition of disempowerment incorporates the internalization of this oppression and the assumption of specific cognitive appraisals: attributions to the cause of the abuse that are internal, stable, and global (Lipinski, 1992). An internal attribution is the causal interpretation of an abusive incident from an internal perspective such as blaming one's self for the abuse, i.e., self-blame. Holding stable and global attributions suggest the cause of an abusive incident as being present across time and across situations in the future. These concepts are elaborated upon in the following section.

Learned helplessness (Seligman, 1975) originated as a conceptual model consisting of a set of responses to victimization (Peterson & Seligman, 1983). Learned helplessness occurs when individuals are not able to perceive results of their actions or efforts to a particular event and quite often results in depression (Abramson & Martin, 1981). When the learned helplessness theory is applied to abuse survivors, it does not mean that individuals learn how to be helpless, rather they may be unable to predict the efficacy of their behavior.

According to Meiselman (1990) children who have been victimized repeatedly may feel defeated and believe they are powerless to stop the abuse, thus lacking the self-confidence to defend themselves against further victimization. Walker (1987) proposed that once learned helplessness is acquired, either through pervasive abusive experiences in childhood or continued abusive situations in adulthood, an individual is more likely to limit behaviors to those that will have the greatest predictability of a known effect. This perspective suggests that children who develop learned helplessness over time may resort to familiar or passive responses in order to survive or avoid more severe abuse. It is apparent that certain responses to childhood sexual abuse satisfy the conditions of helplessness when the following three conditions are met: uncontrollable aversive or negative events occur and precede the behavior; a generalized belief about future uncontrollability exists; and a variety of behaviors or deficits exist in situations unrelated to the one in which uncontrollability was originally encountered (Seligman, 1975).

The original learned helplessness theory was revised to take into account the causal interpretation of the uncontrollable event. When people are faced with uncontrollable situations, they will ask why, and their answer will affect how they actually respond to the event (Abramson et al., 1978). Since attributions are explanations offered to explain why events happen, by definition, they involve individual perceptions of events. Distinctions can be made between types of attributions consisting of cause, responsibility, and blame (Bradbury & Fincham, 1990). Causal attributions are simply explanations given for the occurrence of an event. Attributions of responsibility are concerned with the accountability for an event, while attributions of blame are concerned with an individual's liability for censure or condemnation (Calhoun & Townsley, 1991).

Causal attribution theory has three main dimensions that explain responses. First, the cause of the event may be seen as an internal attribution which is something about the person, or it may be seen as an external attribution, which is something about the situation or circumstances. Second, the cause may be seen as a stable attribution or a factor that will continue to persist across time, or it may be seen as an unstable attribution or a transient one. Third, the cause may be seen as a global attribution that affects a variety of outcomes or it may be a specific attribution that is limited just to the abusive incident.

The revised perspective of learned helplessness integrating causal attribution theory, proposes specific responses to each of three dimensions. The internality of causal beliefs is thought to affect self-esteem loss following negative or aversive events. Thus, a loss of self-esteem occurs if an individual explains a negative event by an internal factor, such as making a statement about blaming one's self. However, self-esteem loss does not occur if an individual explains the event by an external factor such as a statement about the abuse offender.

The second of the three dimensions, stability of causal beliefs, is thought to affect the chronicity of the experience of helplessness and depression following aversive events. For example, maladaptive chronic reactions such as depression will occur when the event is explained by a cause that persists. The reactions are shorter term and less chronic if the event is explained by a transient factor.

Finally, the third dimension, globality of causal beliefs, determines the extensive nature of the deficits experienced following an aversive event. If a global factor has caused the event to occur, then helplessness deficits will occur in a variety of situations, not just to the specific event. However, the deficits are confined if an individual believes that a more specific factor is the cause.

The reformulation of learned helplessness proposes that individuals vulnerable to these reactions interpret the negative events in internal, stable, and global terms, although persons differ widely in their use of causal explanations and their reactions to the same events. For example, not all sexual abuse survivors show emotional numbing and maladaptive passivity (Burgess & Holmstrom, 1974a, 1974b).

In a clinical sample involving 420 women who reported a history of childhood sexual abuse, Conte, Briere, & Sexton (1989) found that internal causal attributions at the time of the abuse was a powerful predictor of later adult symptomatology. This two year national study surveyed women who were in therapy and reported a number of powerful predictors of adult symptomatology including lower adult income, a negative family environment during childhood, and a childhood belief that death would result if the abuse was disclosed to anyone.

In a study by Gold (1986) investigating the long-term effects of victimization in childhood and attributional styles of 191 subjects, women who were sexually abused as children relied more frequently on internal, stable, and global attributions for negative events. She compared a group of women with histories of childhood sexual abuse with a control group and found the attributional style differentiated the two groups. She also discovered that sexual abuse survivors reported greater levels of psychological distress and low self-esteem.

In the area of personal responsibility, Celano (1992) proposed the attributional dimensions of globality and stability be used to identify potentially damaging attributions of responsibility such as self-blame. In another study, Kaslow et al. (1988) reported that children who blame themselves across time periods and situations tend to be at risk for depression-children who hold stable and global attributions. Learned helplessness has been theorized as similar to situational depression (Abramson et al., 1978) and the cognitive disorder of depression (Beck, 1976) has been conceptualized as the result of experiences with uncontrollable negative events (Peterson, Semmel, von Baeyer, Abramson, Metalsky, & Seligman, 1982). Responsibility attributions, learned helplessness, and depression suggest the construct of disempowerment.

Wyatt and Newcomb (1990) conducted a retrospective study of internal and external mediators of women's childhood sexual abuse. Both mediational and direct effects on adult functioning were found in their sample of 111 women. The internal mediator-internal attribution-was one of the most important variables because it explained the impact of childhood sexual abuse on negative outcomes.

Causal attributions may account in part for the differing reactions to victimization. Janoff-Bulman (1979) indicated the dimension of responses may result from unstable and specific causal interpretations. She suggested self-blame directed at one's behavior does not lead to debilitation following negative events, since behavior is generally perceived as flexible, or unstable and specific. In contrast self-blame directed at one's character does result in deficits, since character is fixed, or stable and global. These attributions may be helpful in predicting which individuals are most likely to suffer adversely from child abuse and which types of victimization are most likely to result in traumatic or maladaptive reactions, including deficits in coping.

Childhood Abuse and Subsequent Victimization

The association between childhood sexual abuse and later adult victimization has also been studied (Browne & Finkelhor, 1986; Frieze, 1983; Herman, 1981, 1986; Runtz, 1987; Russell, 1986). Russell (1986) found a significant relationship between childhood sexual abuse and later experiences of sexual assault. McCord (1985) discovered incest victims often had more sexually and physically abusive experiences as adults than non-victims. Walker (1984) revealed that nearly half of all battered women she studied had a history of childhood sexual abuse.

Childhood sexual abuse is an important element that affects recovery from subsequent victimization such as rape. Burgess and Holmstrom (1974b) found that of victims who had experienced childhood abuse, 20% felt recovered and 45% felt they had not recovered, while of those who did not have a history of prior victimization, 47% felt recovered and only 14% did not. Frank, Turner, and Stewart (1980) discovered that adults who had experienced prior victimization had more disruption in their lives and poorer social adjustment.

In a small sample of victims of violent crime an association was found between childhood abuse-categorized as prior victimization-and psychological symptomatology (Lipinski, 1992). Childhood sexual abuse history was a significant variable in predicting traumatic symptoms consisting of dissociation, anxiety, depression, sleep disturbance, sexual problems, and posttraumatic symptoms. Prior victimization was associated with disempowerment and the holding of internal, global, and stable causal attributions regarding the current assault. This finding was similar to previous research that found higher levels of psychological distress for subsequent victimization.

Similarly, Kaslow, Rehm, Pollack, and Siegel (1988) reported that children who blame themselves across time periods and situations tend to be at risk for depression-they have global and stable attributions. Conte, Briere, & Sexton (1989) found that internal causal attributions for childhood sexual abuse experiences were one of the powerful predictors of later adult symptomatology. In related studies, Meyer and Taylor (1986) reported correlations of internal causal attributions consisting of self-blame with adverse psychological consequences for a sample of 58 sexual assault victims. Internal attributions of self-blame were also found to significantly predict negative short and long-term effects of sexual assault in a community sample of 55 women who had been victims of rape or attempted rape (Wyatt, Notgrass, & Newcomb, 1990).

In a study investigating the link between child abuse and revictimization (Runtz, 1987), 291 female undergraduate students with the mean age of 19 years were assessed on four dimensions of victimization and on a number of attitude and psychosocial measures. Childhood sexual abuse was associated with later sexual assault and battery, and with higher psychological distress. Russell (1986) reported that incest victimization was clearly related to much higher rates of subsequent sexual assault and fears of sexual assault in her probability sample.

Individuals who are revictimized may somehow acquire a vulnerability to subsequent assault, due to the function of social isolation (Runtz, 1987; Russell, 1986). Children who have trusted and had that trust violated and exploited through the sexual abuse of their bodies, experience a decrease in their capacity for trust. This process may in turn interfere with the normal developmental stages a child progresses through within interpersonal relationships, contributing to long-term difficulties in ability to trust.

Further studies can explore mediating factors that contribute to disempowerment, psychological dysfunction, and the severity of symptoms experienced by child abuse survivors. Important factors for consideration include causal attributions for childhood abuse, disruptive family environment during childhood, help-seeking behaviors at the time of childhood abuse and their outcome, duration of childhood abuse experience, number of subsequent victimizations, age difference between abuser and abused, and history of other traumatic life crises and their resolution.

Coping Processes

The general reaction an individual experiences in response to violent or abusive behavior has been compared to the psychological response toward a sudden and unexpected loss (Symonds, 1975). The loss may be in the context of loss of control over one's life, one's body, and the course of events (Burt & Katz, 1987), or loss of invulnerability and self-worth (Taylor, 1983). A resolution of the loss does not begin until certain processes are engaged, which may begin with reactions such as denial, fear, anger, or rage, and continue with responses of active or expressive behaviors. All of these processes are methods of coping.

The literature on coping processes, strategies, and styles indicates a relationship between the ways individuals cope with stressful events and their psychological and physical wellness or well being (Burt & Katz, 1987; Folkman & Lazarus, 1980). Coping methods are viewed as adaptive when they serve to modulate, eliminate, or reduce the anxiety of other effects experienced due to interpersonal victimization. Specific types of coping processes tend to emerge for child abuse victims and survivors, with more effective coping methods providing positive outcomes.

Coping has been broadly defined as the adjustment of cognitions, feelings, and behaviors in response to environmental events, including changing the environment if necessary (Moos & Billings, 1982), the combination of methods used to avoid being harmed by stresses in life (Pearlin & Schooler, 1978) ego processing (Haan, 1965; Folkman & Lazarus, 1980), cognitive appraisal (Lazarus & Averill, 1966), the combination of responses to the demands of a certain situation (Holahan & Moos, 1987), and specific to victimization and abuse, as a process of coming to terms with an integrated assumption about one's world and the meaning attached to it (Janoff-Bulman, 1985).

The literature on coping processes, strategies and styles shows there is a relationship between the ways persons cope with stressful events and their psychological and physical wellness or well being (Burt & Katz, 1987; Folkman & Lazarus, 1980; Folkman, Lazarus, Gruen, & DeLongis, 1986; Kobasa, 1979; Pearlin & Schooler, 1978; Taylor, 1983). Koss and Burkhart (1989) believe coping styles that are used during times of overwhelming stress such as childhood abuse experiences, become "stamped in" (p. 36). Responses to subsequent victimization may be rigid, maladaptive, and unsuccessful. Coping generally has two functions, one function regulates stressful emotions and the other function changes the troubled person-environment relation causing distress (Auerbach, 1989; Lazarus and Folkman, 1984).

Coping is usually viewed as either active or passive (Lazarus & Launier, 1978). Attempts are carried out to alter the original stressful event in active coping strategies, while changes are made in the emotional response to the stressful event in passive strategies. Denial is a passive coping strategy that may alter the emotional responses to stressful events.

Runtz (1987) believes that individuals who have experienced childhood abuse and continue to have fear and anxiety may find denial "a particularly effective method of coping with negative emotions that may leave them open to further abuse" (p. 18). The coping task that child abuse victims face may also be overwhelming. Janoff-Bulman and Frieze (1983) argue that the trauma experienced by victims results in negative self-images. They report that self-images are often weak, helpless, frightened, or out of control.

Carmen, Rieker, and Mills (1984) reported in their nonrandom sample of 188 psychiatric inpatient records, that the individuals who had experienced chronic victimization exhibited difficulty in coping with anger and aggression, impaired self-esteem, and inability to trust. The measure of coping behavior focused on the subjects' direction of anger as inward or outward and on subjects' behavioral control of aggressive impulses. They found a higher percentage of abused subjects directed their anger inward in an actively self-destructive manner. The inward direction of anger composed a continuum from quiet resignation, passivity, and depression to self-hatred, suicidal ideation, and self-mutilating behaviors. Carmen et al. (1984) acknowledge the extraordinary task of conflict resolution and coping that victims are faced with, and have recommended a focus on treatment to help victims become survivors, thus empowered.

Coping strategies have been placed within two dimensions-intrapsychic or cognitive modes and direct action (Janoff-Bulman, 1985). The development of posttraumatic stress develops from the shattering of basic assumptions victims hold about themselves and their world. Janoff-Bulman suggested that individuals engage in a range of coping strategies including redefining the event, finding meaning, changing behaviors, seeking social support, and self-blame. Her perspective on effective coping as a process of integrating the victimization experience into one's assumption about one's world and the meaning attached to it focuses on the adaptive nature of the phenomenon of self-blame. She views behavioral self-blame as helpful in rebuilding shattered assumptions in three important domains: invulnerability, meaning, and esteem.

Adaptive coping strategies have also been conceptualized as behaviors that consist of acknowledging and expressing feelings, using social help, engaging in task-focused behavior, exercising, and relaxing (Andrews, 1990). While maladaptive methods are perceived as denial, aggression, suicide attempts, chemical substance use, psychosomatic complaints, and social withdrawal. The differentiation of adaptive and maladaptive coping methods is based on the healthy or unhealthy side effects these may cause.

Conversely, the perception of effective and ineffective coping strategies is taken by Burt and Katz (1987), Janoff-Bulman (1985), Janoff-Bulman and Frieze (1983), and Runtz (1987). Effective coping is seen as the use of techniques that reduce negative symptomatology (Burt & Katz, 1987), as a process of integrating the victimization experience into one's assumption about one's world and the meaning attached to it (Janoff-Bulman, 1985), as the process of coming to terms with a world in which bad experiences happen to oneself (Janoff-Bulman & Frieze, 1983), and coping with negative emotions that may leave one open to further abuse (Runtz, 1987).

The differentiation between an effective and ineffective coping strategy is based on the positive outcome of its use. From a broader perspective, all coping methods are adaptive if they modulate, eliminate or reduce the anxiety or other effects experienced by victimization. However, only particular coping mechanisms or strategies are effective, in that they have a more positive outcome. Briere's conceptualization of tension-reducing behaviors as activities which "anesthetize, soothe, interrupt, or forestall painful affect" (1992, p.63) are adaptive but ineffective coping methods. The adaptive coping methods may include risk-taking behaviors including indiscriminate sexual contacts, alcohol or substance use, self-mutilation, and binge behavior such as shopping, spending, or overeating.

The early perspectives on stress (Abramson, Seligman, & Teasdale, 1978) affirmed that individuals who tend to cope less well experience a sense of help-lessness. While Hobfoll et al. (1991) describe those who cope effectively as having a positive self-concept in-so-far as feeling that one can positively effect one's environment. This can also be called a sense of personal mastery. Similar to Janoff-Bulman and Frieze (1983), Hobfoll et al. (1991) believe that individuals who tend to resort to self-blame for external events, paralyze themselves from coping adequately, and will feel that whatever they do will contribute more negatively to their situation.

Resilience

Resilience is an intriguing concept in the literature. Acknowledging the variations that exist in human nature, this concept suggests a group of factors or a set of evolving processes that may prevent psychological dysfunction and psychopathology, protect persons from developing incapacitating disorders, and allow the completion of developmental tasks in life during times of immense pain, suffering, vulnerability, and potentially overwhelming traumatic experiences.

The complex interplay between biological, psychological, social, environmental, cultural (deVries, 1996) and experiential factors contributes to the development of resilience. A range of coping capacities are also involved in preventing the development of traumatic responses. Vulnerabilities or risk factors such as family history, psychiatric illness, previous traumas, and personality traits (McFarlane, 1996) impact the progression of initial distress to more severe impairments.

Resilience refers to psychological integrity but it may extend beyond one's intrapsychic capacities such as competence, creativity, creative behaviors (Chandy, Blum, & Resnick, 1996), imagination, faith, hope, and acts of altruistic activism. A definitive construct of resilience does not currently exist. Competence (Luthar & Ziglar, 1991) or stress resistance (Werner, 1989) has been the focus in much of the research. More recently a number of resilient themes have been proposed including insight into the abuse or dynamics; independence or emotional or physical distancing from the abuse or family; initiative in terms of taking risks; building relationship with others which may include fantasy figures, dolls, or animals (Dinsmore, 1991); morality evidenced by conscience and expressed through compassion and empathy; creativity; and humor (Wolin & Wolin, 1993). The themes are clusters of qualities that serve as strengths, skills, and strategies. Coping capacities can be identified in this language of resilience, by acknowledging behaviors, thoughts, and images employed while subjected to sexual, physical, or emotional abuse.

Resilience may also be a function of affiliation, meaning the interconnectedness with supportive community resources, restorative compassion from key individuals in one's life, loving or co-existent relationships with animals, kinship felt with figures, symbols, and stories in literature and the arts or a strong spiritual or religious belief system.

There a number of other conceptualizations of resilience. In *Warming the Stone Child*, Estes (1990) tells the story of an internal flame that keeps glowing that can never be extinguished in the face of severe abuse and neglect. In describing the orphan archetype and the abandonment experiences, she hypothesized the internalization or unconscious introjection of an inadequate parent, one that does not tend to fan this internal flame. Nevertheless a glimmer of light remains, which can be accessed in psychotherapy and nurtured into a love, respect, and regard for one's self. This process speaks to the issue of rediscovery, re-empowerment, and "suffering without losing the sense that the situation is somehow workable" (Egendorf, 1985, p.238).

Higgins (1994) proposed a heroic element in the process of resilience when she applied the mythological tale of the Sirens as a metaphor for "overcoming." In Homer's *Odyssey* the potentially fatal Sirens tempt, entice, and captivate all passing mariners in the treacherous seas. The Sirens are viewed as developmental challenges that are faced and overcome by the resilient. When the chorus of Sirens are equated with familiar seductions such as illusions of a harmonious family, denied victimization, or hasty and nonreflective forgiveness, the metaphors serve as challenges to acknowledge and work through. The illusions of the harmonious family and denied victimization function as defensive mechanisms, effectively minimizing or denying the reality of experienced abuse. Higgins suggests that resilient individuals tend to overcome the tendency to deny with acknowledgment of the reality of the abusive experiences "sooner than most" (p.264), learn healthy self-compassion as they perceive and mourn their suffering, heighten their internal sense of efficacy, and participate in healing through understanding and self growth, rather than nonreflective or premature forgiving. In essence, personal characteristics, acknowledgment of abusive experiences, awareness of personal boundaries, intensive recovery, and self growth experiences that may result in altruistic involvement in the world, all contribute to the notion of overcoming and correspond to resilience.

◳ Chapter 9

Perspectives on Violence and Abuse

Our task must be to free ourselves from this prison by widening
our circle of compassion to embrace all living creatures and the
whole of nature in its beauty.

Albert Einstein, 1972

A mericans are well aware of the problem of societal violence. Unfortunately the idyllic image of the family as relatively immune from
violence, a place of refuge or a safe harbor, where a loving family provides
nurturance, sustenance, and care is not a reality for many children. Each year over
one thousand children die as a result of abuse or neglect and many others are
physically, sexually, or emotionally abused and neglected. Research consistently
demonstrates that many women and children are actually more likely to be assaulted
in their own homes than on the streets in the most violent American cities (Gelles,
1997). Perceiving family violence and community violence as interconnected rather
than completely distinct is more pragmatic.

Family Violence

Scholarly endeavors have focused on the qualitative and quantitative differences between men's and women's experience with domestic violence, also categorized as partner abuse, intimate partner violence, interpartner abuse, marital violence, spousal battery, and wife abuse. Notwithstanding the fact that scholars have employed different methodologies and violence has been operationally defined in numerous ways, ranging from one incident of physical abuse to ongoing patterns of psychological terrorizing and beatings resulting in hospitalization or emergency room care, the results report a consistent trend: women constitute more than 90% of partner violence victims reported to law enforcement agencies (Dobash & Dobash, 1977-78; McLeod, 1984; Rand, 1997), are overwhelmingly the injured parties (Kurz, 1990; Langen & Innes, 1986; Tjaden & Thoennes, 2000), suffer more severe consequences than their male counterparts (Morse, 1995; Rand, 1997; Straus, 1993), and are at greater risk for intimate partner violence (Bachman & Saltzman, 1996; Tjaden & Thoennes, 2000).

Straus (1993) and Gelles (1997) indicated their studies found women were 10 times more likely than men to be injured in acts of domestic violence, no matter who may have initiated the violence. Men may tend to underreport their experiences of interpersonal partner violence and have also experienced physical abuse at the hands of their female partners who initiated violence without provocation, but women who are the sole perpetrators of violence appear to be the minority (Adams, 2000). The literature indicates that battered women who use violence employ it primarily in the interest of self-defense (Saunders, 1986) and rarely cause injury when they resort to violence in intimate relationships (Dobash, Dobash, Wilson, & Daly, 1992; Stets & Straus, 1990; Zlotnick, Cohn, Peterson, & Pearlstein, 1998). Moreover, the use of fatal violence is resorted to as a desperate self-defense measure by women (Wilson & Daly, 1992).

In their national survey of more than 6,000 American families, Straus and Gelles (1990) found that of the men who were physically violent toward their partners, 23 percent perpetrated physical abuse and female victims of violence were sometimes the perpetrators of child abuse, and were twice as likely to physically abuse their children than women who were not abused. There is evidence that men who are violent within the home are also violent outside of it and that multiple factors such as peer influence, unemployment, poverty, gun ownership, alcohol, media violence, personality characteristics, and biological factors make contributions to ongoing violence in society. The American Psychological Association's Presidential Task Force on Violence and the Family found that the highest risk factor for being harmed in the family is to be female (American Psychological Association, 1996). The co-occurrence of child maltreatment and domestic violence remains a significant social and psychological issue.

Research on domestic violence began in the 1970's in America and academic courses emerged in the 1980's. The term domestic violence referred to riots and terrorism until the late 1970's (Tierney, 1982) and eventually referred to violence between partners. The mid-80's saw the development of several journals dedicated exclusively to the issues of family and intimate violence, e.g., *The Journal of Family*

Violence, Journal of Child Maltreatment, and *The Journal of Interpersonal Violence*. Interpartner violence and violence against children have been social conditions long before they were considered to be social or legal problems. The 1990's have continued the research expansion into dating violence, abuse among cohabiting partners, interpartner violence among same gender couples, discerning types of violence within intimate relationships, and typologies of batterers (Johnson & Ferraro, 2000). Renzetti (1992) researched violence within lesbian relationships and concluded that power, control, and emotional abuse were contributing issues to the violence. Island and Letellier (1991) estimated that a half million gay men are battered annually. Rates of gay and lesbian partner abuse have been estimated as comparable to that of heterosexual couples (Leeder, 1994; Nisonoff & Bittman, 1979). Random sample studies are needed to estimate current prevalence rates as well as unique differential characteristics. Clearly empirical study is needed to understand the dynamics of family violence across race, class, and sexual orientation.

Constructs of family violence vary, with broad and limiting definitions. One definition conceptualized family violence along two separate continuums: the legitimate-illegitimate continuum represents the degree to which social norms legitimize violence; the instrumental-expressive continuum represents the degree to which violence is used as a means to an end "to induce another person to carry out or refrain from an act" (Gelles & Straus, 1979, p.557) or as an end in itself, e.g., hitting someone out of anger. These two continuums result in a four-cell taxonomy of family violence: 1) legitimate-expressive includes violence as catharsis, reflected in perceptions that spanking children as an external act is preferred over containing one's anger internally; 2) legitimate-instrumental involves the most common type of family violence, including but not limited to, physical punishments of children; 3) illegitimate-expressive acts entail behavior that is widely recognized and publicized as family violence such as child abuse, partner abuse, and murder; and 4) illegitimate-instrumental comprises punishment that society conceptualizes as abuse but that caretakers claim is for a "child's own good" (Gelles & Straus, 1979).

Crenshaw (1992) postulated family violence was one form of social control and oppression, and recommends an analytic perspective from the lens of race, class, gender, and sexual orientation. The social stressors of racism, class stratification, gender inequality, and sexual orientation that exist in American society all contribute and compound the impact of family violence. Given the interplay of these constructs, termed *intersectionality*, family violence is best interpreted from the intersections of sociological, political, economic, and psychological dimensions, moving beyond the tendency to solely assess intrapsychic, interpersonal, or intrafamilial dynamics.

Empirical studies also address the dimensionality of partner violence including sociopolitical aspects of race, gender, economic class, and sexual orientation (Bograd, 1999). "Battery is often precipitated by women's noncompliance with gender requirements" (MacKinnon, 1989, p.178). Dominance, control, and submission become the operational variables regardless of gender, race, or sexual orientation.

Almeida, Woods, Messineo, and Font (1998) encourage therapists to start the analysis and treatment of partner violence at the sociopolitical level and move towards the interior realm of the family including the intrapsychic aspects. Alternatively, holding a both/and position (Goldner, 1992) can be illuminating in cases of marginalized populations including African American, Hispanic American, Asian American, Native American, and gay and lesbian families and partnerships. All individuals impacted by violence deserve benefits gained from ongoing expansive research, acknowledgment, safety, social support, intervention, and preventive measures specific to their socio-cultural contexts.

Limiting family violence to physical aggression also fails to capture the true range of harmful family interactions. For example, child neglect, emotional maltreatment, stalking, and psychological torment can be extremely devastating. Defining and assessing family violence and its impact remains an ongoing controversial area of inquiry. The encompassing construct of family violence includes physical child abuse, child sexual abuse, child neglect, psychological maltreatment, witnessing or being exposed to partner violence, marital violence, marital rape, partner abuse, and elder abuse. Domestic violence is generally defined as physical, sexual, or psychological abuse that occurs between two adult partners in an intimate relationship regardless of sexual orientation.

Conceptions and Misconceptions of Family Violence

A major function of commonly held myths or misconceptions is to reduce fears of personal vulnerability by implying that these kinds of events happen only to others. Myths provide simplistic explanations of complex social issues, although they often contain an element of truth as well. The following are commonly held misconceptions.

The first misconception is that family violence rarely occurs. Family violence is hidden and secretive thus it is difficult to estimate the incidence. However, this should not be interpreted as family violence rarely occurs. In regards to spouse abuse (Straus & Gelles, 1986), 28% of American couples experience at least one act of violence during their marriages, 16% experience at least one act of violence a year, and 6% experience severe violence in any given year. The Child Abuse Incidence Study regularly indicates over three million children experience some form of maltreatment in any given year.

Another misconception about family violence is that it is solely an economic problem and relates to the context of poverty. Studies show economic conditions play a role in violence, in that families living at or below the poverty line had a marital violence rate higher than that of families above the poverty line (Straus & Gelles, 1990). However, the reports of family violence coming to the attention of law enforcement, community agencies, and social service workers are often from the economically disadvantaged. People who are poor and lack other resources may turn to police and other social service agencies more frequently than people who have financial resources.

Misconceptions about the generational cycle of violence abound. Intergenerational patterns of abuse are not complete explanations for family violence. Childhood abuse is neither a necessary nor sufficient cause of adult violence. At best, the data suggest that children who were abused or witnessed abuse or violence, are more likely to be abusive adults. Friedrich (1990) has proposed multigenerational transmission of fear and unresolved trauma as risk factors for abuse. However, the majority of abused children do not grow up to be abusive adults. Social learning theory does hypothesize that aggressive and violent behaviors are learned by children from adults who model violence within the family (Patterson, Reid, & Dishion, 1992).

Child rearing practices and childhood aggressive behavior have been studied by researchers interested in identifying the correlations between the two. Socio-economic explorations and attachment theory allow for hypothesizing about the parent-child relationship in terms of the presence or absence of nurturing behaviors. When parents have few resources and are socially isolated they experience higher levels of stress which can reduce their ability to deal effectively with a child's needs for nurturance (McLeod & Shanahan, 1993). Bronfenner (1986) and McLoyd (1990; 1998) proposed that poverty increases parental distress and diminishes their capacity to be supportive and consistent toward children. The insecurely attached child may develop a personal sense of unworthiness and perceptions of the world as uncaring. The anger and distrust that result from this experience is hypothesized as the groundwork for aggressive interactions with peers and adults (Cicchetti & Toth, 1995).

Data were analyzed in a longitudinal study of abused and nonabused children to determine if developmental differences were associated with children who experienced severe discipline (Herrenkohl & Russo, 2001). Severe discipline was categorized as burning or hitting (to the degree of creating bruising), but spanking was categorized as nonabusive. Children were divided into groups of preschool age, or sixteen months up to the age of 6, and school age, between the ages of 6-11. The study identified three risk factors for the development of childhood aggression: low family socio-economic status, severe physical discipline, and negative parent-child interaction. The negative interactions were a factor in the early preschool years diminishing as children developed. However severe physical discipline increased for children who were classified as high aggression and school age. Herrenkohl and Russo (2001) hypothesized that these school age children, who were responding with anger and aggression to a lack of nurturance, were beginning to explore their environments and were harshly and physically disciplined by parents in their attempts to control them.

Many criticisms exist blaming women for not leaving violent men. Implicit in this assumption lies the inference that something must be psychologically wrong with battered women, that they somehow deserve the violence directed at them, or that they are responsible for their victimization (Berns, 2001). Research does not bear this out. In fact battered women do not come from substantially more abusive homes than those of nonbattered women (Hotaling & Sugarman, 1990), and they are no more alcoholic than nonbattered women, although it has been reported that they may drink in response to abusive episodes (Barnett & Fagan, 1993).

The cycle of violence further explains the complex interpersonal dynamics within battering relationships and the difficulty in separating from the relationship. Walker (1984) hypothesized three distinct phases within the cycle of violence: tension building; an acute episode; followed by the loving respite phase. During the acute episode the expression of violence occurs. Shortly after the battering, a period of contrition and relief may arise, where the relative absence of tension and violence is accompanied by intimate engagement, loving behaviors, and a sense of hope within the relationship. Unfortunately the cycle repeats, the periods of loving respite become shorter in duration, and aggressivity increases.

Moreover, the literature indicates that women are at risk for being killed during their preparation to leave or soon after the successful move (Browne, 1987; Walker, 1989b). Stalking behavior is common among batterers (Browne & Williams, 1989; Dutton, 1995) and is a risk factor for violence and lethality (Walker & Meloy, 1998). Significant lethality factors associated with the escalation of intimate partner violence have been identified: escalating frequency and severity of violence, threats to abuse or kill children, sexual abuse, marital rape, alcohol or drug abuse (Browne, 1987), suicide threats or attempts, presence of weapons, psychiatric impairment, past criminal history, current life stresses, and the presence of a new relationship for either partner (Walker & Meloy, 1998).

Alcohol and Substance Abuse

The abuse of alcohol and other substances has been recognized as a serious social problem in the United States with repercussions within the family and community. When alcohol and drugs are used for self-medication or as coping mechanisms for abusive or oppressive conditions, complex problems may result including addiction. The use of substances may serve a variety of purposes including the avoidance of unbearable emotional feelings and memories or the disinhibition of behavior in cases of intimate partner violence or incest.

A misconception about family violence is centered around alcoholism or drug abuse as the causal factor. Alcohol is implicated in many crimes including one out of four instances of spousal battery. Intoxication may serve as a justification or explanation for the abuse, allowing couples to maintain the belief that their partnership is healthy. Research does indicate that persons who drink are likely to hit each other and to hit their children (Steinmetz, 1987) but the vast majority of individuals who drink do not batter their partners (Kantor & Straus, 1990).

Since alcohol is a significant factor in many acts of interpersonal violence and alcoholism, substance abuse, and other addictions negatively impact family dynamics (Jacob & Johnson, 1997), this is an important assessment when working with couples, families, and abuse survivors. Conversely, addiction treatment programs should assess issues of sexual, physical, emotional, and domestic violence (Beckman, 1994; Finkelstein, 1994). The following excerpt, *Children of Alcoholics: Important Facts*, has been reprinted courtesy of the National Association for Children of Alcoholics (NaCoA, 1998).

Children of Alcoholics: Important Facts

The National Association for Children of Alcoholics believes that no child of an alcoholic should grow up in isolation and without support.

Based on clinical observations and preliminary research, a relationship between parental alcoholism and child abuse is indicated in a large proportion of child abuse cases. A significant number of children in this country are being raised by addicted parents. With more than one million children confirmed each year as victims of child abuse and neglect by state child protective service agencies, state welfare records have indicated that substance abuse is one of the top two problems exhibited by families in 81% of the reported cases. Studies suggest an increased prevalence of alcoholism among parents who abuse children. Existing research suggests alcoholism is more strongly related to child abuse than are other disorders, such as parental depression. Although several studies report very high rates of alcoholism among parents of incest victims, much additional research is needed in this area (Bavolek & Henderson, 1990; Famularo, Stone, Barnum, & Wharton, 1986; Russell, Henderson, & Blume, 1985).

Children of alcoholics exhibit symptoms of depression and anxiety more than children of non-alcoholics. In general, COAs appear to have lower self-esteem than non-COAs in childhood, adolescence, and young adulthood. Children of alcoholics exhibit elevated rates of psychopathology. Anxiety, depression, and externalizing behavior disorders are more common among COAs than among children of non-alcoholics. Young COAs often show symptoms of depression and anxiety such as crying, bed wetting, not having friends, being afraid to go to school, or having nightmares. Older youth may stay in their rooms for long periods of time and not relate to other children claiming they "have no one to talk to." Teens may show depressive symptoms by being perfectionistic in their endeavors, hoarding, staying by themselves, and being excessively self-conscious. Teenage COAs may begin to develop phobias (Ellis, Zucker, & Fitzgerald, 1997; Johnson & Rolf, 1988).

Children of alcoholics often have difficulties in school. COAs often believe that they will be failures even if they do well academically. They often do not view themselves as successful. Children of alcoholics are more likely to be raised by parents with poorer cognitive abilities and in an environment lacking stimulation. A lack of simulation in the reading environment may account in part for the pattern of failure found in COAs compared with non-COAs. COAs are more likely to be truant, drop out of school, repeat grades, or be referred to a school counselor, or psychologist. This may have little to do with academic ability; rather, COAs may have difficulty bonding with teachers, other students and school; they may experience anxiety related to performance; or they may be afraid of failure. The actual reasons have yet to be determined. There is an increasing body of scientific evidence indicating that risk for later problems, and even alcoholic outcomes is detectable early in the life course and, in some instances, before school entry (Caspi, Moffitt, Newman, & Sylvia, 1996; Johnson & Rolf, 1988).

Children of alcoholics may benefit from adult efforts which help them to: develop autonomy and independence; develop a strong social orientation and social skills; engage in acts of "required helpfulness;" develop a close bond with a care-giver; cope successfully with emotionally hazardous experiences; perceive their experiences constructively, even if those experiences cause pain or suffering, and gain, early in life, other people's positive attention; develop day-to-day coping strategies (Werner, 1984).

Maternal alcohol consumption during any time of pregnancy can cause alcohol related birth defects or alcohol related neurological deficits. The rate of drinking during pregnancy appears to be increasing. Prenatal alcohol effects have been detected at moderate levels of alcohol consumption by non-alcoholic women. Even though a mother is not an alcoholic, her child may not be spared the effects of prenatal alcohol exposure. Cognitive performance is less affected by alcohol exposure in infants and children whose mothers stopped drinking in early pregnancy, despite the mothers' resumption of alcohol use after giving birth. One analysis of 6 year olds, with demonstrated effects of second trimester alcohol exposure, had lower academic achievement and problems with reading, spelling, and mathematical skills. Approximately 6 percent of the offspring of alcoholic women have Fetal Alcohol Syndrome (FAS); the FAS risk of offspring born after an FAS sibling, is as high as 70 percent. Those diagnosed as having Fetal Alcohol Syndrome had IQ scores ranging from 20-105 with a mean of 68. Subjects also demonstrated poor concentration and attention. People with FAS demonstrate growth deficits, morphologic abnormalities, mental retardation, and behavioral difficulties. Secondary effects of FAS among adolescents and adults include mental health problems, disrupted schooling (dropping out or being suspended or expelled), trouble with the law, dependent living as an adult, and problems with employment (Gabrielli & Mednic, 1983; Jacobson, 1997; Larkby & Day, 1997). (NaCoA, 1998).

Violence to Animals—The Link

Violent behavior toward animals is generally unacceptable in our culture and has been isolated as a social problem requiring attention, intervention, and prosecution. The oppression and cruelty expressed to animals may also be symptomatic of a much wider problem situated within socially constructed systems of domination. My intention is to validate the suffering experienced by these sentient beings and to expand our perception to the intersecting forms of violence in the domains of domestic violence, child abuse, and animal cruelty.

Cruelty to animals is repeatedly found in homes with domestic violence (DeViney, Dickert, & Lockwood, 1983; McKay, 1994; Sigler, 1989) but is rarely assessed in empirical studies on child abuse. In an examination of the literature pertaining to the intergenerational transmission of violence, violence toward animals was not mentioned (Widom, 1989) and studies on aggression and coercive family strategies did not include the treatment of companion animals (Patterson, Reid, & Dishion, 1992). However, Milner's *Child Abuse Potential Inventory* (1994) does include one item out of 160 on companion animals, another study examined adolescents' perceptions of child abuse and pet abuse (Roscoe, Haney, & Peterson, 1986), and a third study (Raupp, Barlow, & Oliver, 1998) examined the potential for animal cruelty as a component of family violence.

Given the unique and loving connections often made between children and animals, animal cruelty can lead to profound emotional consequences for the children. Children who witness abuse and terrorizing of companion animals, threatened abuse, or the actual killing or mutilation of pets at the hands of their perpetrators may empathically suffer with the animal, endure suffering from their helplessness and inability to protect the pet, experience the abuse as intimately directed toward them, or may be at risk for repeating the abuse they experienced (Felthous, 1980; Kellert & Felthous, 1985).

Animals have been harmed in retaliation against intimate partners and the reluctance to leave a battering spouse has been linked to a concern for the welfare of animals left behind in the home. For this reason, many jurisdictions have developed programs connected with domestic violence shelters that enlist volunteers or local animal shelters to provide safe refuge for the family pets. Animals may be viewed as objects or property by some individuals or as companions that are sentient beings (Hirschman, 1994) by others. Those who provide companionship may be transitional objects for young children as they develop caring relationships. The loss of a pet can elicit a powerful mourning process similar to the bereavement experience in losing a family member (Carmack, 1985). When pets are experienced as part of the self, witnessing their abuse, mutilation, or death may be extremely distressing and stimulate a sense of great vulnerability.

> **Animal Cruelty, Family Violence, and Child Abuse**
> Children witness abuse and terrorizing; Threatened abuse of animals is used as a weapon; Animals used in retaliation against intimate partners resulting in killing or mutilation of pets; Some children are at risk for repeating the abuse while others become protective of the animals.

Quinlisk (1999) surveyed shelters to investigate the connection between domestic violence, child abuse, and animal cruelty. The majority of families indicated the presence of pets within the home. Based on the 72 families who participated in the survey, over two-thirds reported animal cruelty within the home with 68% reporting explicit violence toward the pets. However, of the 18% who reported no animal abuse, coercive threats to kill the animals or release them away were made by the batterers in several cases. The types of abuse included kicking, hitting or punching, torture, mutilation, beheading, and killing. Her study revealed over half the children who had witnessed the violence later engaged in similar behaviors. Conversely a number of children became highly protective toward animals.

In an unrelated survey of 23 families Quinlisk (1999) found 72% of the homes reported animal abuse involving kicking, mutilation, killing, and sexual abuse. Additionally she cited numerous case studies including a father who had beaten his cow to death and threatened to do the same to his family, and a mother who was forced to hold down puppies while her husband sexually assaulted them. This woman later shot and killed her husband.

Integrating assessment questions regarding the presence of animals within the home has been recommended by researchers within the field (Arkow, 1996). Inquiring about their presence, concerns about their welfare, whether anyone has threatened to harm or harmed an animal in the past, and asking about witnessing animal cruelty is suggested (Ascione, 1998). Boat (1999) also recommends asking about any prior pets and their treatment.

Ascione (1990) defines cruel treatment to animals as "socially unaccept-able behavior that intentionally causes unnecessary pain, suffering, or distress to and/or death of an animal" (p.228). Rowan (1999) adds to this definition indicat-ing that animal cruelty involves an intention to harm and the abuser derives satis-faction from the act of inflicting suffering or pain. Rowan distinguishes cruelty from abuse, which he states is motivated by power and control where satisfaction is derived from dominating the animal.

Exhibiting cruelty to animals is a strong signal in a child's life and evidence continues to mount correlating the abusive behaviors with violence expressed toward other humans and non-human animals (Lockwood & Ascione, 1997). Expressing this kind of behavior is a warning sign that has gone unheeded by society for many years. Studies of violent adult criminals and psychiatric patients have reported significant rates of severe animal abuse in childhood (Felthous, 1980; Kellert & Felthous, 1985) and scores of anecdotal reports citing explicit histories of animal cruelty and torture among serial and mass murderers have been offered. Lockwood and Hodge (1986) cautioned that young murderers may initially practice their behaviors on animals prior to killing human beings. More empirical studies on the link between animal cruelty and later violent behavior will help frame prevention and interven-tion programs.

Multidisciplinary intervention programs and interagency collaboration is the suggested mode of responding to cases of animal cruelty and family violence. The combined involvement of veterinarians, physicians, domestic violence shelters, animal shelters, animal control officers, mental health practitioners, child protective service workers, law enforcement officers, and animal welfare groups may be needed to begin the process of animal cruelty identification, risk assessment, inter-vention, and prevention. *Psychologists for the Ethical Treatment of Animals* is a non-profit organization working towards changing the way non-human animals are treated. They have developed an innovative counseling program for those who abuse animals and provide training materials for professionals.

Legislative efforts focused on updating the laws also prove promising. For example, some have argued that sexual abuse of animals should be reclassified as "interspecies sexual assault" because of the similarities to sexual abuse of children (Beirne, 1997). Legislative action has already changed responses to domestic vio-lence in Utah where witnessing violence of pets is considered a serious offense (Ascione, 1999). Recommended interventions range from teaching high risk chil-dren non-violent behaviors and alternatives to aggressive impulsivity to providing individual and family treatments for children who participate in cruelty to animals (Arkow, 1999).

Concluding Remarks

The co-occurrence of partner violence, child abuse, and animal cruelty is a significant societal problem. Domestic partnership violence may take the form of emotional and verbal abuse or escalate into ongoing episodes of physical battering

PART IV

Ariadne's Thread

Interventions

and include threats of violence or sadistic cruelty to animals. Children may not only witness these events which result in severe psychological consequences, but may be the targets of the violence. The significant link between violent behavior and cruelty to animals is an important component in providing services to children who have witnessed or participated in acts of cruelty. Mobilization of services to identify, assess and intervene in the cycle of violence will prevent further abuse and begin to establish roads to recovery and compassion.

Chapter 10

Crisis Interventions

The world offers itself to your imagination.
Mary Oliver, 1992

Ariadne's thread provides us with abundant symbolism associating the mythological story of finding one's way out of the dark and intricate labyrinth with another person's compassionate assistance. The thread contributes a clue out of the current situation connecting one's inner light with an external source. Interventions in child abuse cases range from creating a safe environment, providing crisis intervention, following through on mandated reporting requirements, to providing short and longer term psychotherapy. This section addresses preliminary crisis interventions including suicide intervention, defusings, and critical incident stress debriefing.

Crisis As Opportunity

Two Chinese characters for the term crisis indicate both danger and opportunity. This complex symbolism reflects great potentialities for healing and transformation. Resolution of a crisis leads to an integration of new behaviors, meanings, and identity.

The domain of psychological emergencies is categorized as medical and psychiatric. An emergency, the term derived from the concept of *urgenza* from the Italian literature, is perceived as an acute or intense situation, coupled with a serious or high level of danger, requiring immediate treatment or response. Examples are risk of suicide, risk of physical harm to others, states of seriously impaired judgment in which an individual is endangered-delirium, dementia, acute psychotic episode, severe dissociative state-and situations of risk to a highly vulnerable or defenseless person-abused child, dependent adult, or elder adult.

A psychological crisis, on the other hand, is a disruption of an individual's usual or *baseline* level of functioning, such that the usual coping responses prove inadequate. A crisis is often viewed as a loss of psychological equilibrium, the intrapersonal homeostasis is disrupted and the usual coping strategies become insufficient. Maladaptive coping responses may also be used. This distinction doesn't necessarily imply danger of serious physical harm or life-threatening danger, as in an emergency. Since many crises do involve psychological emergencies, it is important to distinguish between the two in the assessment process, and follow through with the appropriate level of intervention.

Crises involve substantial challenges to one's level of meaning in life, coping strategies, and support strategies (Aguilera, 1994). The nature of the subjective meaning that is drawn from an event will impact the potential development of the crisis. The lack of a support system can cause a moderately stressful event to plunge an individual into crisis. Crises can range from family issues and transitions such as divorce, acts of abuse or violence, alcohol intoxication, attempted suicide, and death, to adjustment to psychotropic medications as well as the development of neurological disorders stemming from head injuries or progressively deteriorating diseases such as Alzheimer's.

Crises call on the therapist to respond compassionately. One needs to assess the circumstances and implement suitable intervention strategies directed toward the patient's safety, although this may include the safety of others also. Responding to crises involves a reliance on the foundations of legal, ethical, medical, community resource, and clinical knowledge.

Crises may be situational or maturational. Situational crises involve unexpected events that are usually beyond the person's control, such as child abuse, natural disaster, sudden death of a loved one. Maturational crises occur during times of transition, for example when a child reaches adolescence, when a parent retires, and during other transitional periods, such as *mid-life* which Jung has addressed so eloquently.

Crisis Intervention Strategy

Approaching a crisis from the perspective of assessment, problem solving or treatment, planning, and termination frames the short-term nature of the work. Establishing rapport or a trusting connection is an important first step. A variety of methods can be used, including the expression of empathy, acknowledging and normalizing feelings, and supportively sharing one's own emotional response to the person or family in crisis. Next, one begins the assessment phase, where an exploration of the current problem or incident begins. Discussing the precipitant event through the use of open-ended questions yields substantial information including the individual's or family's prior level of functioning, coping methods, and identified strengths. Bringing in other sources of support that the family or individual desires is also helpful. Goals of crisis intervention are to assist in the alleviation of symptoms and prevent any psychological deterioration, thus allowing a return to a previous level of functioning, known as pre-morbid adaptive functioning. The planning phase can help the individual or family identify a specific issue to address one step at a time. Professional support can be provided in follow-up sessions and referrals for more intensive work can be given.

Crisis Intervention Strategies

Assess safety and focus on the welfare of the child
Maintain an unbiased attitude
Clarify precipitating events
Provide instrumental assistance and information
Convey concern and willingness to help

Safety is the primary consideration in crises. Assess the current safety of the child and the other children in the home. Maintain an unbiased attitude, avoiding words, gestures, and facial expressions that express or suggest shock and disapproval. If you have the opportunity, clarify precipitating events to this crisis. Focus on the welfare of the child and the parents. Use open-ended questions, such as "How did this occur?" rather than "Did you do this to the child?" Depending on the circumstances, a physician referral may be considered for a physical examination to assess for physical damage caused by abuse and to receive treatment if necessary. Avoid condoning the parents' or caretakers' behaviors. Use statements such as "I understand you were very angry" rather than "Anyone would have felt the same way in that situation." Provide information about the reporting process, the role of child protective services, and the courts. Attempt to reduce shame in the victim by emphasizing that it was good to come forward and make the disclosure.

Assist the victim and family members to clarify their thoughts and feelings through the process of stating responses and labeling feelings. Provide emotional support through encouragement and empathic listening. Convey concern and willingness to help alleviate stress. It is important to keep in mind that children may regress emotionally during times of stress or crisis, so it may be helpful to have a parent, friend, or trusted peer in close proximity.

Assist the family to mobilize their support network. Helpful referrals and adjunctive services include self-help groups, such as Parents Anonymous, Parents United, Adults Molested as Children United, Daughters and Sons United, hotlines, day care. Referrals are noted later in Chapter 12. Some social services programs such as in-home care may reduce environmental stressors that interfere with effective parenting.

If the issue is related to a deficit in parenting, identify strategies to address the difficulties or deficits such as training in parenting skills, or refer to educational programs such as anger management, Parent Effectiveness Training, Systematic Training for Effective parenting. Structured programs often focus on education, child development, and the acquisition of cognitive behavioral strategies in dealing with parenting issues. The integration of new problem solving methods in addition to relaxation training may be helpful.

Suicidal Ideation

Responding to a patient's potential for suicide can be one of the more troubling and intimidating tasks faced by clinicians. A sensitive and comprehensive response is called for. Suicide occurs more frequently than homicide and continues to be a leading cause of death in America (Centers for Disease Control, 1997). Suicide also emerges as one of the leading causes of death for adolescents 10-19 years of age (Borowsky, Ireland, & Resnick, 2001). Becoming familiar with the risk factors is necessary for all clinicians. These risk factors include previous attempts, substance use, impulsivity, presence of lethal means, accessibility to firearms, hopelessness, depressive symptoms, psychopathology, financial hardship, physical illness, and lack of social support.

The potential loss of a patient can evoke immense concerns for the patient and patient's family in addition to serious concerns about the therapist's level of competence or continuation within the profession (Chemtob, Hamada, Bauer, Torigoe, & Kinney, 1988). Comprehensive clinical training in suicide prevention and risk management can provide adequate knowledge and experience to address these crises.

Suicide prevention approaches include action based methods (Bongar, 1992), systematic approaches to assess depression, suicide ideation, suicide plan, self-control, and suicide intent during intake interviews with suicidal patients (Sommers-Flanagan & Sommers-Flanagan, 1995), and integrated models combining affective and action-based interventions (Rosenberg, 1999). Additionally, *Dialectical Behavior Therapy* (Linehan, 1993) can be used as a treatment protocol to treat individuals with self harming tendencies and suicidal behavior who meet the criteria of borderline personality disorder. This approach synthesizes cognitive behavioral, feminist, and Zen theories with an emphasis on dialectics, the holding of simultaneous conflicting perspectives.

Suicidality is measured through a comprehensive clinical interview, review of ancillary information from previous outpatient and inpatient records, and psychological testing or use of assessment instruments such as questionnaires (Maris, Berman, Maltsberger, & Yufit, 1992). Beginning with a thorough clinical interview, suicidal risk can be measured on a continuum from mild, moderate, to severe. When suicidal ideation is present, a number of aspects can be systematically evaluated: the intent and motivation to die, precipitating factors, details of the plan, and the means being considered. Inquiries can be made of the suicidal thoughts, feelings, and the frequency, intensity, and duration of these.

The intent of suicide is a risk factor to consider. Having patients rate their intent from 0 to 10 can provide a sense of the imminence. "Intent can be rated as absent, low, moderate, or high" (Sommers-Flannagan & Sommers-Flannagan, 1995, p.45). When a plan has been made, the specific details, methods, and time frame being considered will be important. Inquiring about the means of suicide reveals the depth of contemplation the patient has given and provides more clues to the overall risk of suicide. If the patient considers a weapon, rope, or taking an overdose it is essential to know the accessibility of these.

Suicide Risk Factors

Hopelessess	Intent
Physical Illness	Substance Use
Accessibility to Firearms	Lack of Social Support
Depressive Symptoms	Financial Hardship
Previous Attempts	Lethal Means
Psychopathology	Impulsivity

Higher rates of completed suicide are correlated with intent and more lethal methods, including firearms, strangulation, and overdose. These are considered significant risk factors (Centers for Disease Control, 1997). The availability of firearms is correlated with suicide among children, e.g., Zwillich (1998) reported that guns figured in the suicides of 53% of children aged 1-14 years and 61% of children aged 15-18.

A history of previously attempted suicide is a significant risk factor (Olin & Keatinge, 1998) for suicide. Almost 80 percent of completed suicides were preceded by a prior attempt in a study by Schneidman (1975). Borowsky, Ireland, and Resnick (2001) found previous attempts to be the most important correlate in their longitudinal study of adolescents. Gay or lesbian orientation also emerged as a risk factor among 10-19 year olds, that cross cut gender and racial/ethnic groups.

Additional risk factors include the patient's sense of hopelessness, depressed mood, cognitive distortions, impaired thinking, impulsivity, intoxication, and judgment capacity. During times of depression, suicide risk increases when the mood shifts and the individual becomes anxious, agitated, or angry, indicating potential energy and increased motivation to carry out the suicide. Physical illness is also a contributing factor to risk, as is a history of psychiatric inpatient hospitalization (Olin & Keatinge, 1998; Pope & Vasquez, 1998).

Protective factors or deterrents to suicide are equally important to consider when a patient is contemplating suicide. Significant deterrents involve the presence of support systems and the patient's willingness and capacity to seek these out. The presence of parent-family connectiveness was found to be an important protective factor for adolescents in Borowsky, Ireland, and Resnick's studies (2001). Threats to family cohesion may emerge during times of involvement in the legal system, disclosure of child abuse, and domestic violence incidents. Continued employment, financial resources, religious values, and spiritual beliefs also function as deterrents to suicide.

Protective Factors and Deterrents To Suicide

Presence of support systems
Willingness to access support
Religious values
Spiritual beliefs
Continued employment
Financial resources

When a patient is imminently suicidal, providing safety and structure is essential. Safety measures may include the consideration of voluntary or involuntary hospitalization. When suicidal ideation is present but the risk is low, support systems can be mobilized, psychiatric or physician referrals can be made, and a number of clinical management measures can be taken. Noting the protective or life enhancing aspects of the patient's self such as the desire for help and a desire to live has been indicated as a helpful response (Rosenberg, 1999), as is working toward the elimination of the chosen means. Intensifying treatment by increasing the frequency of sessions, establishing a no-suicide contract, providing emergency or crisis line numbers, and addressing the underlying thoughts and feelings of suicide (Schneidman, 1992) such as emotional pain, despair, and hopelessness experienced by the patient (Rosenberg, 1999) are supportive measures. Longer range goals may center around the continued resolution of ongoing issues including the consequences of abuse, substance abuse, and depression.

Defusing

Defusings were developed as interventions to use immediately after traumatic events (Mitchell & Everly, 1996). A defusing is a small group process initiated after any traumatic event or critical incident powerful enough to overwhelm the coping mechanisms of the persons exposed to it. The timing of this response differentiates it from a critical incident stress debriefing. It usually occurs as early as possible after the event, immediately if possible. The focus of the defusing is on small groups of people that usually work together, for example after a hostage crisis at a high school, one defusing may be engaged in with teachers, one with counselors, another with students in each respective classroom.

There are generally four goals to a defusing: moving toward a reduction of the intense reaction to the traumatic event; normalizing the experience so that everyone can return back to their work or duties; re-establishment of the social network; and assessment of the individuals involved to determine if a full critical incident stress debriefing is necessary.

Critical Incident Stress Debriefing

A critical incident is defined as any event with enough impact to produce significant emotional reactions in people immediately or at a later time. This is an event considered extremely unusual in the range of ordinary human experiences. The incident may be the foundation of the diagnosis of posttraumatic stress disorder if not resolved effectively in a timely manner.

A critical incident stress debriefing is a group process employing methods of crisis intervention and educational processes, aimed at mitigating or resolving the psychological distress emerging from a critical incident or traumatic event (Mitchell & Everly, 1996). This type of group intervention can provide psychoeducation and reassurance about the range of normal expected reactions to serious traumatic situations. It also gives clinicians the opportunity to suggest ways of coping with secondary stresses, traumatic reminders, and losses. As originally designed, a debriefing may take from two to three hours without a break, with one or two facilitators. The optimal time frame for a debriefing is from 24 to 72 hours after the critical incident. Debriefings are best held in functional workgroups also.

A primary goal of debriefing is to mitigate or alleviate the impact of the critical incident on those who were directly traumatized by the event. Debriefings are also appropriate for secondary victims, such as emergency services personnel who witnessed or managed the traumatic event, or tertiary victims, family and friends who may learn about the event from the primary victims.

A second goal is to accelerate the recovery processes in people who are experiencing normal stress reactions to these abnormal traumatic events. Additional objectives are to educate about the range of stressors, stress reactions, and provide information on methods of survival, allowing for an opportunity for emotional expression or ventilation. Mitchell and Everly (1996) reported participants benefit from reassurances that the stress responses are controllable and that recovery is likely. It is also helpful to foreshadow signs and symptoms which may emerge in the near future. A debriefing establishes a positive contact with mental health professionals, screens for people who need additional assessment or therapy, and provides referrals for counseling or other services.

Critical incident stress debriefing interventions have seven phases: introduction, fact, thought, reaction, symptoms, teaching, and re-entry. A brief summary of each phase is included. The introduction phase centers around introducing the facilitators, process, setting ground rules and expectations such as safety and confidentiality. The facilitators introduce themselves as the debriefing team and describe their intent, to work toward alleviating the impact of the traumatic event. Participants are asked to stay in the debriefing room. No cameras or recorders are permitted and the process is described as differing from psychotherapy and that the aim is to discuss the event in the presence of their peers. The step by step debriefing process is described, and the debriefers ask the participants to state who they are, what their role in the incident was, and what happened from their perspective. Each person is provided an opportunity to share.

The next step is the fact phase. Of all the elements of a critical incident, facts are often easier to initially discuss than attempting to talk about how one feels. The debriefing team asks questions about the participant roles or jobs during the incident and the events from their point of view. Emotions are not elaborated upon in this phase, but if emotions are expressed, they are acknowledged by the facilitators and the group is reassured that emotion is expected. The pacing is important so as not to emotionally overwhelm the participants in the early phase.

The thought phase follows the fact phase. This phase begins with the facilitators asking the participants to state what their first or most prominent thought was once they were not longer functioning in an automatic mode. The thought phase serves as a transitional phase between the factual and emotional, between the cognitive and affective domain. The next phase is the reaction phase, often the most emotionally powerful of the seven phases. The stimulating or trigger question centers on the worst thing about the incident for each individual. For example "What was the worst thing about this event for you personally," "What part of the event bothers you most," or "What elements of the situation cause you the most pain?"

The lengthy reaction phase is followed by the symptom phase, which moves the group back from the emotionally laden material into the cognitively oriented material. Participants are asked to describe any cognitive, physical, emotional or behavioral experiences they may have encountered while they were working at the scene of the incident (e.g., trembling hands, inability to make a decision, excessive silence or feelings of anger). Then the group talks about the various ways in which they experienced symptoms of distress while working at the scene.

After the symptoms phase, the group moves into the teaching phase, which naturally begins with a review or summary of the symptoms. The symptoms are normalized and described as commonly expected after the type of critical incident they experienced. This phase is cognitively designed in order to move the participants further away from the emotional intensity of the reaction phase. To close this phase, facilitators may ask what may given the participants some hope in the midst of their pain, or if there was something during the incident that made it less chaotic or painful.

The last phase of re-entry is an opportunity to clarify issues, answer questions, make summary statements and return the group to their normal functions. This phase brings closure to the discussions which have occurred during the debriefing. The debriefing team answers questions, reassures and informs as needed, states any feelings which are suspected to be present but were not mentioned, provides appropriate handouts, makes summary comments.

While crisis interventions address initial responses to overwhelming life experiences, longer term treatment may be necessary for resolution of underlying issues of childhood abuse. The following chapters suggest additional intervention methods.

◈ Chapter 11

Treatment as
Care of the Soul

In the world of psyche, it is your *work*, rather than your
theoretical ideas, that builds consciousness.

Robert Johnson, 1986

Much of the work described in this section on tending soul focuses on the
work of individuation as a way of enhancing community in the sense
that each individual "presupposes a collective relationship, the process
of individuation does not lead to isolation, but to an intenser and more universal
collective solidarity" (Jung, 1953, p.152). The individuation process is embedded
within the culture and may easily clash against collective norms when societal
adaptation is unwarranted, inappropriate, or oppressive. Psychological work is not
separate but situated within the collective culture, affecting the culture as well as
the individual. Psychotherapeutic treatment becomes a collaborative adventure with
immense potentialities for cultural transformation.

Please Call Me By My True Names

Do not say that I'll depart tomorrow
because even today I still arrive.
Look deeply: I arrive in every second
to be a bud on a spring branch,
to be a tiny bird, with wings still fragile,
learning to sing in my new nest,
to be a caterpillar in the heart of a flower,
to be a jewel hiding itself in a stone.
I still arrive, in order to laugh and to cry,
in order to fear and to hope.
The rhythm of my heart is the birth and
death of all that are alive.
I am the mayfly metamorphosing on the surface of the river,
and I am the bird, which,
when spring comes, arrives in time
to eat the mayfly.
I am the frog swimming happily in the clear pond,
and I am also the grass-snake who,
approaching in silence,
feeds itself on the frog
I am the child in Uganda, all skin and bones,
my legs as thin as bamboo sticks,
and I am the arms merchant,
selling deadly weapons to Uganda.
I am the twelve year old girl,
refugee on a small boat,
who throws herself into the ocean after being raped by a sea pirate,
and I am the pirate,
my heart not yet capable of seeing and loving.
I am a member of the politburo,
with plenty of power in my hands,
and I am the man who has to pay his "debt of blood" to my people,
dying slowly in a forced labor camp.
My joy is like spring,
so warm it makes flowers bloom in all walks of life.
My pain is like a river of tears, so full it fills the four oceans.
Please call me by my true names,
so I can hear all my cries and laughs at once,
so that I can see that my joy and pain are one.
Please call me by my true names,
so I can wake up,
and so the door of my heart can be left open,
the door of compassion.

Reprinted from *Call Me By My True Names: The Collected Poems of Thich Nhat Hanh* (1999) by
Thich Nhat Hanh with permission of Parallax Press, Berkeley, California.

W e have so much in common with each other even in light of our differences. Compassion can become "the bridge, the spiritual foundation for peace, harmony, and balance" (Tulku, 1977, p.39). All of us have experienced degrees of suffering, isolation, fear, and shame by virtue of our humanness. We have also expressed intentional or unintentional disregard, insensitivity, harm, or disrespect toward others. These ways of being are inescapable.

Psychological Perspectives

Knowing our roots is important. Etymologically the term *psychotherapy* emanates from two derivatives, *psyche* and *therapeuein*. According to Edinger (1997) the original meaning of *psyche* referred to *soul* or *life spirit*. The term *therapeuein* meant to tend, to render service. "The original usage of the word was to render service to the gods in their temples" (p.10). The practice of psychotherapy has historical roots in a practice that was medical, philosophical, scientific, artistic, and transpersonal. These historical roots are helpful to keep in mind when doing the work, connecting us with something much larger than ourselves.

My theoretical orientation is psychodynamic with a Jungian foundation, while my clinical practice can be described as integrative. The early training I received was in feminist and psychodynamic theory, community organization, systems theory, phenomenology, existentialism, and ethnography. During the past twenty years I have been further informed by archetypal psychology, trauma focused therapy, social constructivism, gestalt, self-psychology, cognitively oriented theories, and behavioral methodologies. An integrative perspective begins with an understanding that psychotherapy is both a science and an art. The blending of the two suggests the importance of learning this practice in an academically rigorous form of study along with clinical supervision of the practice providing support, feedback, guidance, and encouragement to develop ones' unique or creative skills.

The term *depth* augments the term *psychotherapy* alluding to the belief in the existence of the unconscious. This elaboration speaks further to the integrative orientation. Additionally, I find the practice of psychotherapy is a profound privilege (Edinger, 1997) with great responsibilities. Few professions allow opportunities to work with psyche and witness so intimately the range of human suffering and transformation. The responsibilities are many, given the nature of the private elements of our work, the unequal balance of power, and the potential harm that could be done. Thus the importance of striving for integrity and remaining devoted to a range of basic values.

Throughout this work, the terms *patient* and *client* are used interchangeably. The historical derivations of the term *patient* refer to one who endures, tolerates, or bears suffering (Oxford Dictionary of Etymology, 1966). This resonates more closely with my view of the profound transformative process of psychotherapy. Psychotherapy has been described as assisting the patient learn how to authentically bear suffering and to "acquire steadfastness and philosophic patience in face of suffering" (Jung, 1954, p. 81). However, I hesitate to privilege this term in a text on child abuse, which is also a societal problem. Being highly sensitive to the power of social oppression through language and other-imposed labels, my intention is not to medically pathologize the intrapersonal and interpersonal experiences of those who have endured childhood abuse, but to highlight their potentialities, strengths, and sense of selves in the context of these experiences.

Given that *patient* is a term that has medical connotations, the modern term *client* may be preferred by many practitioners. Unfortunately this alternate term speaks to the role of being a customer, as in "one for whom professional services are rendered" (Webster's, 1984, p.270). My dream is that a new term comes into being or is socially constructed, repairing the dualistic split in consciousness, meeting the needs of the psychological profession in describing those we provide services to and the needs of those receiving the services. In addition to the terms *individual, person, victim,* and *member of the community,* some other terms that have been adopted include *survivor, thriver,* and *consumer.*

Healing and the Mysteries of Antiquity

To fully appreciate healing perspectives and symptomatic manifestations of soul, a foray into the traditional mysteries of antiquity is made. In those times, it was customary to make a pilgrimage toward a healing place. This was undertaken with intention, relinquishment, purification, and often with great suffering or personal cost (Kerenyi, 1967).

In Greece I had the opportunity to travel on the Sacred Road to Eleusis, the precise road that ancient travelers journeyed by foot. After careful preparation and purification, initiates would begin at the Acropolis in Athens, the home of the temple to Athena, and endure this arduous twenty-six mile journey to their destination, Eleusis, the site of the mysteries. Others would travel to Epidauros to the abatons, the sleeping or incubation pits, in which Asklepian dream rituals would unfold (Meier, 1959). We see remnants of these ancient methods and processes alive within psychotherapy today. A process of purification, cathartic experiences, a focus toward interiority, incubation and reflection periods, and the presence of healing dreams continue to be a part of the healing process.

Asklepios, the god of healing, was the son of Apollo and Coronis, who was raised by the centaur Chiron. Chiron was half horse and half human, known as the most wise, virtuous, and fair creature on earth. He embodied the best of horse nature: strength, endurance, and potency, and the best of human nature: the capacity to speak, a caring heart, and great wisdom. Asklepios learned from Chiron and eventually surpassed his knowledge and ability in the healing arts.

Asklepios was considered a prominent healer. Psychological healing was held in reverence during these times in antiquity. Healing was frequently depicted by the image of Asklepios and his daughter Hygeia, whose name refers to a system of principles for preserving health, as in our modern day *hygiene.* She was considered the goddess of health. The symbolism of the feminine and masculine image has not escaped my eye. When we view these representations as energies existing within each one of us, not concrete genders, we see a blending of wisdom and insight, containment and action, being and doing, yin and yang. A complementary and dynamically oriented element. "The dynamic universe, both natural and social, is in a state of dynamic balance, with all its components oscillating between two archetypal poles" (Capra, 1983, p. 312).

Depictions of Asklepios show him holding a staff and caduceus. Jung (1963) made a distinction between these two symbols. The symbolism of the sacred serpent can be seen as the autonomous healing properties that emanated from the gods while the caduceus, representing Mercurius, indicated the power of healing situated within the hand of the individual holding it. As though the gods were bestowing the individual's hand with the power or secret to healing "in the hands of the physician lie the magic remedies granted by God" (p.228). I understand messengers and ambassadors of peace were once called caduceatores.

I find this distinction fitting with my efforts to understand the profound elements that underlie healing. Healing as a renewal process that is free, having an existence of its own, outside of any personal containment, in particular, the therapist. The therapist does not hold the healing powers for the patient but serves as a conduit or medium for the healing to come forward, the healing potential that resides within the patient. However, the therapist does need personal ego strength and a capacity to hold the mix of issues including transference and countertransference within the therapeutic container in order to assist the patient. This creates a *temenos* or sacred container.

Jung (1974) ventured into this realm of the unconscious in an expansive manner seeking to understand the gifts of healing from a transformational, alchemical, and mysterious perspective. These methods invoke a receptivity and attendance to many aspects allowing subtleties to emerge. In the process of psychotherapy the patient and therapist are affected and may be transformed. "Genuine healing is a journey, facilitated by a healer, into a broken and hurt self, the purpose of which is to encounter a depth of humanity deeper than the tragedy of any illness" (Kaptchuk, 1989, p. 105).

The healer-patient archetype provides an illuminating perspective. This archetype emerges in the presence of illness (Guggenbuhl-Craig, 1971) and constellates within the patient and therapist as well as between the two. For example a patient who has been traumatized and is experiencing a range of symptoms seeks out a therapist. The patient has an inner healer in addition to the illness. The therapist, as the healer, has an inner patient, or the repository of his or her own wounding. This image of the wounded healer provides us with a template to understand the inevitability of our own wounding. It points to the importance of accepting and living with our own wounds and the need to focus on their healing. A process of continual renewal and healing is symbolized. As Kleinman (1988) noted "Healing, as a sacred or secular ritual, achieves its efficacy through the transformation of experience" (p.134). The mysteries of healing shed light on the need for a guide or partner in this process, the importance of witnessing human drama, and the necessary periods of quietness, reflection, solitude, interiority, preparation, incubation, collective participation, and transformation.

Images of Nature

Sullivan (1989) uses the imagery of nature in expressing her perspective on healing. "An approach that seeks the fecund compost of wholeness rather than the aridity of perfection begins by recognizing that illness and death are intrinsic elements in life, in psyche, indeed in every experience" (p.85).

A graceful resonance exists within these metaphors. Hillman (1983) recognized the power of imagination as the root of healing. This infusion of metaphor becomes a convocation or invitation to healing. I have witnessed many allusions to the germination, darkness, light, dryness, fertility, and blossoming of the interior process experienced within psychotherapy. In his articulate characterization of healing Levine (1987) also described a psychotherapeutic process "a blossoming fed by deep roots extending into the dark, moist soil of the previously uninvestigated mind" (p.4). This perspective is situated within a constellation of nourishment, akin to a human community.

I believe the matter of the garden has become a universal metaphor that allows us to get back in touch with nature and what we may have carelessly disregarded in our high paced technological world. These allusions to nature address a cyclical process and a hopefulness of what is yet to unfold, provided care and proper attention is given. Growth processes within the garden incorporate life, death, and rebirth. A tending of the soul that does not remove wounds but contains them in a process that eventually becomes internalized. In speaking of the work one's soul must have, Alice Walker (2000) characterized her mother's gardening, as "ordering the universe in the image of her personal conception of beauty" (p.231).

Gardening or working the soil as the soul's work is an eloquent way to illustrate the process of soul making or *poiesis*. Theoretical constructions of the self are broadened when the mutual connections we have to the earth are considered, an ecological "self-world connection" (Conn, 1995, p.166). "Poetically, we dwell on this earth" (Downing, 1992). One can also respect the contributions of dreams, creativity, and art in potentiating healing experiences, both for the therapist and patient.

Mythological Reflections on Psychotherapy

The process of psychotherapy contains inherent saturnian and melancholic aspects. This frame allows for a certain structure to the work incorporating the need for broadening the tolerance for the pace and assisting patients do the same. A lugubrious or heavy energy is often teamed with melancholia. The more difficult processes within therapy are comparable to traveling into a dark forest or bog. Woodman (personal communication, February, 1993) shared her way of addressing some of the very difficult work within psychotherapy, by lighting a candle within her consulting room. This served as an anchor for the patient to be accompanied by light as he or she re-experienced some of the darkness from the past.

The mythology of Medusa provides a template for understanding how some issues are addressed within the healing process. A formerly beautiful Medusa was turned into a hideous monster by Athena, with serpents emanating from her head, writhing, moving, and reaching beyond her. One can view the serpentine energy as repressed or unconscious energy which is spilling over, but not seen by the patient. Medusa's eyes are glaring and filled with rage, capable of turning anyone into stone and paralyzing them with fear. To avoid destruction, Perseus discovered a way to confront her which was indirect, by looking at a mirrored reflection of Medusa. Eventually the winged horse of creativity, Pegasus, was released from Medusa's body (Woodman, 1982). This indirect confrontation is a powerful metaphor

112

for the more difficult processes within psychotherapy, particularly those which focus on energies that create a daunting or paralyzing fear if confronted directly. All the characters of this myth are parallel to the events within psychotherapy, where a patient is assisted by a reflection of self, through the therapist, who becomes an internalized Perseus, able to release and free the creative life forces. Self-injurious behavior, the range of addictive and sexually compulsive behaviors, and a host of tension-reducing behaviors are represented by this story.

Stories and storytelling are integral elements in oral history. Historicizing is embedded within anamnesis, a remembering and recollection that occurs within psychotherapy. "A ritual recall of our lives to the images in the background of the soul" (Hillman, 1983, p.42). Participating in anamnesis through the expression of images, thoughts, drawings, stories, and behaviors embeds current symptoms and disorders within a context. This historicizing contributes to psychological healing through the process of making meaning of the events in our lives. Perhaps the term psychological poiesis more accurately reflects this process, given that poeisis literally refers to *making*. Psychotherapy fundamentally becomes a meaning making and soul making process.

The goddess of memory, Mnemosyne, assists in this process. The Greek term *mnemonikos* refers to "of memory, mindful; pertaining to, aiding or intended to aid the memory" (Webster's New Riverside, 1984, p. 760). Mnemosyne is invoked in the historicizing process within psychotherapy, supporting the therapist and patient in the meaning making process. The Nobel Prize winner Toni Morrison once said our culture didn't encourage dwelling on the past or coming to terms with the truth (as cited in Lorenz & Watkins, 2000). These words on the pressures American immigrants face to erase the past and start over are resonant with the experiences of child abuse survivors. The pressures to move on, forget, and begin anew are experienced externally and internally. Yet coming to terms with the truth about the past is central to the healing process. Chopra defined healing as "the restoration of the memory of wholeness" (1993, p.20). This is an intriguing concept when one imagines the process of remembering or bringing the fragmented pieces together toward wholeness.

Pre-Hellenic stories from mythology provide motifs that represent the individuation process often witnessed in psychotherapy. One version of the Sumerian myth of Inanna (Perera, 1981) provides a model for healing, recognizing a tumultuous descent and complex return to wholeness. Inanna was a Sumerian goddess of heaven and earth who chose to travel to the underworld in order to attend funerary rites of a relative. As she descends she comes upon seven consecutive gates, where she must remove an item of clothing at each juncture, essentially giving up her earthly connections. When she reaches the underworld she learns she must remain, in death. Prior to her travel, Inanna wisely left instructions with Enki, a god allied with emotion, to secure her release if she did not return in three days. Enki responds by sending two creatures into the underworld who restore Inanna to life. On her ascent Inanna returns through the seven consecutive gates reclaiming her clothing from the gatekeepers. However, the return is not without sacrifice, for she must leave someone in her place to dwell in the underworld. Her partner Dumuzi meets his fate in the form of this sacrifice, ultimately sharing this burden with his sister Geshtinanna, who had lovingly offered to spend six months in his place each year.

A dark journey to the underworld is initiated either willingly or involuntarily. This can occur in response to trauma or sudden loss and at passages into challenging developmental phases. The Homeric myth of Demeter and Persephone offers a story of descent that is engaged involuntarily, as Persephone is abducted and disappears into the underworld. Persephone is kidnapped and separated from her mother Demeter, the goddess of grain. While confined in the afterworld in order to become the bride of Hades, she partakes of the pomegranate eating only the seeds. While Demeter grieves for Persephone nothing grows on the earth. The mighty god Zeus intervenes and sends his messenger Hermes to retrieve Persephone and reunite daughter with mother. Once united with her mother, she discovers she is eternally fated to engage in seasonal underworld descents since she had eaten something while confined in the underworld. During these cyclical descents the earth would lay dormant as it continues to do so during the winter season.

This dark journey can be experienced as a descent into the depths of one's instinctual self or center. The descent is characterized as a dark night of the soul where depression is a companion who provides no revelations about the length of time one will dwell in the darkness. Suffering, despair, pain, confusion, self-doubt, intensity, and fear may accompany the time of confinement in the underworld. In this dwelling place transformative energy can be elusive, yet it is often in close proximity. "If we can hold long enough, a tiny light is conceived in the dark unconscious, and if we can wait and hold, in its own time it will be born in its full radiance" (Woodman, 1992, p.115).

The ascent evokes images of emergence, change, transformation, termination, initiation, and a renewed sense of self. Thresholds are crossed, identities are formed, and new relationships develop. Both stories address the profound sacrifices made in these transformational processes, leaving something of ourselves behind. Each story engages other persons along the journey who witness, support, impede, provide direction, guide, burden, wait, or actively assist. At the conclusion of the myths enduring commitments to the underworld remain. These connections acknowledge the significance of psychologically embracing, holding, and integrating the darkness along our continued journeys toward wholeness.

Several versions of the Demeter and Persephone myth recount the rape of Persephone by Hades in the underworld (Downing, 1996). From this perspective Persephone feels betrayed by her mother Demeter for failing to protect her adequately. Her father Zeus, although not the perpetrator, is the instigator of the rape. This version can be helpful for sexual assault and incest survivors, fathers, or mothers who identify more literally with this aspect of the story. The dramatic elements involving the parents accepting responsibility for the events and acknowledging guilt can parallel a parent's healing process or provide an imaginal framework to situate oneself in. Most significant is the realization that all are immeasurably changed by the events.

Memory Controversies That Inform Clinical Practice

Memory becomes central to those who have been required to renounce their perceptions in order to remain safe, survive, or avoid danger. This is true for trauma survivors including children who have experienced the helplessness of ongoing fear and numbness from emotional, physical, and sexual abuse. In Taylor's (1997) study of the military dictatorship in Argentina she categorized this damaging and dehumanizing type of renunciation as *percepticide*. Percepticide "blinds, maims, kills through the senses" (p.124). In cases of child abuse, whether one is the victim, offender, or witness, coming to know the truth, acknowledging what has occurred, no longer denying or avoiding, and transforming the numbness becomes a challenge in the healing process. Percepticide is also a societal practice that must be transformed and overcome in order to prevent abuse, neglect, and other forms of violence.

Issues relating to memory have been hotly contested in clinical, academic (Berliner & Loftus, 1992; Enns, McNeilly, Corkery, & Gilbert, 1995), and legal circles and received sensational media coverage during the 1990's (Jarof, 1993; Safran, 1993). The escalation of conflict between professionals is largely unprecedented although it evokes images of the debates that ensued at the turn of the last century when Freud publicized his patients' reports of sexual abuse. Writings on repressed memory, false memories (Loftus & Ketcham, 1994), delayed memory, memory retrieval, and lawsuits against therapists accused of implanting memories (Pope & Caudill, 2000) have appeared. Psychologists have also been sued by third parties, individuals accused of abuse by the therapist's patients.

The context of these debates is compassionately addressed in an article regarding the cultural backlash against professionals engaged in raising societal awareness about child abuse, specifically sexual abuse (Enns, 1996). The author analyzed the development of this backlash and its function in shifting the focus from the continuing realities of oppression, childhood abuse, and violence. Wylie (1993) noted that our societal reaction to terrible news is instinctually denial or dissociation "societies dissociate their knowledge of trauma—massive injuries, torture, genocide—preferring to live in the 'bleached present' of conventional disbelief and logical denial" (p.43).

Much of this debate has been credited with the clarity developing around standards of practice, given the professional consensus that childhood abuse and traumatic response impact the memory process (American Psychological Association, 1995). For example, caution is recommended when using hypnosis to address memories, audiotaping or videotaping sessions dealing with memory retrieval is advised, and accurate record keeping is suggested. Therapists are advised to become intimately aware of their own biases and begin to understand potential legal vulnerabilities in the therapeutic process.

In terms of competent and ethical practice becoming familiar with the literature is essential. Myers (1989, 1992) offered extensive recommendations for professionals serving as expert witnesses in child sexual abuse litigation, Melton and Limber (1989) addressed the numerous pitfalls in forming professional opinions on memory processes when relying on non-empirical data, Pope (1996) addressed the scientific research on recovered memory, and Pope and Brown (1996) wrote a comprehensive text on the forensic and clinical aspects of recovered memory.

Of significance is the research on traumatic amnesias and the uniqueness of traumatic memories (van der Kolk, Blitz, Burr, & Hartmann, 1984). Traumatic memories may be encoded differently than memories of ordinary events lacking extreme emotional arousal (van der Kolk, 1994). Fragmentation of memory (Burgess, Hartmann, & Baker, 1995) and amnesia of the abuse or original traumatic event have also been reported in the literature (Briere & Conte, 1993; Williams, 1994). An innovative treatment approach capable of attending to these differences shows promise in the research literature, Eye Movement Desensitization and Reprocessing, EMDR (Shapiro, 1995). This approach uses rhythmic eye movements coupled with images or somatic memories of the traumatic experience, and strives to reduce the frequency and intensity of intrusive recollections from trauma.

Attending to the evolving standards of practice serves to enhance knowledge and clinical interventions. First, when using any new methods, therapists become educated, trained, and competent with the method prior to integrating it, e.g., hypnosis, guided imagery, or dream analysis. Informing the patient about the limitations and risks of the intervention and providing sufficient time for processing the material at the conclusion is important. When using hypnosis experienced therapists videotape or audiotape the session, after receiving written authorization from the patient, or prepare detailed written records of the events. Some states require such documentation for later criminal court proceedings specifically dealing with information discovered while under hypnosis. It is also important to be mindful of the types of questions asked and the phrasing used within the questions, so as not to lead the patient.

Therapeutic methods that are generally accepted by the mainstream professional community are preferred by psychologists who have been involved in the legal system. Limiting the use of controversial or experimental methods and obtaining informed consent for each method, explaining the risks and benefits becomes a sound practice. Presenting or recommending potentially controversial reading material to patients can also include information about the risks and benefits. Earlier editions of *Courage to Heal* (Bass & Davis, 1988) generated considerable controversy. This was partly due to its assumptions of childhood sexual abuse in persons who held suspicions of their sexual abuse and exhibited a constellation of specific symptoms. Recent editions include exploration of the memory debate and provide information on how to attenuate flashbacks and reduce dissociative states in the face of intrusive recollections. This inspiring self-help text is one example of the evolution of knowledge in the field of trauma and the benefits from constructive analysis, reflections from professionals in the field of child abuse, and feedback from survivors. It continues to be an important contribution to the self-help abuse literature.

When a patient begins to describe an abusive event, allow the information to be revealed at the patient's pace and in his or her own words. Using open ended questions is the suggested manner. Respecting and valuing the patient's timing is an overall critical issue in therapy with abuse survivors. This does not mean colluding with silence or avoidance of material, but respecting a patient's stated need or preference to proceed slowly. Sharing observations when a patient begins

116

to stop speaking or dissociates from a memory when beginning to express it, can be highly supportive. This acknowledges the distress without challenging the patient to elaborate or go more deeply into the discomfort at that moment. This clinical practice "follows the psyche" by acknowledging the necessary and important defenses that have been built, without prematurely removing them. In fact, these adaptations may never be removed but may be slightly modified. I strongly believe in respecting the patient's timing and capacity to consolidate the progressively revealed information.

Therapists indirectly influence or bias the process of therapy or memory emergence based on beliefs about the pervasiveness of abuse or that abuse can be affirmatively assessed based on specific memories or behavioral cues. Multiple traumatic symptoms can result from a wide range of circumstances including sexual abuse and other types of interpersonal victimization such as rape or assault (Finkelhor, 1995). Legal advisors caution that therapists become vulnerable professionally when quick assumptions are made about the causal relationship between current symptoms and past events.

Memories may also represent fragmentary realities that haven't been integrated such as flashbacks. They may appear within the unconscious as images, smells, somatic or sensory sensations, impressions, or waking dreams. The research on state dependent learning (van der Kolk, 1989) indicates that some memories may only be accessible during the experience of similar or parallel emotional states. Memories may suddenly arise when similar emotional states are experienced, such as anxiety, fear, terror, or confusion, while engaging in reminiscent sexual behaviors, or during ongoing psychotherapy that is gradually built on trust and safety. It is also likely that full recollection of the early childhood abuse experiences may never be reached.

Since I do not engage in memory retrieval processes per se, my work with patients in this area has focused primarily on increasing affective tolerance for the memories that do arise. This assists patients in responding to and processing the painful memories in conscious, intentional, and therapeutic ways, decreasing their impact on daily functioning. Self-soothing and self-nurturing techniques are employed or taught as alternate ways to address aversive stressors and memories. The increased tolerance progressively leads to an eventual replacement or cessation of automatic dissociative responses, impulsive behaviors, or tension reducing acts, including self-mutilation. This type of transitioning is rarely short term, since relapse to the earlier tension reducing behaviors may occur. After time patients discover a renewed personal power and experience greater versatility in their responses, no longer held prisoner to the emotionally intense and painful memories that intruded upon, constricted, or prevented the experience of living life to capacity.

Chapter 12

Spinning Lead into Gold
Clinical Interventions

I came to explore the wreck . . . I came to see the damage that
was done and the treasures that prevail.

Adrienne Rich, 1973

The alchemical process of transforming lead into gold provides a framework in which to view the healing process. The alchemical process is known
as the *opus* or the work. The therapeutic work begins with the heaviness of
leadened matter which exudes toxicity and tends toward bitter corrosion. Attention, focus, continued work, and occasional impedance ultimately coagulates into
the splendor of gold. Another way to look at this is to imagine raw, disconnected,
or unraveled threads becoming a full cohesive tapestry. Although the internal work
is individual, it is a "world creating process" (Edinger, 1985, p.9). Witnessing this
restorative process is truly some of the most fulfilling work one can do. This chapter suggests the parameters of treatment with children and adults, offers intentions
in this work of restoration, and presents selected clinical interventions.

Initial Concerns

Discussing the limits and parameters of psychotherapy is an important step in setting the initial frame for therapy. Initiating this discussion indicates how one tends to work, demonstrates an interest in discussing the facts of therapy, begins to build a safe container or *temenos* for treatment, and serves to invite questions or concerns the patient may have about the process of psychotherapy. Limits to confidentiality including the duty to warn are essential elements to cover. Briere (1989) suggests specifying regular appointment times, being mindful of beginning and ending times in sessions, allocating a limited amount of time for each session such as one hour, refraining from contact outside therapy such as luncheon engagements, and not holding a session if the patient arrives intoxicated, except in an emergency centering around danger to self or others.

In my experience working with children and adults who were abused, I have developed a conservative approach to touch. Although a reassuring touch can be a facilitative gesture for certain patients at important times within the treatment, I explicitly discuss this with patients clarifying my philosophical perspective on respecting personal boundaries. The seemingly harmless act of touching the knee or shoulder may have initiated sexual advances leading to sexual abuse during childhood, or the patient may have experienced countless bodily violations in the past including therapist-patient sexual intimacy. The range of prior behaviors and the meanings attached to them is not known at the beginning of treatment and may be misinterpreted or sexualized. Until the meaning and function of physical contact has been explored and understood by both of us, I refrain from touch and hugs.

This discussion also raises the fact of the power differential that exists in psychotherapy. Philosophically I acknowledge this differential and in practice, validate the patient's perception of inequality, respect the patient's autonomy, and equalize the relationship as much as is practicably possible through open discussion. The therapist who is compassionate, responsible, nonexploitative, and consistent will strive to be aware of any potential abuses of power and address them as early as possible. Addressing these can be in the form of discussing the therapeutic process, being clear about the parameters of therapy, clarifying the roles involved, and inviting disagreement and expression of discomfort with any aspect of the psychotherapy. My view encompasses a partnership with the patient.

Therapeutic environments that support honesty, respect, nonexploitation, and foster self-awareness and self-acceptance can be highly empowering for patients. The qualities of authenticity and consistency are no small matter within psychotherapy and become precious in work with abuse survivors. "Chronically traumatized clients have an exquisite attunement to unconscious and non-verbal communications" (Herman, 1992, p.139) bringing these capacities to bear on the therapeutic relationship.

The characteristic of caring becomes a central element in light of the term cure which comes from the Latin *cura* meaning care and is associated with the term *curious* (Lockhart, 1977). Cure and healing are two distinct words and are usually interpreted differently. *Heal* is related to the terms whole and health. Heal-

119

ing, wholeness, and caring are often associated with the psychotherapeutic process and highlight several important threads in the work. These etymological roots provide insights to the cure or healing process that emanates from a caring relationship. I propose that caring on the part of the patient is similarly important, particularly self-care and self-acceptance, however I look at these qualities as aspirational rather than conditions that need to be present when initiating psychotherapy. Self-care strategies may need to be acquired progressively throughout the course of treatment. "Seemingly small and simple self-care issues may have major traumatic associations and may not resolve easily" (Courtois, 1997, p.488).

Since therapists carry values and biases into sessions, which impact their therapeutic decisions, and are likely to influence the direction and outcome of the therapy, it is essential to be aware of personal values, determine how they affect or interfere with clinical practice, and discuss those values that are part of the treatment approach, whenever appropriate. A strong bias can be expressed as a tendency to be inappropriately directive on some issues such as whether or not to seek prosecution, to carry to term or abort a fetus conceived during sexual abuse or incest, or to civilly sue an abuser, etc. Sometimes therapists are also unaware of being influenced by biases such as gender role stereotypes or strong beliefs that mothers should be primary caretakers of children. A recognition of these biases becomes paramount in treatment.

Coping and the Process of Restoration

Individuals often experience great psychological tolls in attempting to cope with abusive events, significantly damaging assumptions about self and the world (Janoff-Bulman and Frieze, 1983). One of these fundamental assumptions is based on personal invulnerability. Anxiety develops when one's sense of personal invulnerability is threatened and may lead to a type of immobility or paralysis. Another primary assumption suggests the world is a meaningful and comprehensible place. An abusive incident shakes this perspective. The last assumption is based on a positive self-image, often altered when one is victimized. With these factors in mind, therapy focuses on the eventual restoration of the patient's positive self-image during the process of coming to terms with a world in which these experiences occur. Integrating an understanding that these painful life events can occur in one's own life is part of the healing process and contributes to a broader world perspective as well as the individuation process. This perspective incorporates the experience of abuse into one's cognitive assumptions about the world (Janoff-Bulman, 1985). This view continually needs expansion for those who experience repeated victimization in adulthood and live with cultural oppression.

New strategies in therapeutic work with survivors of abuse may be necessary to address the psychological effects that result from victimization. Rather than focus on adjustment as the goal for psychotherapy, or a return to pre-morbid functioning, comprehensive healing and re-empowerment is a more inclusive and complete outcome. Disempowerment may be prevented or reversed through the assistance of self-help groups, group therapy, social activism, or the process of individual psychotherapy, where an individual becomes psychologically strengthened and empowered through additional competence training and skill-building activities (Walker, 1989a).

Future research and clinical focus on this process of re-empowerment, including the optimal methods for victims to re-empower themselves, will prove useful to child abuse survivors in their healing and recovery process. Working through and integrating the abusive experience, from victim to survivor, thriver, or other self chosen term, within a supportive framework (Schechter, 1982) will help individuals in the validation of their perceptions and in the development or rediscovery of a belief in their own power and capabilities. I also believe in the affirmative power of social, political, and legislative activism in the later stages of healing, as an immensely empowering method to prevent future cases of abuse and to help others by contributing to necessary changes in the investigative, prosecutorial, legislative, or rehabilitative process. Through these actions the realities of abuse also become less invisible in the world.

Intentions in Treatment

An understanding of the complexity of child abuse as a community problem is an important approach in assessment and treatment. Conveying and holding an attitude of positive intention to the work rather than bias about the cause of abuse is essential, acknowledging the myriad of potential causal factors including psychological, social, cultural, environmental, and socio-economic.

In our post-modern culture it is very difficult to raise children when there is no extended family, when the parents are teenagers themselves, when alcohol and drug abuse exists within the family, or where homelessness or joblessness is an issue. Many of these issues are risk factors for child abuse and neglect. Skilled psychotherapists approach this issue with the recognition that most parents hold positive intentions toward their children and have no intentions to hurt them.

Some parents who do harm their children experience remorse but may have insurmountable personal difficulties that contribute to their behavior. These difficulties may involve their own abuse or neglect issues, attachment deficits, family factors such as marital discord, possessing extremely poor parenting skills, substance abuse, or geographic isolation. Parental interventions include psychotherapy in conjunction with teaching parenting skills, coping strategies, and communication skills.

Holding a foundational belief in the capacity for people to change their behavior and continue their emotional and social development is generative. Exhibiting a quality of respect toward all persons we work with is an important constant. Otherwise we engage in counterproductivity and may find ourselves unable to continue the work, blaming parents or the victims of abuse.

In addressing the adolescent psyche Frankel (1998) recognized that the behavior of adolescents has an inherent purpose and reveals many facets of an adolescent's tumultuous experience of development into the world. He suggests we view the present culture of adolescents to understand the new archetypal patterns that are emerging, the images underlying them, and the fresh vision that arises. He does not believe the difficulties adolescents experience are entirely rooted in childhood trauma, but that the adolescent emerging spirit hungers for experience through variable and dynamic states of being.

Adolescent behavior reflects back on the culture at large, responding to the receptivity or denigration experienced. If the response to this emerging spirit becomes receptive, life affirming, and nonpathologizing, acknowledging the inherent meaning and vitalizing quality of the behaviors, no matter how frightening or volatile they may appear to adults, a dramatic shift may occur. This kind of welcoming and compassionate holding environment allows for the presence of the adolescent's developmental passages without an authoritative emphasis on prohibition but rather on self-discovery and responsibility.

Trauma Focused Cognitive Behavioral Therapy for Children

Many treatments for abused children have been modified from effective treatments for adults and from interventions used with anxious or depressed children (Cohen, Mannarino, Berliner, & Deblinger, 2000). Empirical support exists for the effectiveness of trauma focused cognitive behavioral therapy with children in reducing trauma specific symptoms. These approaches incorporate discussion, recollecting the abuse experience and various distressing details, processing of the experience, addressing and changing cognitive distortions, and increasing coping methods through stress management, muscle relaxation, and deep breathing techniques. Debriefing group interventions are also cognitively based initial treatments that involve gradual recollections of the traumatic event, along with processing of the elements that were most startling and memorable. Debriefing has been used with adults and children alike.

Cohen and Mannarino (1993) developed a treatment model for sexually abused preschoolers and their parents, focusing on direct discussion of the range of traumatic issues. This is a gradual exposure model where children initially describe less distressing aspects of the trauma and gradually progress by sharing more uncomfortable events in response to questions from the therapist. The therapist begins by asking the children to share anything about the abuse incident, then slowly begins to ask more detailed questions. This process incorporates artistic expression, drawings, and verbal articulation. At the end of each session the therapist checks in with the patient to see how he or she felt describing the events in order to assess the child's tolerance to this exposure. Deblinger and Heflin (1996) developed a manual for treating sexually abused children and their nonoffending parents that incorporates similar gradual exposure techniques.

Imaginal flooding exercises have been used with children to decrease intensity of intrusive recollections related to posttraumatic stress symptomatology. Saigh, Yule, and Inandar (1996) applied the techniques of imaginal flooding to treat children exposed to traumatic experiences. This approach involves the development of a hierarchy of anxiety producing images related to the abuse experience. The work begins with an in depth clinical interview where the scenes are identified, followed by sessions that intentionally incorporate scenes that create more discomfort. The child imagines these scenes in detail and rates the degree of distress experienced. The theory behind this approach relates to the behavioral mechanisms of extinction, reciprocal inhibition, and habituation (Wolpe, 1990), involving repetitive exposure to an ongoing stressor that becomes less emotionally difficult over time. Apparently there is no empirical evidence that successful treatment always requires the use of these repeated exposure techniques with children, and it is recommended only for apparent posttraumatic stress symptoms (Cohen, Mannarino, Berliner, & Deblinger, 2000).

Stress management methods incorporating muscle relaxation and breathing techniques have been used effectively with children to decrease anxiety and hypervigilance. Learning to relax tense muscles through the use of progressive relaxation, beginning with the feet and slowly working up through the body to the head, can reduce emotional and physical tension. Massage therapy was evaluated as a potential treatment for anxiety reduction in a study by Field, Seligman, Scafedi, and Schanberg (1996). The massage therapy improved levels of anxiety and depression. Deep abdominal breathing techniques can be applied to successfully reduce or alleviate anxiety. These techniques may be incorporated with other methods, taught within a psychotherapeutic session, and assigned as homework.

Cognitive interventions have been applied to various attributions of the abuse experience. As cited earlier, characterological or behavioral self-blame is a frequent consequence of abuse. As children seek to understand the reasons for the abuse or attempt to make meaning out of their experiences, they may look to their behavior and believe they were to blame or caused the abuse, thus believing they have some control over preventing the abuse in the future. This and other cognitions and attributions centering around worldview, global nature of abuse, and aspects pertaining to the perpetrator can be addressed thoroughly within psychotherapy by examining beliefs, uncovering the reasoning process, gaining clarity about who was responsible for the abuse, and acknowledging they may have engaged in behavior that contributed to but did cause the abuse (Cohen, Mannarino, Berliner, & Deblinger, 2000).

Integrated Treatment Approaches with Children

Many treatment approaches rooted in specific theoretical schools are used with abused children. Friedrich (1996) described the major goals of integrated approaches focusing on individual, group, and family therapy. These approaches emanate from three orientations: attachment theory, dysregulation theory, and self-theory. An integrated model is derived from these three approaches.

Attachment has become central in understanding the internal disruptions resulting from abusive experiences, trauma, and disturbed bonds with caregivers (Main & George, 1985). Incorporating attachment theory into individual therapy creates a focus on the formation of the therapeutic alliance, creating safety, acceptance, and correcting the internal working model of attachment. Group therapy emphasizes the development of cohesion, maintaining boundaries, creating safety, and developing empathy, while family therapy involves identifying similarities among family members, goal setting, creating rapid treatment gains, and home visitation.

The dysregulation model focuses on the capacities of self-regulation of thoughts and feelings including modulating arousal. Emotional regulation includes learning to self-soothe, focusing attention, and differentiating powerful internal feelings (Katz & Gottman, 1991). Individual therapy begins with explaining the process of therapy, establishing specific goals, modulating the intensity of treatment, and continues with psycho-education approaches including the teaching of self-soothing techniques, and the use of cognitive behavioral strategies for anxiety and posttraumatic stress. Group therapy establishes safety, reduces agitation, and provides opportunities for practicing the respect of boundaries and interrupts victim/abuser dynamics. Family therapy creates safety, reduces sexualized behavior, sets goals, and utilizes behaviorally based methods (Friedrich, 1996).

Self theoretical approaches differ from the two previous models in that individual therapy identifies and processes feelings, focuses on competency, externalizes the problem outside of the child's control, and confronts the accuracy of self-perceptions (Harter, 1988). Group therapy provides children with opportunities to broaden their self-perceptions by understanding the perceptions of others, while family therapy normalizes personally unacceptable feelings, addresses parenting behaviors, explores negative projections, re-empowers the parents who were previously victimized.

Abuse focused therapy is not associated with a particular theoretical perspective and integrates techniques from cognitive, behavioral, systemic, and dynamic therapeutic approaches (Chaffin, Bonner, Worley, & Lawson, 1996). The phenomenological exploration of a child's victimization is emphasized with an integration of methods addressing affect modulation and attachment, utilizing modalities of group, individual, and family treatment. In cases of incest, parental support and belief have been powerful predictors of recovery from the incestuous abuse (Everson, Hunter, Runyan, Edelsohn, & Coulter, 1989). These models emphasize the importance of drawing upon varied approaches in order to meet the therapeutic needs of children.

Creative Expression and Play Therapy

Artistic expression, sandplay, and play therapy are wonderfully creative modalities that are often used in work with child abuse victims and survivors. Artistic expression within therapy vitalizes, enhances, potentiates, and complements therapeutic work. Creative engagement expresses the inexpressible, reveals what is not yet visible, and provides a context for healing to occur. Many have proposed that creativity is ontological (May, 1975), necessary to our being (Estes, 1991), and inseparable from the conditions of the world (Winter, 1978). The numinous or sacred can be evoked in the process of creating. The inspired person expressing the creative art may be shaped as much as he or she shapes the art. Shulman (1997) reasoned that creativity was the "crucial ritual of healing" (p.204).

The reworking of childhood trauma within creative work (Terr, 1991) is evidenced by the works of well known artists, writers, dramatists, sculptors, and dancers. The safe containment of this reworking process can also take form in psychotherapy. Serving as a participant-observer rather than playing along can be highly therapeutic for clients working through the trauma. There are many forms of art allowing for a range of authentic communications and expression including drawing, painting, sculpting, writing, dancing, movement, singing, poetry, music, dramatic representation, and playing.

Play as an expressive and symbolic representation is "an activity of the spirit that allows full expression" (Gadon, 1989, p.292) of one's total being. Play is usually unstructured, pursued for its own sake, and is not goal directed. Play has also been centrally involved in the work of therapy with abused children (Gil, 1991; Oaklander, 1978) and has among its merits the quality to transcend the conscious and unveil unconscious processes. Winnicott (1971a) viewed play as a creative mode to express the whole personality leading to a discovery of the self. Anna Freud used play as a tool for diagnosis in her work with children, Melanie Klein incorporated play in her psychoanalytic treatment of children, and Margaret Lowenfield integrated play in the form of the world technique, a forerunner to the sandplay method.

Working with abused and neglected children who have special therapeutic needs requires understanding of the range of psychological issues they may be experiencing. Porter, Blick, and Sgroi (1982) indicate the importance of being aware of the potential depression, guilt, repressed anger, hostility, impaired abilities to trust, blurred boundary or role confusion, and the sense of being *damaged goods* that many sexually abused children feel.

An instructive handbook on play therapy with abused children, *The Healing Power of Play*, demonstrates sensitivity to the phenomenological experience of the child (Gil, 1991). Gil encourages individual therapy with all children to provide them with the "one-on-one experience with trained professionals" (p.47) in addition to group or family therapy especially when reunification is planned. She uses therapeutic stories, puppet play, sandplay, video therapy, feeling cards, and items such as telephones and sunglasses.

Another important contribution to therapy with children is *Windows to Our Children* (Oaklander, 1978) written with an immense respect for children as our greatest teachers. The author covers drawing, fantasy, creating things, storytelling, poetry, puppetry, play therapy, sensory experiences, enactment, and draws attention to specific problem behaviors.

Creative imagery can be used effectively with children to elicit relaxation, enhance their capacities of self-expression, meet with inner figures of wisdom, and cope with stress (Murdock, 1987). Drawing, painting, sculpting, and playing with figures provide non-intrusive ways to self disclose conflicts. These are unique opportunities to work through issues in a psychological context (Allan, 1988) allowing for emotional expression, explorations of relationships and perceptions of individuals within one's life, and containment of affect. Incorporating artistic expression or art therapy within psychotherapy provides a means to express difficult emotions safely and to be heard or understood (Case & Dalley, 1992).

Many years ago Winnicott (1971b) developed the squiggle technique for use with children in initial consultations. This projective technique is still used by therapists today. The therapist invites the child to participate in the sguiggle drawing game by drawing a squiggle, a straight, curved, or spiraled line or lines that the child forms into a picture of his or her choosing. Children elaborate on the completed picture with stories that communicate their thoughts, feelings, concerns, wishes, inner conflicts, and external challenges. Claman (1993) suggests starting the stories with the expression "Once upon a time, far, far away, a long time ago" (p.181). The therapist asks questions to deepen the telling of the story, then takes the next turn elaborating on a squiggle the child draws for the therapist. However, the therapist is guided by the child's initial narrative in creating a story about this new squiggle drawing expressing understanding of the child's situation and progressing toward the suggestion of possible solutions. This model provides many opportunities for developing a therapeutic alliance, expressing empathy, and presenting various themes about assertiveness, dealing with fears, coping methods, and the value of exploration of feelings. From his extensive practice with children Bettelheim (1976) offered a detailed commentary on the significance of communication through stories and the uses of enchantment with fairy tales. Becoming familiar with these methods expands one's repertoire of applied interventions.

Seeing the World in a Grain of Sand

Sandplay as a primary therapeutic mode of treatment for children and adults was developed by Dora Kalff (1980). This creative method involves active imagination and symbolic play, facilitating the individuation process. In my experience with sandplay, I have found children magnetically drawn to the container of sand, often placing their hands into the sand to begin the creative process. On the other hand, adults have been somewhat reluctant to sift through the sand so readily. After an introduction and explanation of the therapeutic process both adults and children discover enthusiasm about this dramatic and highly creative process.

Sandplay employs a precisely dimensioned container of sand (19 1/2" x 28 1/2" x 3") representative of one's world, and an array of miniature objects and figures that are chosen and arranged by the client within the tray. Preferably an additional container is offered to introduce water onto the landscape. In the free and protected space, energy is expressed outward, representing the interior worlds of the individual. The work is witnessed respectfully by both the therapist and client and spontaneous connections to the experiences of the past may be made by the client. The therapist's interpretation is generally not part of the process.

Several guidebooks on sandplay include photos of sandplay worlds and commentaries by therapists. Stewart (1990) addressed the developmental psychology of sandplay in his work with young children and Bradway (1990a) illustrated the developmental stages in children's sand worlds highlighting the three stages of development initially proposed by Kalff: animal-vegetative, fighting, and adaptation to the collective. Bradway (1990b) also demonstrated the healing value of sandplay in her presentation of one woman's individuation process from the creation of 70 sandplay worlds.

Accounts of the creative power of sandplay are depicted along with eight children's worlds in another work (Dundas, 1980). In this work the importance of the symbolism of the bear and owl were noted, two figures chosen repeatedly by children and adults for sandplay. Dundas proposed associations to the instinctual bear with the "perilous part of the unconscious which needs healing" (p.144), the cyclical nature of retreating from the external world, ferociousness, motherly love, and the connection to qualities of endurance, strength, and courage. The owl may have associations to isolation, abandonment, terror, fear of the unknown, as well as insight, wisdom, and protection "the poetry and spiritual beauty of the night" (p.146). The contradictory nature of these associations suggests the symbolic meanings that play a part in initiating the healing process and eventually reuniting the opposites.

Interventions for Children Who Witness Domestic Violence

Unfortunately, very few children caught within the complex of domestic violence receive treatment unless they are seen at a shelter. This type of treatment is often crisis intervention or short term group counseling. Children may also receive treatment when their conduct calls attention to disruptive behavior in a school setting through acts of truancy, assault, theft, or drug use.

In conducting clinical assessments of children, it is important to keep in mind that some children develop symptoms in the clinical range and others may demonstrate various strengths in social competence and adjustment. Safety is the initial primary concern when working with children. It is important to evaluate the plan for the child's psychological and physical safety. If working within a shelter for battered women, the location is kept confidential for the safety of all residents. Developing a plan for safety if the marital violence recurs is helpful in identifying safe havens for the child within or outside the home. Helping the child refrain from functioning as an intermediary in stopping the violence between the parents is a powerful intervention. Keeping the child safe also involves conducting an assessment of lethality in order to avoid any revictimization of the child when it is likely that the family members will be brought together for therapy.

In taking a family history, assessing risk factors such as depression or antisocial behavior among family members provides potential information about the child's symptoms. Becoming aware of the stresses faced by the family, including financial or economic constraints, cultural, and language factors sheds light on the dynamics that may be present. Understanding the child rearing and discipline standards applied within the family are essential.

The child's developmental level is a major component in the assessment since an infant's needs will differ from a school age child's, as will the capacity to process information, and the reactions to trauma within different age groups vary. During times of acute stress the usual coping processes are severely challenged and prior self-calming or soothing methods may prove to be inadequate.

When creating a treatment plan, issues to consider include the potential length of intervention required, whether the symptoms are the result of long term exposure to multiple stressors or prolonged trauma, which family members need treatment in what constellation, and the co-occurring disorders such as depression, conduct disorder, and attention deficit disorder. It is also important to assess the broad range of coping behaviors, tension reducing behaviors, and characteristics of competence and resilience.

Group counseling for children is often the treatment of choice within shelters, outpatient social service agencies, and family court. Common goals are to develop safety skills, label feelings, express hopes and wishes about the family relationships, identify ways to obtain social support, develop self-concepts, increase levels of competence, and begin to understand the dynamics of family violence including the recognition of one's lack of responsibility for the parent or the violence.

In situations where the mother has taken refuge within a shelter and opportunities exist to work with the mother, helping her learn to respond effectively to her children's needs will strengthen her ability to provide support to them. This occurs after the physical and medical needs of the mother and children are met. The mother's individual psychotherapeutic treatment will support her, allow for time to evaluate her options, express her feelings, thoughts, and concerns, and will serve to empower her.

Specific treatment needs of the parent may involve assessment, development of a safety plan, addressing the psychological effects from the battering, meeting any medical needs, and resolving long-term consequences of the abuse or unresolved issues from childhood. Rarely is conjoint family therapy with the battering spouse recommended at this early phase in the treatment due to realistic and grave concerns of safety. However, conjoint therapy is recommended in the family reconstructionist approach which proposes the violence is maintained by reciprocal processes in the family. Lachkar (1998) described one such process, the dynamic of dual projective identification that exists in mutual cycles of projections and identifications. The systemic method includes gradual therapeutic work with individuals within the family, moving toward combined mother-child therapy, to conjoint therapy, and eventually family therapy. But it is very important to keep in mind the necessity for partner lethality assessments and the timing of this approach since premature conjoint therapy and family counseling can lead to further violence.

Partner Abuse

Various offender typologies have been proposed with the most recent empirical, clinical, and anecdotal data placing the behaviors into three specific groups: individuals who have abnormal power and control needs, restricting their violence within the home; individuals possessing these control needs and suffering from serious psychological problems; and those who engage in criminal or psychopathic behaviors outside the home (Walker & Meloy, 1998). Psycho-educational treatment is the treatment of choice for most offenders while longer term psychotherapy, medication management, and incarceration may be needed for others.

A number of treatment approaches exist for intimate partner violence from differing theoretical perspectives. The macrotheories view battering as a societal problem and espouse a resocialization approach where power and control tactics are abandoned and biased attitudes toward women are changed (Wyatt, 1994). The microtheories emerge from cognitive behavioral perspectives holding assumptions that individuals who batter can benefit from developments in learning theory and behavior modification. Cognitive techniques involving thought and belief restructuring, reinterpretation of events, and righting cognitive inversions are utilized (Barnett, Miller-Perrin, & Perrin, 1997). The cognitive inversions are distorted

perceptions such as believing one is not the batterer but a ʼ
sible for battering behavior. Individuals who batter may ʼ
nize verbal and psychological abuse as abusive behavi
change these kinds of behavior. The therapeutic work
intimidation and sets goals to stop the nonphysical as weⅡ ᴀ _
relationship. Anger management approaches are also utilized wheℕ
manage adverse arousal, methods of appropriate assertive behavior, and pɪⱷ
solving skills.

In general, systemic theories view partner violence as a reflection of faulty interaction within the dyad and value the reunification of the family. Couples therapy is incorporated, techniques are taught to improve communication, and marital or partner satisfaction is sought. Male and female co-therapists are utilized to model nonviolent behavior. Integrated approaches incorporate macrotheory, microtheory, utilize marital therapy approaches, and address problems with alcohol and substance addiction.

Sexual Abuse Offenders

One of the first broad based treatment models for incest and sexual abuse of children was the Giarretto model (1978). This multi-dimensional model incorporates self-help methods with the involvement of professionals who facilitate groups, and offers programs for offenders incarcerated for incest. The model includes groups for offending spouses, non-offending spouses, couples, multiple family groups, children's groups, adolescent groups, and adult survivor groups. Advanced groups allow opportunities for a combination of individuals, including offenders, non-offending spouses, and survivors to deepen their recovery process through interpersonal confrontation and support.

Research indicates both males and females are vulnerable to incestuous abuse and that men and women perpetrate the abuse. Girls may be most vulnerable when they are the oldest female child in the home (Russell, 1986) or have assumed parental roles and responsibilities such as caring for other children in the home (Meiselman, 1990). Men are more frequently the perpetrators of child sexual abuse and tend to engage in more severe or traumatic behaviors (Finkelhor & Russell, 1984). Women who sexually abuse children are more likely to abuse males and may function as active or passive co-offenders in the abuse of females (Meiselman, 1990). Same gender incest is viewed as symbolic identification and may be more representative of narcissism than homosexual orientation.

Typologies of child abuse offenders have focused heavily on pedophiles and incest offenders. Initially Groth, Hobson, & Gary (1982) proposed a dualistic typology of child molesters, placing individuals into the fixated or regressed groups. This theory held that the fixated offender had a primary sexual orientation to children, had pedophilic interests that began during adolescence, pre-meditated and planned his offenses, and held a persistent sexual interest followed by compulsive behavior. The regressed type possessed a sexual orientation to adult age mates, had pedophilic interests which developed during adulthood, experienced precipitating stressors prior to the sexual abuse of children, and had epi-

offenses toward children. The fixated offender tended to choose males as victims while the regressed chose females. The fixated offender was characterized as an individual who identified closely with the victims and had little or no sexual contact with adults. The regressed offender had sexual contacts with adults and children and lived a more traditional lifestyle.

While this theory was initially helpful in developing a theoretical understanding as to the differences between some offenders, the discrete categories have not proven valid in many circumstances, such as with adolescent sexual offenders. A number of additional theories have been proposed that involve an array of complex factors. One classification system elaborated upon Groth's typologies by dividing the fixated-regressed dimension into two categories, intensity of pedophilic interest and the existing level of social competence (Knight & Prentky, 1990). Another model, the Four Factor Model of Child Molesting (Araji & Finkelhor, 1994) postulates the interplay of factors consisting of emotional congruence, sexual arousal, blockage, and inhibition. Emotional congruence relates to issues of immaturity, low self-esteem, mastery of trauma through repetition, an attraction to children based on dominance, and identification with aggression. The sexual arousal theory encompasses a heightened sexual arousal to children and conditioning or modeling from early childhood. The blockage theory suggests a difficulty in relating to adult women, inadequate social skills, sexual anxiety, disturbances in adult sexual relationships, and the holding of repressive norms about sexual behavior. The disinhibition theory relates to impulse disorders and use of alcohol.

Cognitive behavioral models have also been proposed (Becker & Kaplan, 1993; Conte, 1985; Marshall & Barbaree, 1988) focusing on degrees of arousal, social competence, cognitive distortions, empathy for victims, general sexual functioning, and identification of high-risk situations. These approaches report promising outcomes. Treatment approaches including cognitive behavioral components (Marshall & Barbaree, 1990) confront cognitive distortions which include minimizations, justifications, and rationalizations for sexual offending. Accepting responsibility for the offense and moving past denial is an integral function of treatment and is a necessary component for current treatment models.

Sexual offender programs for adolescents doubled in number within a ten year period (Bonner, Marx, Thompson, & Michaelson, 1998). Adolescent offenders have become the focus of significant research and clinical work resulting in the development of extensive assessment and treatment methods. As with adult offenders, comprehensive psychological testing is recommended, with a focus on cognitive ability, sexual behavior, personality, and psychopathology. Family functioning, social skills, self-esteem, and self-concept are also assessed. Instruments such as polygraphs are utilized to measure changes in physiological functioning when asked about sexual behavior and plethysmographs are used to measure sexual arousal in both male and female offenders (Lane, 1997). Research has indicated the majority of adolescent sexual offenders are not sexual abuse victims (Benoit & Kennedy, 1992) but do live within disruptive homes where physical abuse, spouse abuse, and alcohol or substance abuse are predominant (Graves, Openshaw, Ascione, & Ericksen, 1996).

Individual treatment approaches have largely been developed from the models used with adults (Becker & Kaplan), integrating techniques aimed at reducing deviant sexual arousal. Cognitive behavioral group treatment remains the most common treatment for adolescent sexual offenders centering around discussion of the offense, modifying cognitive distortions, assertiveness, anger management, sexual education, and relapse prevention.

Relapse prevention frameworks confront denial, identify risk factors, decrease distorted cognitions, increase empathy for victims, decrease the deviant sexual arousal to children, and increase social competency (Murphy & Smith, 1997). Ward and Hudson (1998) proposed a comprehensive relapse prevention model incorporating cognitive, behavioral, and affective factors, with motivation, and contextual pathways (Ward, Louden, Hudson, & Marshall, 1995). Their model attempts to assess the particular offending style, the degree of violence involved, the specific time, place, and circumstance involved for each offender, acknowledging the heterogeneity of the offending population.

Multisystemic therapy appears to the most promising treatment approach to address the known risk factors for adolescent sexual offending (Swenson, Henggeler, Schoenwald, Kaufman, & Randall, 1998). This approach is a social-ecological model focusing on the multiple factors correlated with offending, including the environments of family, peers, school, and community. The model incorporates a focus on the grooming behaviors that facilitate abuse, clarify the placement of responsibility on the offender, involve the family in the treatment in order to reduce risk and establish safety, and work toward family reunification. Since some adolescent offenders also have been sexually victimized, this approach integrates trauma focused treatment as well (Cohen & Mannarino, 1996; Veronen & Kilpatrick, 1993). Empirical research, provider outcome studies, and comprehensive assessments of sexual offenders will continue to refine treatments, address the specific deficits, alter the behaviors, and impact future sexual predatory behavior.

Adult Survivors

The symptoms that bring adult survivors into psychotherapy may center around issues of identity, attachment, difficulty with relationships, lack of self-soothing capacity, violations of personal boundaries, and affect regulation. Seven components of recovery have been articulated in work with survivors of childhood trauma: authority over the remembering process, integration of memory and affect, affect tolerance, symptom mastery, self-esteem and self-cohesion, safe attachment, and meaning making (Harvey, 1996). This is a multidimensional model of empowerment.

During the course of treatment, the issues of pacing, timing, and the development of stability in the survivor's life are important considerations. Briere (1989; 1992), Courtois (1988; 1997), and Meiselman (1990) addressed these issues in their inclusive treatment manuals and provided theoretical perspectives on the dynamics within incestuous families. Saakvitne, Gamble, Pearlman, and Lev (2000) also developed a comprehensive treatment protocol *Risking Connection: A Train-*

ing Curriculum for Working with Survivors of Childhood Abuse, that provides numerous case history examples and suggestions for assessing countertransference within a relational trauma therapy framework.

In treatment with adult survivors of incestuous abuse Courtois (1997) proposed four sequenced phases: pretreatment assessment; a preliminary phase of alliance building, safety, and stabilization; a middle phase for mourning and resolution of the trauma; and a last phase allowing for further integration. The primary goal is to gain stability and perspective through a treatment process that progresses at a manageable pace, allowing for integration and assimilation of the range of experiences and resultant emotions. Hosting the imagination in the healing process can be done during all of these phases. Kane's (1989) work with incest survivors is centered in the imaginal complementing her view of incest as a denial of freedom, feeling, and imagination.

During the trauma resolution phase Herman (1992) encourages letting go as a goal of treatment rather than forgiveness. A letting go that occurs internally and allows the victim role to dissipate. She believes the best use of the term *victim* is temporary, signaling the dynamic nature of the recovery process leading to transformation. The identification with the victim role is a form of internalized oppression with the potential for abusing oneself as well as others. Helplessness and fantasies of revenge emerge when the victim archetype takes over, constellating personal disempowerment and does not contribute to healing. Courtois (1997) encourages therapists to learn about the range of enactments that occur within treatment and to recognize when the roles of victim, victimizer, and rescuer, known as the victimization triangle, are projected or protected against. As patients increase awareness of these unconscious roles they experience a range of new behaviors within intrapersonal relationships.

The integrity of the psyche is witnessed repeatedly in psychotherapeutic work. When I become aware of incongruencies in the therapeutic process or notice unstated disturbing dynamics, I tend to *follow psyche* at these moments and bring this explicitly into the consulting room by articulating what I have become aware of. I may see tears when a specific relationship is discussed, notice a constricting gesture or posture that seems incongruent with the topic, or experience direct avoidance of an issue. When the patient is not able or willing to address the issues I will respect his or her desire, or resistance, in not pursuing this issue or behavior at that time. An aspect of the current internal conflict or symptom has emerged, perhaps just enough to be held by the patient's awareness at that moment. In my experience I have seen this re-emerge at a later date when the patient has greater capacity to work through it. This appears to be an important protective mechanism that needs to be respected and trusted. Kalsched (1996) proposed the concept of the archetypal self-care system referring to a protective constellation or structure that prevents a violation of the "personal spirit at the core of the individual's true self" (p.12).

Given the general focus of therapy as integration, a striving toward wholeness, and making meaning from experiences, when dissociation emerges in psychotherapy, one is very aware of the disintegration that is being signaled. Dissociation may be used during psychotherapy, to psychologically vacate, as it may have been used as a coping strategy during the abuse. Dissociation is a powerful defensive process and is received with respect and an acknowledgment of this unique survival strategy. Patients may not be aware of the role that dissociation plays or may be interested in limiting it to more appropriate circumstances. Helping the patient become aware of and decrease the dissociative behaviors can be extremely empowering. Providing feedback about the behaviors observed within the sessions will assist the patient to regain control of some of the unconscious behaviors.

Dissociation may be viewed as a continuum, with subtle disengagement or detachment at one end and psychological withdrawal or repression at the other. Briere (1989) describes customary forms of dissociation ranging from primitive to more sophisticated forms, including disengagement, detachment or numbing, observation, postsession amnesia, as if, shutdown, and total repression. Some of these dissociative experiences are quite common human experiences, such as daydreaming or disengaging for a few seconds within a classroom or detaching from emotionally laden situations that reduce stress. The extreme toll of detachment may be experienced as numbness of feeling, being unaware or void of emotions, or eventually shutting down. Many adult survivors describe the sense of being outside looking in and somehow observing what is happening as in depersonalization experiences. Discontinuity may be experienced from one session to the next where the patient has not remembered a significant or particularly difficult part of the previous week's work. The more extreme forms of dissociation may result in extensive periods of memory lapses, chronic disturbing dreams, compulsive behaviors, a tendency to become involved in destructive or degrading relationships, and unexplainable reactions to films or books about sexual abuse (Briere, 1989).

Survivors of childhood abuse may engage indirectly or directly in self-injurious behavior. Direct engagement may involve intentional cutting behaviors, burning of the skin, and other acts of self-mutilation while indirect engagement in self-injury may be the omission of self-care. These behaviors are viewed as tension reducing behaviors (Briere, 1992) and attempts at self-regulation (van der Kolk, 1996) that serve adaptive functions, attempting to preserve life or help the individual remain grounded during overwhelming affective experiences or embodied experiences of intrusive memories. This ongoing wounding of the body is very significant. In work with survivors, it brings my attention to the embodiment of the original violence experienced in childhood. This may also be a way of remembering the disparate experiences and the way out of the oppression. This is a symptom that cries out for exploration within a safe environment. The consulting room provides a safe place in which to explore the meanings of these behaviors.

Goals in treatment are centered around identifying the behaviors, understanding their adaptations, assisting the patient in broadening his or her capacity to tolerate feelings, and slowly introducing alternative behaviors that are less harmful. The behaviors may allow the patient to feel, to avoid feeling, to express anger or rage, to become grounded, or to punish. Connors (1996) proposed guidelines for therapists in responding to these behaviors. She emphasized the importance of not shaming or labeling the behavior as "crazy or manipulative" (p.209) and encourages practitioners to become familiar with their own reactions or level of discomfort to the self-injurious behaviors in order avert unconscious blaming of the patient.

I have witnessed many involved in the healing process comment on a novel sense of experiencing *home* for the first time. This is a discovery of a new found sense of self, coming into contact with the core of one's being within a supportive community. A regeneration, renewal, or even reformation (Gadon, 1989). A sense of acceptance, acknowledgment, and a recognition of imperfection may accompany this new hospitable environment. Home embodies a self-nurturing capacity, serving as a turning point within psychotherapy, allowing for the presence of the disparate life experiences. One may no longer be striving, hungering for the external home that was either destructive in childhood or elusive later in adulthood. The despair, sense of void, and rage may begin to subside. Grieving may accompany the process, with an unfolding awareness of the work that is still ahead.

Referrals

In the practice of psychotherapy, where the process of assessment is ongoing, providing the most comprehensive treatment includes the use of additional resources to meet your patient's needs. Referrals may be either essential, such as medical referrals during emergency situations, or complementary to the treatment process. Complementary referrals enrich the treatment process and may include training or coursework in parenting skills, group work as an adjunct to the individual treatment, family treatment in addition to individual work, traditional healers or religious practitioners, physically supportive services such as chiropractic or massage, and self help programs for addiction.

In making a referral consider which specific person, community agency, or service is qualified to assist the patient and the patient's readiness or willingness to access the referral. Any limitations, cultural barriers, or constraints that would make it difficult for the patient to gain or benefit, e.g., inaccessibility, unaffordable cost, or language should be known in advance. Some referrals may be directly accessed by the therapist, depending on the therapist's setting, such as within a shelter, and the timing within the treatment, while others can be given to the patient, allowing her or him to make the contact with the referral source. This can be highly empowering and may also be the favored clinical dynamic with some referrals.

The following listing provides a host of potential adjunctive services that will enhance one's ability to respond to the needs of the individuals or family members being treated, strengthen one's case management ability, and provide resources for future work with patients.

Crisis Referrals
- Emergency Room: Immediate medical or psychiatric assistance
- Police or Other Law Enforcement Agency such as Sheriff's Department. May be used when making a child abuse report or for protection of the patient
- Hotline: Information; Support for patient or family members
- Rape Crisis Center: Counseling, support, partner assistance
- Domestic Violence Shelter: Safe respite; Shelter for homeless or battered women and children
- Social Services: Child and adult protective services; assistance with money, food, clothing, and shelter.

Clinically Related Adjunctive Referrals
- Clinical Psychologist: Psychological or neurological testing
- Psychiatrist: Psychopharmacological consultation
- Child Psychologist: Special expertise in working with children
- Sex Therapist: Sexual dysfunction that you are not qualified to treat
- Vocational Counselor: Occupational testing; Career counseling
- Guidance Counselor: Guidance in vocational opportunities
- Group Therapy: Adjunctive or sole treatment
- College Counseling Centers: Patients who are students
- Residential Treatment: Structured and specialized

Religious or Spiritual Referrals
- Rabbi, Priest, Minister
- Pastoral Counselor or Clergy
- Traditional Healer or Spiritual Leader
- Shaman, Curandero, Espiritista, or Indigenous Healer

Legal Resources
- Attorney or Legal Clinic or Legal Assistance Center
- Patients' Rights Advocate: For violation or denial of rights
- American Civil Liberties Union
- Attorney General's Office
- Family Violence Legal Center or Battered Woman's Legal Office
- District Attorney's Office
- Victim-Witness Services of the County
- Licensing Boards or Professional Associations: To register ethical complaints with board or association
- Insurance Company

Educational or Occupational Resources
- School Systems: Pupil personnel service; Attendance counselors; Nurses; Special education services; Services for students with disabilities
- Library: Resources for information
- Child's School: Principal or teacher for school related child/family problems
- Employment Development Department: Employment services
- Social Services: Welfare services, employment assistance
- Employment Agencies: Job recruitment, placement, and training
- Employee Assistance Program: Employee services for issues interfering with job

Medical Referrals
- Emergency Room Assessment and Treatment
- Family Physician: Physical exams to rule out organic causes;
  consult with eating disorder team
- Neurologist: To assess and diagnosis organic mental disorders
- Veterans Administration (VA) Hospital
- Psychiatrist: Consultation and Medication Evaluation
- Urologist or Gynecologist
- HIV Testing Center; AIDS Projects
- Physical Therapy; Bodywork; Massage
- Sleep Disorders Diagnostic Clinic
- Detoxification Center
- Registered Dietitian

Self-Help and Support Groups
- Survivor Groups such as Incest Survivors: Daughters United,
  Daughters and Sons United; Incest Survivors Anonymous;
  Men's survivor groups.
- Survivor Groups (other Traumas): Children of Holocaust Survivors;
  Survivors of Disasters such as plane crashes; Political Prisoners of War
- Parents Groups: Parent Effectiveness Training (PET);
  Systematic Training for Effective Parenting (STEP); Parents United
- Support Groups for Patient's Families
- Coming Out Groups; Gay Men's Groups; Lesbian Groups
- Twelve step programs such as Alcoholics Anonymous; Al Anon;
  Alateen; CoDependents Anonymous; Cocaine or Narcotics Anonymous
  (*currently over 150 Anonymous groups*)
- Thirteen step programs such as 13 Steps of Women for Sobriety
- Adult Children of Alcoholics treatment groups
  ACA groups, ACOA workshops
- Sex Addicts Anonymous
- Dream Work Groups
- Eating Disorder Groups: Overeaters Anonymous
  Specifically focused group therapy.
- Smoking Cessation Groups
- Specific Racial or Ethnic or Cultural Support Group
- Singles Groups: Parents Without Partners for single parents; community
  organizations such as YMCA, YWCA, churches

Referring a Case Out

There are a number of circumstances that necessitate referring a case out prior to beginning the treatment process or disengaging from the case while it is in progress. Seeking peer consultation, supervision, or professional consultation can assist in the determination process of when to refer the case out in complex situations. For example, when countertransference reactions are interfering with one's ability to provide psychotherapy, such as personal wounds that emerge for the first time in the course of treatment that become overwhelming, and one is unable to resolve these through supervision, consultation, or personal therapy, it is in the patient's best interest to refer to another practitioner. Another situation is when a strong erotic countertransference emerges and the therapist is unable to contain it, process it, or utilize it to the benefit of the patient as potential clinical information.

When the case is outside one's scope of practice or the course of therapy is outside one's level of training and experience, it is prudent to refer the case. Similarly if a professional relationship with the potential patient already exists, or one personally knows the individual as a friend, relative, neighbor, student, or the individual is in a family, friendship, or intimate relationship with an existing patient causing unresolvable boundary or confidentiality issues, then referring is recommended.

Closure or Termination Process

Closure or termination remains an integral part of the therapeutic process. Termination may evolve organically after the client has experienced a range of personal gains, implemented support systems, resolved conflicts, and integrated new behaviors. While the termination process may consolidate and summarize the treatment process, and provide the client with opportunities for further developmental growth, individuation, and empowerment, it can also restimulate abuse related issues.

The responsibility to engage in a termination process belongs to the therapist and is addressed explicitly within many profession's ethical codes of conduct. Planning a considerable amount of time for termination and closure issues with abuse survivors is preferred to a brief ending. The number of termination focused sessions is highly dependent on the length of the therapeutic relationship and the context of the treatment. If a therapist is working with clients on a time-limited basis, a referral to an appropriate provider would be given, but if the client is in the midst of a crisis at the pre-specified end of therapy, the therapist addresses those needs until the crisis is resolved.

Sensitively welcoming the potential issues associated with this transition includes inviting the range of feelings that may emerge including any restimulated abuse related issues. Clearly dependent upon the relationship, the circumstances of the termination, and the amount of time devoted to the termination, grieving the loss of the intimate therapeutic relationship with the therapist may be necessary and expressions of anger at the perceived abandonment may occur. Further opportunities for growth abound during this process within the safety of the therapeutic relationship.

In some circumstances, the client may express a desire to end the therapeutic process either directly or indirectly. The client may explicitly state that she or he is interested in ending therapy-perhaps prematurely in your professional opinion-or the client has reached a point where it would be helpful to terminate and the original agreed upon goals have been reached. In these situations, validate the client's stated desire, invite the patient to express and acknowledge feelings, thoughts, or images about terminating, and work toward an acceptable resolution.

The resolution may consist of a vacation or break from therapy, a full termination, or a referral to another practitioner or form of treatment.

I have learned that honoring the client's stated desire to end treatment at this juncture far outweighs my initial interest in wanting the client to continue in treatment. Since I view the treatment process as a collaboration, I customarily express my support of the client's wish, inquire further into the desire, and share my clinical perspective. I believe in taking breaks from the therapeutic process when time is needed to consolidate gains made. An explicit discussion about the termination may also reveal undisclosed wishes or needs of the clients that were not raised earlier. For this reason it can prove to be highly empowering and may even move the treatment into a deeper arenas.

Moving toward closure the therapist can effectively address unfinished questions or concerns, including unstated feelings between the patient and therapist, the patient's perception of the therapy process, especially if this hasn't been done throughout the therapeutic process, and evaluation of the positive aspects and possible disappointments concerning the therapeutic process. The termination phase allows the therapist to acknowledge the client's personal growth, summarize gains and successes, identify major "learnings" for both patient and therapist, discuss possible areas for future work, and recommend future therapy alternatives if the client is interested.

▨ Chapter 13

Meridian Assessment Paradigm

Dream the myth onwards and give it a modern dress.
                                                    Jung, 1969

The following section presents an assessment and treatment model that grew from my studies in Jungian psychology, traditional healing practices, phenomenology, and empirical assessment methods. I have relied on it as a guiding framework when meeting with individual patients, couples, and families for initial assessments, ongoing treatment, and dreamwork. It also has applicability as an instrument for the therapist's development and self-care.

Traditional psychological assessment has focused on psychopathology from the perspective of the medical model, viewing deficits and problematic affect, thoughts, and behaviors as symptoms to alleviate or cure. Assessment results are reported as diagnostic labels or in terms of actuarial scores. The Meridian Assessment Paradigm, a depth psychological assessment approach, provides a comprehensive and collaborative heuristic model in which to view both the suffering of the soul and the pathways to healing. *Heuristic* comes from the Greek *heuriskein*, meaning to discover or to find. This model relies upon a discovery or unveiling process.

The term *meridian* refers to the period of greatest elevation of splendor or the highest point achieved, as in a specific place or circumstance distinguished from others. In the Eastern healing system known as Chinese Traditional Medicine, meridians run vertically and horizontally through the body, just as the longitudinal and latitudinal lines run on the earth's sphere. In this traditional practice and philosophy, the meridians transport Chi, the vital life energy to the organs helping to maintain harmony in mind-body-spirit. Meridians serve as channels in which this life force flows. This is an appropriate metaphor for the potential of the meridian assessment paradigm to open unacknowledged, unknown, or stifled life sustaining energy.

The meridian assessment paradigm presents eight fields of inquiry: material, ecological, relational, interior, deportmental, imaginal, archetypal, and numinous. The fields are extensively interconnected and represent a balance between these elements of human existence, like the threads within a tapestry. This model is not linear but circular, ordered around intuitive reasoning.

As a practicing psychologist I am acutely interested in the function of symptoms. Many are relatively straightforward and provide a direct means to the presenting problem and treatment. Clearly others require a meandering approach to slowly reveal their meaning or function. In times of antiquity symptoms were perceived as messengers from the gods, sent to heal aspects of self or psyche. Taking an inductive reasoning approach, from the specific to the general, symptoms can be viewed as healing messengers or healing messages that call for understanding. Striving for understanding contributes to the process of making meaning from the symptoms.

In this tradition, the meridian assessment paradigm is offered as a path to experience the meaning of authentic suffering and enter into the reality of the patient's life and life view. This is an active collaborative process engaged with intention, curiosity, and reflection. The process may be experienced as the initiation of a labyrinthine journey, calling upon a certain degree of faith, not knowing what may emerge or present itself along the way. Bachelard (1969) likened the structure of the soul with "the image of the labyrinth" (p.113).

The process begins with a focus on mater, the Material, of or pertaining to the body. Mater is also defined as mother, another beginning place. These are the manifestations of the body and the physiological aspects belonging to it. "The body is a language, a gesture, a sign, and a form of speaking in and to the world" (Slattery, 2000, p.19). In conducting an assessment, organic aspects are noted, such as the presence of health, illness, and specific symptoms causing distress or pain. The senses are contemplated: visual, auditory, olfactory, taste, and kinesthetic. The pleasure or displeasure one receives from the body is also evaluated. Secondarily, assessing the matter taken into the body is essential, such as food, medications, and non-nutritive substances. Eating disorders are evaluated in this dimension. Matter covering the body such as clothing or adornments become tertiary elements. Also, the felt sense of being in this body, of living within the body is assessed. When applying this to patients who are healing from abuse, one also looks at the overall residual effect that prevents the individual from living life fully and the impact on the body. Physical structural issues may need to be addressed, such as the need to release muscle tension through relaxation exercises, physical exercise, progressive relaxation, body treatment such as Feldenkrais, movement therapy, massage, or chiropractic care.

The next facet is the Ecological. This is the landscape and environment, the ecosystem, the territory one dwells in. The relationship or connection to nature is evaluated here. The presence of and association with companion animals, pets, farm animals, and wild animals is considered. "A view of nature that stresses its interpenetration into all areas of human experience" (Hayles, 1995, p. 465). This ecological focus includes the geography, the place one is actually situated, the context in which one lives and works. Explorations of the landscape, the setting one is customarily in or *at home in*, such as a house, apartment, separate room, or the outdoors. The context may be urban, crowded, spacious, rural, country, desert, forest, oceanscape, wilderness, suburban, in wealth, poverty, polluted, fresh and clear. Aspects to consider are cultural, cross-cultural, economic, and political as well. This would include the combined attributes of the community, tribe, or group the individual is part of.

To understand the full sense of the ecological one needs to know the climate the person lives in, both literal and metaphorical. The metaphorical season and climate may be winter, summer, humid, dry and arid, hot, cold, or a temperate zone. The environmental conditions are also factors such as snow, rain, storms, gale forces, lightning, thunder, peaceful serenity, moonlight, darkness, sunshine, or daylight. Note the associations made to the sounds, odors, tastes, or fragrances contained there. These externals can be quite remarkable. When using the ecological dimension with survivors of abuse, note where the abuse occurred, e.g., the actual physical setting, and the client's current relationship to this setting, the avoidance of it, or the continued involvement with it. Awareness of the felt sense of this place today will yield more information. The developmental stage and age at the time of the abuse is also explored.

The next step is to look at the Relational and interpersonal aspects. Noting the relationships with those who are living, recently deceased, or ancestral. The sexual, erotic, and other loving relationships are assessed. The existence of connections with family, friends, acquaintances, coworkers, strangers, and creatures is noted. Assess what lives in the field between self and others–tension, fusion, separation, enmeshment, abandonment, compassion, care, or nurturing. In terms of abuse, all of these aspects of the relationship are assessed, with a specific focus on the prior and current relationship with the individual or individuals who perpetrated the abuse. The presence of any enlightened witnesses or supportive persons would be highlighted and the impact on relationships today are considered including the therapeutic relationship.

The next sequence is Interiority. This is the inner life or intrapersonal dimension of the person focusing on the intraverted aspects. Secondarily, this involves the inner lives of any figures, characters, or persons within images and dreams. The intuitions, personal judgments, moods, passions, desires, and feelings are reviewed. In terms of affect and intensity, the range of qualities are assessed which may include surprise, distress, shame, fear, enjoyment, disgust, anger, or interest. Specific feelings or thoughts may become outstanding through this process. Becoming aware of the relationship to self is essential in this dimension. Noting a quality of peace, tranquillity, contemplation, solitude, or chaos, frenzy, haste, or foreboding provides insight into the phenomenological world of the client. Accessing the internal qualities that are not ordinarily exposed to the outside world provides important insights. In relating this interior dimension to the abuse experience, the personal thoughts, feelings, and psychological responses to the abuse are considered. Thoughts and feelings about self, level of confidence, competence in life, capacity to modulate one's internal state, and the ability to self-soothe are all interior factors.

Deportment or demeanor is the next realm. The term deportment is from the Latin "deportare" referring to how one carries oneself in the outside world. This dimension is descriptive of behavior and involves a range of extraverted behaviors, movements, conduct, and personal carriage. Behavior is revealed in the presence and quality of gesture, tone and pitch of voice, how one walks, and speaks, and appears to perceive. How one carries the body and appears to others externally is important, especially if character armor is present. This is an opportunity to focus on descriptions of behavior and all accompanying extraverted actions. Mobility, movements, and dance may be considered. Actions may be spontaneous, compulsive, repetitive, familiar, unusual, or physically exhaustive. Behavior may be explosive, implosive, or frequent physical accidents may occur. In terms of the abuse experiences the impact on one's exterior presentation is comprehensively explored, noting changes that may have occurred or that occur in certain situations. Insights may emerge when asking whether the current behavioral representation feels in line with one's interior sense of self.

The domain of the Imaginal focuses on the experience and quality of the imaginal life "the imagination is the real and literal power of soul to create images" (Kane, 1989, p.25). Spontaneous images, dreams, and recurring symbols are tended to. Any obvious, clear, or hidden symbols, signs, primordial images, mandalas, or artistic expressions are noted. Figures or elements may exist indicating symmetry, fragmentation, or polar opposition, containing conflictual inharmonious aspects. Drawing, painting, or sculpting the images may allow the dimensionality of the images to be experienced. Becoming aware of the size, color, and weight of the images is helpful. Images may be of the dark side, of the subterranean lower depths, or of brilliance and light. "The image dwells in depth, in depths created by shadows and reflections, depths that can be dived into and treaded amongst" (Watkins, 1984, p.128). The images from dreams, flashbacks, and nightmares may become central in work with the abuse survivor. Images of darkness, the absence of light, the presence of a black hole or black sun (Kristeva, 1989) may accompany the healing process of abuse survivors.

The next realm is Archetypal. The universal patterns, mythological themes, legends, and stories of one's history and family history are addressed here. "Particular myths, at least, will be living themselves out in one's life" (Edinger, 1994, p.3). Narratives provide insight into the dramatic structure, including the beginning, the presence of impasses or conflicts, resolutions or catastrophes, culmination, and outcome. Becoming familiar with the traditional movements within the genre of the epic, lyric, comic, or tragic work provides another lens through which one sees the overall drama. The muted, invisible, inexpressible, or subtle manifestations are also explored. Perhaps a particular myth or folktale resonates with personal experience. A new story can also be created that is more fitting for the changes made throughout the restoration and healing process. In working with abuse survivors themes of resilience or strength can be woven into stories of survival.

The domain of the Numinous is honorably distinguished by appearing last in this continuum, ensouling the entire meridian paradigm. The "approach to the numinous" (Jung, 1973, p.376) is seen as central to the healing process and involves the sacred dimension of our physical and spiritual lives. The capacity for wholeness is embodied within the numinous. The numinosum has been described as the alterations in consciousness that emerge from contact with transpersonal psychic energies (Otto, 1958).

These numinous aspects often co-exist with spiritual or religious experience, mysticism, synchronicity, epiphany, metaphysical experience, the presence of visions, ancient traditions, ritual, oracular divination, and devotional practices. "Epiphany thus interrupts the everyday flow of time and enters as one privileged moment when we intuitively grasp a deeper more essential reality" (Milosz, 1996, p.3). Religious observance, near death experiences, and synchronistic events are also explored in this dimension. Divine, reverent, or holy figures may emerge in the imaginal realm or an awareness of the daimonic, a guiding force, or demonic may be prominent. Associations and amplifications can be made to these numinous aspects. In work with abuse survivors, coming to terms with the abusive experiences in the context of enduring or forsaken religious and spiritual beliefs may become central in the therapeutic work.

Although the numinous concludes the meridian assessment paradigm, it truly belongs to the epenthetic realm, with subtle permeations in the preceding dimensions of this continuum. "For an approach to divinity that has personal relevance, it is necessary to focus on its manifestations within the psyche, in the body, in relationships" (Corbett, 1996, p.2). Jung also referred to the association of intense affect with archetypal and numinous experiences. Matter can be conceptualized as the concretization or manifestation of spirit. From this perspective, the circumambulant nature of the meridian assessment paradigm becomes apparent.

With the meridian assessment process the patterns emerge, predominant images arise, conflicts are highlighted, problematic areas or deficits become known, wishes and desires become apparent. One intention is "to make visible the otherwise invisible dynamics of the unconscious psyche" (Johnson, 1986, p.23). Opposite and conflicting modes of being may present a *tension of the opposites* that will orient the healing process.

There are several overlays that can be utilized in engaging the meridian as an assessment tool. One has to do with joys and fears. This yields abundant information about the perceived strengths, passions, and weaknesses, providing a glimpse into the areas of delight, satisfaction, and joy as well as the constricted and limiting qualities that may not be nurtured. In terms of matter, questions focusing on the joys of the body and the fears it holds can elicit strengths and perceived limitations. Sometimes asking the right questions can lead to transformative experiences (Estes, 1992). Approaching inquisitively and curiously is a suggested method.

The process of the meridian assessment paradigm is to look, to slow down, to sit with the impressions and themes. Intentional engagement in this work mitigates the effects of the cultural proscriptions of solitary individualism, isolation, and detachment from community, given that we live in "an age which regards as real only what goes fast and can be clutched with both hands" (Heidegger, 1959, p.206). Keeping a journal becomes a chronicle and living document of the process.

The *ways of knowing* articulated in this chapter are non-chronological and nonlinear, representing a close approximation to a spiral or circular process, where each realm is not entirely distinct from the other, but contains overlapping elements. Each dimension has connection to another. The elaborate image of the spiral, perpetually turning in on itself, expanding and contracting, sustains discovery, association, and amplification.

One can begin this meridian process with a reconstruction, literally recording and recollecting, looking at events, making associations to images, connections with personal issues, conflicts, psychological or spiritual development, or life circumstances. Allowing time for incubation, inspiration, and meanings to emerge. Throughout this process one discovers foremost that images function as profound gifts revealing more than they represent.

PART V

The Poetics of Tend-
ing Soul

Figure 3: Hygieia
Statuette of Aphrodite-Hygieia with Eros, Marble, AD 100-200.
Reprinted by permission of The J. Paul Getty Museum, Malibu, California.

Chapter 14

Prevention
Stop the Bloodshed

On the side of the dreamer, constituting the dreamer, we must
then recognize a power of poetization which can well be
designated as a psychological poetics; it is the poetics of the
psyche where all the psychic forces fall into harmony.

Gaston Bachelard, 1969

Cultural change and systemic prevention are preferred modalities to individual remediation. Although prevention as a concept has roots in prehistory, when communities came together using prayers and rituals to ward off disaster or catastrophe (Schmolling, Youkeles, & Burger, 1997), it has not received the same scholarly attention in the field of psychology as individual problem resolution, dysfunction, or distress (Holden & Black, 1999). Community psychology and social work training programs are the exception as they are philosophically and historically aligned with community prevention endeavors or institutional change.

The professions of psychology, marriage and family therapy, medicine, and social work all make significant contributions to the culture in their prevention efforts spanning research, practical application, and advocacy. The field of depth psychology has recently emphasized the importance of archetypal activism, working within communities to address issues affecting individuals, groups, communities, and society at large. These efforts emphasize a collaborative approach within communities holding respect for cultural norms and beliefs.

Prevention was recently situated as a focal point in psychology, evidenced by the president of the American Psychological Association declaring prevention as the theme of the 1998 annual conference. Conceptual models of prevention have been proposed including advocacy across the lifespan, preventive developmental interventions, prevention in the workplace, intervention with youth and older adults, and health promotion (Brown & Lent, 2000).

Public health prevention efforts devoted to physical health have been categorized into three levels: primary, secondary, and tertiary (Caplan, 1964). Primary prevention methods reduce the number of new instances of a disorder, while secondary efforts target an at-risk group in order to reduce the rate of prevalence of a disorder, and tertiary prevention efforts are aimed at decreasing the disabling effects of an existing disorder. Both the secondary and tertiary prevention methods integrate remediation or treatment, however, in practice, the distinctions between all three levels of prevention are more difficult to differentiate, and may not be as beneficial for examining psychologically relevant programs. For example, when a coping skills class is offered within a school setting, it can be classified as primary, secondary, or tertiary prevention depending on the students in the classroom: primary prevention for students with no dysfunctional coping habits; secondary prevention for students at risk for dysfunctional coping such as alcohol or drug use; and tertiary prevention for students who may already rely on drugs or alcohol in order to cope.

Romano and Hage (2000) broadened and expanded upon the three tiered prevention categorization adding two risk reduction strategies. They proposed five dimensions of prevention interventions: 1) primary prevention which stops a problem or behavior from occurring; 2) secondary prevention, delays the onset of a problem; 3) tertiary prevention, reduces the impact of a problem; 4) health promotion or personal well-being prevention, strengthens knowledge, attitudes, and behaviors that promote emotional and physical well-being; and 5) social and political change initiatives to improve environments where individuals live, learn, and work. The health promotion dimension includes teaching skills that inoculate against potentially harmful events or lifestyle behaviors such as training in life skills, wellness strategies, and stress management.

The fifth dimension emphasizes institutional change rather than individual change, and supports governmental, institutional, and community policies in efforts to promote well being (Romano & Hage, 2000). An example of this is the international support and implementation of the Convention on the Rights of the Child. As presented earlier in the text, this convention articulates a vision, incorporating the concepts of human dignity, the best interests of the child, nondiscrimination, maximum survival and development, and respect for children as human beings who are the subject of their own rights. Another example is the national public health agenda to improve health, contribute to the quality of life, and prevent disability, disease, and premature death in America, Healthy People 2010 (US Department of Health and Human Services, 2000). This document targets ten health indicators including mental health, substance abuse, and violence, specifying improvements within a ten year period.

Prevention of Child Abuse

Preventing child abuse requires multidisciplinary efforts originating from multiple levels. Prevention includes education, skills training, problem solving modules, and other efforts to prevent abusive behaviors from occurring. Delaying the onset of psychological problems and attaining a reduction in the incidence of child abuse is another prevention goal. Reducing and addressing the traumatic and stressful consequences associated with the experience of child abuse and neglect constitutes a form of prevention referred to as treatment. Health promotion efforts that strengthen knowledge, attitudes, and behaviors considerably impact overall well being and may contribute to the development of competence and resilience. Social and political change initiatives are also necessary as society evolves in more sophisticated and flexible ways to address child abuse.

One of the initial steps needed to prevent child abuse and neglect is to become aware of the problem, acknowledge its existence, and understand the psychological, social, and economic consequences. Re-evaluating the local, community, and national systems in place to address child maltreatment by assessing the functional and dysfunctional aspects, or conducting outcome studies can yield meaningful information and provide insight into the historical attempts at preventing child abuse. In addition to program evaluations, conducting needs assessments to ascertain the specific requirements of a group of children, a school, or community will prove beneficial prior to the implementation of any program.

Collaborating within a community and maintaining sensitivity to ethnic, racial, and cultural norms will increase the effectiveness of preventive measures. Failure to do so limits the effectiveness considerably (Schinke, 1994). Collaboration between agencies and across disciplines maximizes the exchange of information, pools resources, and refines the development of programs. Professional or parental training programs can be cosponsored by business leaders, tribal and non-tribal agencies, hospitals, churches, and schools. Court advocates, students, and interns can be recruited to volunteer their efforts. The achievement of common goals becomes a coordinated and cooperative endeavor.

Targeting the risk factors that contribute to child abuse and neglect through prevention programs is a strategy used by many community agencies. Education efforts aimed at increasing parenting skills or teaching child development can in turn increase a parent's level of competence, knowledge, and care, reducing abusive behavior. Creating educational programs to address animal cruelty and developing opportunities for children to experience regard and kindness expressed by animals (Dillman, 1999) are ways to emphasize the values of trust and respect for life. Companion animal farm programs and science programs can teach the value of non-human animals in our lives and instill compassion in the children who have opportunities to care for them. Animal assisted therapy programs (Fine, 1999) have been applied to a range of physical disabilities and psychological impairments, to teach socialization skills and expand well-being.

When designing child abuse prevention programs it is essential to assess the needs of the given community, implement the program within that community, and follow up to evaluate the effectiveness of the program. The project incorporates the unique cultural sensitivities and differences of the particular community. For example Zambrana & Dorrington (1998) cited the social, economic, and family structure variables that have contributed to risk for Latino subgroups creating vulnerability for abuse and neglect. The studies reviewed showed Latinos were more likely to have larger families than non-Hispanic families and less likely to have both parents in the home. They recommended that services to strengthen the families promote economic and social integration within the larger society.

Efforts to prevent physical violence toward children have ranged from parent education, free telephone consultation services to parents, information on child development, creation of social support networks, and the development of a wide range of services for parents. Home visitation, observation of interactions, and modeling of appropriate behavior has been gaining interest as a mode of physical abuse prevention. School based prevention programs and child assault prevention curricula situated within elementary and high schools have been developed to address sexual abuse and identify students at risk for developing behavioral or emotional problems. Parent support and outreach groups have formed bringing together fathers or mothers to empower and support each other in positive parenting efforts.

Violence prevention and community programs which integrate outreach, education, and empowerment are also necessary. These programs raise awareness of the cultural beliefs and practices of violence in order to change attitudes and behavior. Participants identify, practice, and incorporate a wider range of responses to solving problems, getting one's needs met, and dealing with stress.

Revisioning Psychotherapy

Psychotherapy has a place in prevention as well. During the last several years, the consciousness of many professional communities has been raised in the direction of a more active form of psychotherapy, taking into account the individual's or family's ecological framework including the community lived in. Beginning to perceive the individual seated within the psychotherapeutic consulting room as more than one person with an internal psychic life, but an individual living within a context, a web of life interacting with friends, family, coworkers, peers, children, etc. Clinical training programs are increasingly integrating a family and societal perspective into coursework, and the focus expands beyond the individual.

Doherty (1995) suggests promoting moral responsibility within psychotherapy given the current moral center of society is no longer maintained. He believes the American cultural values of economic and psychological private gain are out of balance with community values. The initial six decades of psychotherapy's history promoted morality, then shifted due to the growing awareness of psychology's potential contribution to individual oppression arising from outdated cultural norms. Forty years later the norms are shifting again and in turn psychology needs to respond differently or lead the way into a new direction.

Hillman and Ventura (1992) cited psychotherapy's general contribution to the erosion of human community through the process of ignoring social and political realms while venerating the personal and private domains. The focus on self-interest to the detriment of political or community interest was the dominant model of psychotherapy for many years. Clearly this model is in need of revision and has been undergoing a radical shift in some circles. "Swimming in a sea of culture that is both given to us and continually reconstituted by us is a vision filled with equal parts awe, terror, and hopefulness" (Cushman, 1995, p.352). A shifting and revisioning has appeared within depth psychology through scholarly work reflecting the integration of complexity theory (Shulman, 1997), liberation psychology (Lorenz & Watkins, 2000; Watkins, 2000), postcolonial analysis (Lorenz, 2000) and the paradigm of the interdependent self (Watkins, 1992).

Psychotherapy's heritage is rooted in Freud's early work, which has been called the first force in psychology. Cushman (1995) noted that Freud's influence went well beyond transforming psychology, and influenced advertising, popular culture, and capitalism. While there have been many dynamic and controversial developments in the science and art of psychology that could feasibly be enumerated, Locke (1992) proposed the second force in psychology was behaviorism, the third humanistic psychology, and the fourth multiculturalism. I believe the latter perspectives continue to inform our work in exciting and relevant ways and have the potential of transforming psychological practice in this new millennium.

Seeing our therapeutic work as informed by a larger community situated within a political context can provide a more expansive perception. Feminist and cross-cultural scholars have contributed much to this area of psychology during recent years. Acknowledging the erroneous reliance of research results on white male adults and extrapolating the findings to all persons, women and men within differing economic, cultural, ethnic, and racial groups, was a foundational first step. Gilligan's early work exploring female moral development (1982), Hare-Mustin's focus on feminism and family therapy (1978), and Sue's (1995) work on multicultural counseling and competence, provide a more inclusive convergence.

Assisting an individual to become well, to find one's own voice, discover one's personal power, to learn new coping strategies, to be free of destructive relationships, and to heal from abuses, are distinguishing characteristics of psychotherapy. And all of these aspects are best grounded within the social and cultural context each individual lives, works, and thrives in, keeping in mind the individual differences within and across cultural groups. Our responsibilities to become aware of the cultural contexts our patients exist in along with our own internalized societal attitudes and values are called for. Respecting and appreciating the differences, being comfortable with the differences, and having the ability to change any false beliefs we may hold are all necessary components in the process.

Broadening Environmental Contexts

Contexts also involve the environment. Developing environmental sensibilities, renewing interest, or establishing commitments to our communities and ecological terrains are relational ways to increase our connections early in life. These are also ways to know the world we reside in and to know ourselves through the world. In *The Dream of the Earth*, Berry (1988) comments on the lack of excitement in the current teachings about human existence in schools, encouraging the origination of stories that unite personal meanings with "the grandeur and meaning of the universe" (p.131). This is one way to become intimate with the interconnectedness of humans and nature.

Some cultures have relied on folktales, mythology, and traditional historical stories to explain these connections in passionate and direct ways, including the Native American and Australian Aboriginal cultures. While in Australia during my sabbatical, I learned the Dreamtime or the Dreaming is the spiritual domain holding a connection with all creation including one's ancestors, spirits, and animals, "there is kinship between people and all animals. Such is the Law" (Mowaljarlai & Malnic, 1993, p.132). Stories about the Dreamtime recall the omnipresence and non-separateness of all of these relations and view the hills, rivers, and mountains as evidence of this. This is related to the concept of panempathy, an "empathy with all sentient life" (Fox, 1996, p.119).

Bringing enchantment into the world can be done quite easily, but may need to be explored and cultivated with intention. "If this fascination, this entrancement, with life is not evoked, the children will not have the psychic energies needed to sustain the sorrows inherent in the human condition" (Berry, 1988, p.131). An extraordinary recommendation for developing these necessary capacities. In Perlman's (1995) work on reforesting the soul, the rejuvenating power of trees, the persistence of trees in life, and the profound role their restoration plays in establishing human re-connection, solidarity, and kinship was presented. "If you stay close to nature, to its simplicity, to the small things hardly noticeable, those things can unexpectedly become great and immeasurable" (Rilke, 2000, p.34).

Investing resources in our children is an important prevention effort, although it may not be perceived as a prevention effort directly. Increasing funds to provide quality education for all children rather than prioritizing monies for the building of larger prisons or increasing national defense technologies is a significant shift with powerful and rewarding consequences. Valuing and encouraging more opportunities for families to play together and enjoy games or safe outings needs to be integrated into our societal value system. Replacing competition with collaboration in many sports and popular television shows, or developing opportunities to work on teams toward a common shared goal builds interdependent awareness. This differs greatly from the popular and manipulative reality game shows that center on individual competition. Increased community involvement in terms of social support of single parents or economically struggling parents enhances the child rearing process and reduces the stresses that often exist when raising children under adverse conditions.

Expanding Academic Courses on Child Abuse

Many professional licensing agencies including the Board of Psychology and the Board of Behavioral Science Examiners require coursework in Child Maltreatment as a prerequisite to licensure for independent practice. These courses usually include information on prevention, assessment, reporting responsibilities, and treatment. Unfortunately the length of most courses is minimal (seven hours in California) compared to other offerings in an academic curriculum, and does not allow for the optimal depth of learning. Information on the range of issues children face developmentally in preschool, grade school, and high school, and the long term consequences of abuse that adults endure are important elements to address. Identifying the varying presentations of post traumatic stress disorder at different developmental stages is integral to assessment. Training in sexual abuse treatment and learning how to deal with disclosures (Alpert & Paulson, 1990) is central to the development of competent therapists.

Becoming familiar with the research and clinical resources available to enhance one's immediate and longer term psychotherapeutic treatment with young children, adolescents, and adults requires focused time and critical analysis of the various approaches grounded in family systems perspectives, psychodynamic theories, cognitive and behavioral therapies, crisis intervention, and pharmacotherapeutic interventions. Understanding the construct of resilience, the range of adaptive coping mechanisms, and tension reducing behaviors is applicable to assessment of mediating factors and the creation of treatment goals.

Relevant instruction on research and successful treatment approaches for perpetrators of abuse including young adolescent sexual offenders is essential. Comprehensive coverage of the psychological, neuropsychological, developmental, biological, cultural, and socio-economic theories of psychopathological disorders is warranted. Forensic aspects of child abuse are highly relevant, including conducting forensic evaluations for civil and criminal proceedings, available empirically validated assessment instruments, preparation for court testimony, and extant research on diagnostic tools.

A child abuse course affirmatively focused on therapist self-awareness and self-care is justified given the high percentage of individuals in the mental health profession who have themselves experienced childhood abuse (Elliot & Guy, 1993; Pope & Feldman-Summers, 1992). In my teaching experience from 1990 to 2000, I found more than half of psychology graduate students in the child abuse courses reported experiences of childhood sexual or physical abuse. Experientially knowing the consequences of abuse, neglect, and other trauma allows practitioners to access deep levels of empathy for their patients and alternatively, may prove challenging when faced with issues that resonate with personal experience. The use of one's self within psychotherapeutic treatment draws on these experiences of parental neglect, abuse, abandonment, and loss.

A significant focus on self-awareness is meaningful due to the unsettling or disturbing nature of course readings. Course material may also serve to restimulate previous traumatic responses or long hidden memories of abuse or perpetration. This process may be experienced as an invitation to re-engage in psychotherapy, assisting in the ongoing healing process. Given the range of potential responses, a sensitive and compassionate focus on the mental health professional is paramount. Since a high incidence of child abuse is found among clinical populations, expanding a child abuse course beyond the minimum required hours provides great benefits for students and professionals, allowing for comprehensive understanding and development of skill.

Training in Disaster and Critical Incident Intervention

The increase in community violence in the United States along with the recent airline crashes of TWA flight 800 near New York, the Alaska Airlines flight in 2000 off the shores of California, the Oklahoma City federal building bombing, and the occurrence of deadly school shootings have heightened the importance of training mental health professionals in disaster response and intervention. Disaster response training typically involves education in the immediate psychological consequences to disaster as well as prevention, evaluation, and treatment of traumatic stress. Integrating this information into academic programs for psychologists, marriage and family therapists, social workers, and psychiatrists will strengthen the knowledge base of clinicians and will allow them to competently address the issues arising from traumatic events such as disasters, kidnappings, hostage situations, or homicides. Increasing a clinician's sensitivity to the range of events that may exacerbate current traumatic symptoms of abuse will serve to strengthen the response.

If disaster response or critical incident intervention training is not provided within one's academic programs, there are many organizations that host this type of training or provide it for free in exchange for one's services. The American Red Cross and the American Psychological Association entered into an agreement to train professionals in the mental health needs of disaster survivors several years ago. This resulted in the Disaster Response Network. The American Red Cross provides a two day training module in disaster mental health response at no cost to participants. Chapters are located in counties of each state. The International Critical Incident Stress Foundation also provides basic and advanced certification in critical incident stress debriefing and management. Similarly, the National Organization for Victim Assistance sponsors week long trainings in community crisis response assistance. More specific to victims of interpersonal violence, the National Victim Assistance Academy provides a 45 hour university based comprehensive training to victim advocates. Please refer to the Resources in the Appendix.

Educational Resources

Many resources are available to learn more about child abuse prevention and intervention. There are journals devoted to the study of trauma and interpersonal violence such as *Child Maltreatment, Child Abuse and Neglect, Journal of Traumatic Stress, Violence and Victims, Journal of Child Sexual Abuse, Journal of Interpersonal Violence*, and *Journal of Family Violence.*

The American Professional Society on the Abuse of Children, APSAC, is an interdisciplinary organization that publishes a monthly newsletter, hosts professional trainings and colloquiums on child abuse assessment and treatment, and cosponsors the annual San Diego Conference on Responding to Child Maltreatment. Attendance at professional conferences and continuing education courses provides opportunities for networking with other therapists and updating one's skill level and knowledge base.

Inspirational Prevention

Preventing child abuse and neglect is a complex problem. A problem that will not be ameliorated in a simple manner through the creation of one prevention program or expanded resources within a social service agency. As previously stated, this is a societal problem requiring large scale culturally relevant interventions that target multiple dimensions. Although these problems will take time to address, each one of us can effectively contribute in our own manner, through education based programs, skills training, academic teaching, program evaluation, individual or social advocacy, scholarly research on early childhood risk and protective factors, participating in long-term longitudinal follow-up studies, crisis intervention, psychotherapeutic treatment, or social and political activism.

I believe it is our obligation to respond and heed the call to intervene and prevent child abuse. One's unique background, societal interconnections, creativity, personal experience, culture, academic training, financial resources, felt sense of responsibility, and commitment will all determine the form of the response. It is my hope that scholars and practitioners of psychology will continue to think beyond the medical model rooted in curing disease and develop innovative and creative ways to transform these social problems involving collective energy and vision.

Inspiration and motivation for social action projects can be drawn from religious and cultural communities. The Jewish tradition of Tikkum Olam which encourages a mission to repair the world is one example. In an article on the importance of instilling this desire in teens, Schwarz (1999) cited the importance of five critical principles that are integral to this effort: comprehensive societal information that instills moral outrage, empowerment that channels the moral outrage into constructive engagement, inspiration from passionate role models or mentors, motivation that comes from deep human connection with others who are different, oppressed, or marginalized, and contextualization whereby the social action is seen as a noble expression of the religion. Tikkum Olam provides a way to begin the process of creating solutions in society (Kline, 2000).

The Jesuit priest, academic psychologist, and revolutionary intellectual Ignacio Martin-Baro saw no political distinction between his religious and psychological work. He gave his life to the advance of dialogue and a liberation psychology (1994) that hosted a belief in personal and cultural transformation through the dialectical process of dialogue. He was assassinated along with seven others by Salvadoran security forces in 1989. His evolved vision of psychology was rooted in the core process of praxis, where the socially and personally constructed self is known through the world and through relations with others, an interdependent paradigm. Kovel (1996) referred to this consciousness as socially transformative. Through the consciousness of interdependence, liberation psychology provides a vision for effecting structural change within all dimensions of society. These potentialities instill a hope in a vision for a restored future. A future that hosts communities of involved, active, non-marginalized, and empowered members.

The practice of dynamic compassion known as *Ahimsa* is another way to effect change in the world and create the society that we desire. The way of dynamic harmlessness is a philosophy Mahatma Gandhi adopted, inspiring many to integrate or aspire to this spiritual approach to life. Ahimsa is a term having origins in Sanskrit and ancient roots in East Asian cultures including the Jaina, Hindu, and Buddhist traditions (Chapple, 1993). A practice dedicated to nonviolence, truth, the active expression of compassion, a deep understanding of personal responsibility, achieving peace through peace, and perceiving the ends and the means as "one and the same" (Altman, 1980, p.102). This active reverence for life can be expressed on many levels, and may be familiar as nonviolent personal action or respectful acts of civil disobedience. Ahimsa also inspires daily acts of compassion in thought, language, and relationship with others, situated within the larger community. This practice of compassion "necessitates a dialogical relationship between self and other, human and nature, human and animal" (Chapple, 1993, p.117).

Dialogical Methods

As this work on prevention comes to a close, I would like to share two additional perspectives, dialogue and council, that invite information from a variety of sources encouraging creative and collaborative learning. Dialogue is a process that allows for meaning to be shared and received by a group. Dialogue grew from Bohm's (1985) work in quantum phenomena as he searched for ways to effect cultural transformation. Bohm traced the roots of the term *dialogue* to the Greek *dia* and *logos* which means *through meaning*. Situating oneself in a group of people committed to dialogue is a frame for building community and collective meanings. Isaacs (1999) conceptualized dialogue as the profound process of thinking together and embracing different points of view. Ellinor and Gerard (1998) also expanded on this dialogue method bringing the process to varied business and work environments.

The methods of dialogue have empowered groups, created collaborative partnerships, inspired creativity and novel problem solving, and allowed for extremely difficult issues to be heard. Dialogue creates cultures of shared leadership and cooperation increasing partnership and inclusion. The fundamental values that form the deeply honoring perspectives within dialogue are the convictions that all members within a group have important contributions to make, a balance between inquiry and advocacy is held, the focus is on learning from others, and role or status is suspended. The intention of learning emphasizes understanding, relationships, the suspension of judgments, and making assumptions visible. This focus eliminates power over others, supports the discovery process, and synthesizes disparate points of view. Competition falls away and true community collaboration develops.

The council process has also been a remarkably successful and authentic group method established in inner city schools, spiritual centers, and businesses, resulting in cooperative communities (Zimmerman & Coyle, 1996). Family councils have been created, in effect strengthening, invigorating, and building family connections through focused listening, speaking from the heart, lean expression, and spontaneous emotional sharing. The council process is engaged within a ceremonial environment akin to tribal circles and councils. A talking piece is chosen, representing the intentions of the council through its organizing symbolism. The talking piece is held by each individual who speaks, supporting the deep listening process. A shared silence may also be held during these times.

Perhaps as families, teen school groups, elementary and high school teachers, parent groups, disparate work teams, mental health professionals, government employees, and community workers become intimately familiar with the empowering and generative capacities of respect, honor, and inquisitive exploration through methods such as dialogue and council process, these emergent cultures will synergize grass roots prevention efforts creating communities that children and adults thrive in. This kind of accessible and revolutionary vitalization embodies the potential to animate cultural transformation. A saying from the oral traditions of the Jewish Talmud exquisitely highlights our responsibilities as compassionate professionals: *It is not our responsibility to finish the work but we are not free to walk away from it.*

◈ Chapter 15

Challenges to Psyche in Trauma Treatment

Compassion, the knowledge that comes from suffering with
others, is a tremendous gift. It comes from deeply and truth-
fully recognizing your own suffering and pain, valuing it for
its truth, its thereness.

Polly Young-Eisendrath, 1996

To follow one's calling into the psychotherapy profession can lead to
profound satisfaction, fulfillment, and unexpected encounters with chaos,
external and internal. Many challenges to psyche can be experienced within
this vocation. Working in the area of trauma can evoke feelings of uncertainty and
vulnerability as well. Shulman (1997) cogently addressed related issues in *Living
at the Edge of Chaos: Complex Systems in Culture and Psyche*. She conveyed the
disequilibrium that lives at the intersection of chaos and disruption. Such immense
fertility and potentiality exists within this rupture. Integrating the image of the

crossroads and the tremendous power associated with coming to this place can normalize one's uncertainty, serve to broaden perspective, and allow for an infusion of renewed energy.

Learning to acknowledge and tolerate ambiguity is a task most psychotherapists are faced with at some time. Broadening one's ability to deal with ambiguous and even dissonant information may begin early in life or at certain crossroads such as graduate school, and continues throughout life's work. Confronting and making peace with the emergent anxiety when one does not know the right answer is one way to practice this. After all the alleged right answer seldom exists and multiple points of view are more common. "Try to love the questions themselves" (Rilke, 1984, p. 35) is perhaps an appropriate framework for these issues. Cultivating a tolerance for ambiguity is a framework of not knowing, learning to bear anxieties, and remaining non-defensive with uncertainty. This way of being can open doors of possibilities, responses, and actions. I see this as divine ambiguity, a fitting dimension of psychotherapeutic practice.

Eros and the Experience of Countertransference

I believe it is not unusual to experience a deep prizing, love, or attraction toward a patient during the course of treatment. In fact this experience or the lack of it, can serve as a powerful assessment and therapeutic tool revealing a depth of clinical information not available in another form. Unfortunately this topic is often perceived as taboo, relegated to the shadow, perhaps among practitioners who have not received training or instruction in how to address these human emotions and experiences when they emerge during psychotherapy. On the contrary, this needs to be a topic that we seek to understand, openly discuss, willingly consult about, and examine mindfully.

Eros emerges within psychotherapy and may be present throughout the entire treatment process. In Greek mythology Eros the god brought individuals together within a community, was considered a god of attraction, and was honored for inspiring passion. Eros signified a sexual love in ancient times, in distinction to agape, an altruistic love, or philia, viewed as brotherly love or friendly affection. Jung (1960) broadened the modern understanding of eros by accurately interpreting this concept as life force energy and creative power. If viewed as creative power and life force energy that can also manifest sexually but does not do so exclusively, eros becomes less threatening or fear invoking. Indeed many therapists experience cognitive dissonance when faced with a discussion of eros and its misunderstood expression within the therapeutic setting. Eros and the experience of countertransference, or erotic countertransference, remains both a goldmine and minefield (Hedges, Hilton, Hilton, & Caudill, 1997).

The presence of eros, a creative power, vitality, and life force energy can be viewed as a foundational element within the psychotherapeutic process. Eros as a contributor to the archetypal field psychotherapy is contained in. Eros as an *animating* quality, a soulful force. This pertains to a form of human connection, engagement, love, an inspiring empathy, a passionate creativity, within this process. It resides in a liminal space between the individuals, within the intersubjective field, in the imaginal realm, in the therapeutic consulting room and serves a therapeutic purpose. But neither individual becomes identified with it, overpowered by it, or possessed by it. This speaks to a soulful resonance or interpersonal connection. Samuels' (1989) concept of *embodied countertransference* as the physical, actual, material, and sensual expression within the therapist of something in the patient's inner world seems to speak to this realm beautifully. Schwartz-Salant (1984) wrote on the *subtle body*, a phenomenon that exists outside the usual sense of time within the imaginal realm, that allows a flowing of attention through one's heart toward another person. These are generative qualities that invoke the presence of eros and not sexual enactments or transgressions of boundaries.

Therapists are trained to assess and analyze the transference and may be more comfortable with this perspective in distinction to a focus on countertransference. Learning to tolerate transference responses such as strong attachments, dependency needs, and idealization are important skills. These attachments, needs, and idealizations may also generate countertransference reactions within the therapist that benefit from exploration. The capacity to become aware of and monitor responses serves our patients well.

Maintaining sensitivity to the consequences from the earlier boundary violations experienced by the patient and respecting appropriate boundaries remains integral to the treatment of abuse survivors. Covert or overt sexualization of the relationship is not engaged in (American Psychological Association, 1992) and self-disclosure is used when it is in the best interest of the patient (Brown, 1991). The manner of the self-disclosure, the context, and the benefit to the patient are all important elements (Guttheil & Gabbard, 1998).

Hayden (1996) astutely observed that a patient's erotic feelings may be only a small part of the entire range of intense feelings that are transference based. In noting the power struggles that may emerge within psychotherapy, she indicated the communication of sexual feelings always took place in a context of interpersonal power. Therapeutic work with adult survivors of childhood sexual abuse may restimulate earlier "confusions about how affection, dependency, vulnerability, sexuality and power are intertwined" (p.13). Thus, feelings of sexual arousal may exist for patients who are feeling heard or are experiencing a sense of deep connection. The sexual arousal may result in shame based or angry feelings. When patients are not able to tolerate these feelings, they can be projected onto the therapist who may experience great discomfort or projective identification. Mindfully discerning these countertransference reactions and sensitively processing and framing responses or interpreting the transference may lead to invaluable insights about prior abusive relational dynamics.

In terms of eros as sexual attraction, studies indicate the phenomenon of sexual attraction to patients is statistically normal (Pope & Bouhoutsos, 1986) and "may be a completely natural part of the therapist's reaction to some patients" (p.36). However, acting on the sexual attraction and engaging in sexual enactments is not. Additionally sexual involvement is both ethically and legally prohibited, although these restrictions have not served to persuade some therapists against betraying the trust of their patients.

In place of allowing these issues to remain in the collective shadow, defending against, denying, fleeing from, or avoiding the emergence of eros within psychotherapy or the erotic nature of the work including sexual attraction, we can look mindfully, explore consciously, sensitively, and clearly at these complex feelings including the absence of them. This process of *seeing through* can lead to a profound understanding of the patient, the therapeutic process, and of ourselves. In this way we are relying on eros as a therapeutic resource.

Baur (1999) examined how the psychotherapy profession has responded to the intricacies and ambiguities of love in psychotherapy. She implied that we may be fearful about learning more about ourselves, or of being like our patients, thus exposing our vulnerability. Schamess (1999) encouraged therapists to recognize erotic content within therapy as "an important, but not necessarily central component of treatment" (p.26). This added dimension serves to enhance, broaden, and expand one's clinical work. "It encourages us to see our patients as more fully human, and to be more fully human ourselves" (p.26). Remaining mindful of the patient's psychological well-being in psychotherapy is essential, as is understanding and exploring the fullness of their images, cognitions, and feelings.

When psychotherapy is provided to child sexual abuse survivors and the erotic countertransference is concretized through sexual involvement, the therapeutic container is irreparably shattered, the therapeutic trust betrayed, and the patient revictimized through the current violation. The sexual enactment becomes extremely damaging for the patient and is also damaging for the therapist personally, professionally, legally, ethically, and economically. Holroyd and Brodsky (1977) found that therapists who had sexualized therapy with one patient often repeated this behavior with others. In fact the behavior recurred in 80 percent of the cases. In another study Pope, Keith-Speigel, and Tabachnik (1986) found 86 percent of therapists who became sexually intimate with their patients did so once or twice, but 10 percent did so between three and ten times.

This issue is raised in order to bring light to the devastating outcomes of this behavior and to encourage therapists to turn to colleagues, consultants, supervisors, or distressed therapist assistance programs such as the Colleague Assistance and Support Program within the California Psychological Association, to address their fears or ethical breaches prior to acting on them. Likewise, professionals are encouraged to become concerned and directly address their colleagues' diminished capacities and symptoms of impairment such as alcohol or drug addiction, faulty clinical judgment, untreated and debilitating emotional distress or mental disorder, isolating behaviors, burnout, and attentional or memory disturbances in the aim of preventing any further tragedies. All of us within this profession have a duty to our colleagues and patients, regardless of any reluctance to breach these topics.

Gifts From the Archetypal Wounded Healer

In classical mythology the centaur Chiron, half horse-half human, was endowed with the gift of healing and initiated Asklepios. An important characteristic of Chiron was his woundedness. Although Zeus endowed him with the gift of healing, he was fated to be mortally wounded. Thus, rather than die from this mortal wound he was restored to his full health, but the restoration was an ongoing process since the wounding continually resumed its destructiveness.

This image of the wounded healer provides us with a template to understand the inevitability of our own wounding. It signals the importance of accepting and living with our own wounds and the need to focus on their healing. A process of continual renewal and healing is symbolized.

Another way to understand this myth is to see our wounds as providing us with an entrance into a deep understanding of the suffering and pain that is part of our human nature, allowing us to empathize with others more easily, and possibly giving us a window into healing. The wound serves as a great teacher. To elaborate further, the myth speaks to the divine interventions that are needed for our healing to occur. Perhaps through mindful focusing, becoming aware of the meaning of the wound, experiencing the suffering emanating from the pain, and learning how to bear it, we create an opening for connecting to a divine healing potential, a source greater than our self. Sardello (1988) recounted an experience he had while tending an illness "I believe there was importance in servicing the disease as my teacher. Medical diagnosis has the effect of isolation, of restricting one's illness in such a fashion that it is quite impossible to fully experience an illness as soul-making" (p. 15).

Last, Chiron's wound continued to wound him. The wounder and healer were one. This piece of the myth speaks to two issues: the inevitable wounding that we all participate in as humans, whether it is intentional, conscious, or unconscious and the internalized wounding that we may live with based on prior experiences of being harmed by others. The former aspect sheds light on accepting the imperfection that exists in human nature, and the need to take responsibility for our actions when we injure others. The latter speaks to the need for our own self awareness, growth, and continued individuation process. We need to work with our internal wounds, not only for our optimal health, but to impede the process of inadvertently hurting others from an unexamined place. This has also been conceptualized as the management of risk factors.

Erosions of Empathy

We are trained to be empathically available to patients and may even suffer with patients "the sympathia" (von Franz, 1980, p.68). The capacity for empathy is integral to this profession, as the capacity for self-care is essential to a therapist's emotional competence (Koocher & Keith-Spiegel, 1998). Emotional competence is required in order to successfully contain and tolerate difficult clinical material, to assess bias, and to become aware of those anxiety-provoking experiences that signal one's subtle transgressions. Empathic or compassionate engagement may slowly shift or erode due to the context of trauma work. Witnessing compound losses and immense suffering through our work with children, adults, couples, and families who have experienced or participated in severely intrusive psychological, physical, or sexual assaults can prove to be very challenging.

Once aware of these erosions or unsettling changes, we can employ heuristic methods (Moustakas, 1990) to investigate and discover the particularities. This involves self-search, self-dialogue, and self-discovery. Many theoretical formulations have been proposed to describe the constellation of responses professionals experience. The concepts of burnout, secondary traumatization, compassion fatigue, and vicarious traumatization attempt to capture the phenomenological experiences of professionals who work in this field.

Burnout (Freudenberger, 1974) describes the physical, emotional, and mental exhaustion that impacts professionals in the negative manner in which they perceive self and other including colleagues and patients (Maslach, 1982). Burnout may develop insidiously and be unconscious. It is associated with a progressive deterioration in energy level resulting in extreme fatigue and a diminishment of one's prior idealism. It often occurs over a length of time where one is chronically exposed to stressors, but it can also develop from intensive concentrated activity. Emotional exhaustion is prominent, depersonalization in the treatment of patients, and the lack of a sense of personal competence in the face of stress are the factors frequently associated with burnout.

The concept of compassion fatigue has been addressed in the traumatic stress literature by Figley (1995). Compassion fatigue is an acute reaction manifesting in physical or mental exhaustion. This exhaustion impacts one's ability to express empathy or compassion and has been categorized as a form of burnout developing into secondary traumatic stress (Stebnicki, 2000). Unlike burnout, compassion fatigue does not deter most therapists from working, rather, the work is continued while the empathic capacities further erode. From the perspective of eros, one experiences *erosion*, a loss of connectedness and passion.

Pearlman and Saakvitne (1995) developed the term vicarious traumatization to refer to therapists' responses and reactions to their work across time and across patients. Their focus was originally on the therapist treating patients working through issues of incest. "We do not believe anyone, however psychologically healthy, can do this work and remain unchanged" (p.295). Over the days, weeks, months, and years of doing this work, listening deeply, empathically engaging, confronting, containing uncomfortable material, and assisting with problem solving, the therapist is affected, over time, across patients. This impact on values, beliefs, and worldview can occur for therapists treating other populations as well. For some therapists, this may result in a slow, debilitating disempowerment, for others a hubris, no longer seeking consultation from others, believing they have all the knowledge and insight needed to do the work successfully. Both of these extremes result in profound changes that lead to unfavorable consequences, personally and professionally.

Becoming involved in activities of the professional community provides opportunities for collaboration, participant sharing, and leads to the formation of an extended network of colleagues. Addressing and preventing burnout, compassion fatigue, and vicarious traumatization may involve joining a professional association (see Resources), becoming familiar with the monthly literature, reading journals, attending conferences or workshops, and seeking consultation or engaging in personal psychotherapy when faced with the inevitable discomfort that may accompany some of the therapeutic work. Participating in peer groups such as supportive weekly consultations, vicarious traumatization groups (Pearlman & Saakvitne, 1995), lunchtime support gatherings, and clinical supervision have also been recommended.

The institutionalization of mentoring programs for newer members of the profession is a unique way to support therapists in their professional development over time, effectively modeling a range of beneficial coping mechanisms. From a self-psychological perspective (Kohut, 1984) modeling can lead to the process known as transmuting internalization, or simply stated, integrating one's therapist or supervisor as a self-object. Holding an internal therapist or internal supervisor (Casement, 1991) can provide an extremely helpful referent in some circumstances. An active and effective internal supervisor is vital to our work, continually enhanced or modified based on successive experiences.

The erosion of connectedness, passion, and loving energy must be addressed. Referring to the process of restoration Leonard (1989) reminds us "accept the descent into the dark abyss, acknowledge the fall to the bottom . . . surrender to the greater powers that be" (p.243). The process of surrender may be extremely painful and difficult to experience, but may also initiate our own healing. I conclude with words from Rainer Maria Rilke's (1984) counsel to a young poet: "for these are the moments when something new has entered us, something unknown, and the new which no one knows, stands in the midst of it, and is silent" (p.74).

◈ Chapter 16

Tending Soul as Self-Care

> When we cannot communicate, we get sick, and as our
> sickness increases, we suffer and spill our suffering on
> other people. We purchase the services of psychotherapists
> to listen to our suffering, but if the psychotherapists do not
> practice the universal door, they will not succeed.
> Thich Nhat Hanh, 1993

Appreciating the mysteries in life, thriving in relationships, participating in vital activity within our communities are all life sustaining involvements. Cultivating a sacredness toward these daily activities is care of the soul (Moore, 1992). Therapist self-care is another facet of tending soul. It is curiously viewed as an innovative topic in clinical practice yet is necessary to ethical practice. The standard of self-care evolved from the theory that lack of self-care leads to ethical and legal transgressions, including boundary violations such as dual relationships (Lerman & Rigby, 1990). Recognizing and acknowledging personal limitations and seeking assistance is generally seen as a sign of strength, contributing to a therapist's growth and professionalism. In this context, self-care serves three primary functions: protects the patient by reducing risk factors, models growth and well-being, and protects the therapist against miscalculations and burnout (Porter, 1995).

Pope and Brown (1996) conceptualized two types of therapeutic competence: intellectual and emotional competence. Intellectual competence is the knowledge and experiential base, including the assessment, treatment, and intervention skills possessed by the therapist. This area is traditionally encompassed by one's scope of education, training, and experience. Emotional competence refers to the ability to contain and tolerate the range of clinical material that emerges in treatment (Koocher & Keith-Spiegel, 1998), the ability to assess one's bias, and the capacity to engage in self-care.

Situating the capacity for self-care alongside the central and necessary capacity for empathy within the psychological profession solidifies the importance of therapist self-care, diminishes the risk management emphasis, and highlights the duty we have to emotional competence as a prevention effort. Self-care can be further broadened beyond emotional competence, incorporating a striving for emotional, psychological, physical, and spiritual well-being. In light of the potential development of burnout (Freudenberger, 1974), the progression of compassion fatigue (Figley, 1995), or the inevitable changes from vicarious traumatization (Pearlman & Saakvitne, 1995), a focus on self-care is indispensable.

Self-care can also be viewed expansively integrating the perspective of self and culture Martin-Baro (1994) referred to as communitarian. He spoke of the receptive and egalitarian aspect of the self as an opening "toward the other, a readiness to let oneself be questioned by the other, as a separate being, to listen to his or her words, in dialogue; to confront reality in relationship to and with (but not over) him or her, to unite in solidarity in a struggle in which both will be transformed" (p.183). Viewing self-care in this context is a way to integrate back into the community, to underscore the fluid connections to others, and to see the self as truly situated within community. The notion of self-care becomes a responsibility and commitment toward maintaining community.

Active engagement in self-care can provide balance in one's life, improvement in personal relationships, and a renewed commitment to one's vocation, chosen career, or community. A definitive focus on self-care integrates both external and internal realities, involving relationships and activities with friends, family, and colleagues, in addition to spiritually, physically, and psychologically enriching endeavors, such as creative and artistic activities or appreciations, i.e., drawing, painting, writing, sculpting, dance, movement, drama, music, connecting with nature, contemplation, and meditation. Taking breaks from the intensity of the work, refocusing one's vision and commitment, and actively engaging in stress management speak to this explicit focus.

Regaining one's vision

A focus on self-care becomes indispensable during times of inordinate stress. At times it may seem as though the work is too challenging, testing commitment, or confusing one's direction. One may experience life inside the darkness of the labyrinth, not knowing if one is traveling forward or backward, east or west. Seeking consultation, taking time away from the work, renewing one's spirit may all contribute to the restoration of one's initial vision. Shifting one's perspective of work as contemplative practice, where one provides service without a sacrifice of self may prove rejuvenating. Remaining open to the potential and excitement of learning from all experiences without judging them as difficulties, hardships, or impossible hurdles reframes the challenge. Shifting our imagination from fear toward a "perception of more beauty" (Sardello, 1999, p.209) may be one way to address this process.

It may be helpful to identify a vision of one's optimal professional life or flow (Csikszentmihaly, 1990) through visualization or guided imagery. If you like, take a few moments at this time to reflect on your original passion and excitement about the field of psychology. Think back to a time when you initially identified psychology as your profession, or when others in your life encouraged you to follow this path given your natural talent, compassion, or interest in serving. Perhaps you recall the sense of vocation, a calling to do this work, and are able to identify a moment in time where this became very clear to you. Get back in touch with your early feelings, images, and thoughts about how you expected to apply your training and skills. During graduate school, as you learned about psychology, research, and psychotherapy in depth, you refined these aspirations and expectations. How does your current practice integrate your hopes, desires, and vision? What developments do you imagine will be ahead in your future? What steps will you take to implement your vision today?

Just as a unicursal labyrinth will eventually lead to light, this type of contemplation can provide insight and renewal. Attending to one's personal needs, exercise, scheduling time for enjoyable activities, spending quality moments with friends and family, engaging in humor, and restoring one's vision will all contribute to a greater sense of well-being.

Research and anecdotal reports suggest animals can promote humor, laughter, and play in people (Cusack, 1988). Matthew Fox (1990) proposed a number of spiritual lessons we can learn from animals in his book *A Spirituality Named Compassion*. The lessons include the joy of being an animal, experiencing ecstasy without guilt, playing with no justification for the behavior, remaining open and exhibiting broadened sensitivity, humor-considered a "radical celebrative awareness of dialectic and paradox" (p.167), the power of non-verbal communication, the grace of beauty, sensuousness, and silent dignity in acknowledgment of one's self worth and pride. These are valuable lessons to incorporate into our lives.

Self-Care and Coping with Stress

For the most part, stress is a companion to be embraced not defended against, for it is a natural response to threatening, difficult, or challenging events or circumstances. A survival mechanism that alerts us to danger and activates protective functions. Modern day stress also motivates, inspires, invigorates, and encourages us to develop our capacities. It may push us toward accomplishment in endeavors we might otherwise never attempt. Stress also maintains our awareness, contributes to alertness, and generally keeps us alive.

However, when stress becomes unrelenting, extreme, or chronic, its benefits recede being replaced by obstacles or impairments. Many of us are all too familiar with the physical and emotional toll chronic or excessive stress can take including the contributions to cardiovascular disease, interference with thought processes, cessation of creativity, disruption of relationships, prevention of sleep, and the development of addictive behavior. Conversely the absence of stress can be symptomatic as well, resulting in feelings of boredom, fatigue, apathy, loss of purpose or mission, and lack of challenge, and loss of flow.

The art of stress management is seeking a balance between the poles of stimulation and relaxation and taking responsibility for making beneficial changes and implementing stress reduction techniques. This becomes a unique process of discovery, focusing on what, when, how much, and how. Noticing what creates the stress and what the stressors are the initial steps in this process. Assessing the conditions, times of day, month, or season that contribute to the stress is the second step. Becoming aware of understimulation as well as the amount of stress that is optimal for one's functioning will reveals one's stress parameters. And last, exploring, investigating, and experimenting with effective stress reduction methods can present novel and relaxing experiences.

Recognizing that a stress reaction is one's personal response to a stressor or accumulation of stressors is essential, since stress is not the actual situation, such as a particular job, issue, role, supervisor, or patient. This recognition is supported by Frankl's (1994) severe experiences in concentration camps and his comment that one's attitude toward the incident or trauma is the factor that impacts one's ability to cope. This distinction speaks to the variability of human experience in that each one of us responds to stressors differently. Our personality characteristics, way of being, and access to support systems, and willingness to reach out for assistance all affect the way we respond to events.

Simple remedies exist for addressing stress on a daily basis. Taking a walk away from the chaos in one's office or job can provide moments of awe strolling through a garden, a park, or down a path. Stopping to watch birds, experiencing the scent of a flower, gazing up into the sky, or noticing the breeze on one's neck are all ways to open up the senses differently. Deep breathing techniques serve calming functions and may be integrated into brief interludes during one's day. Laughter or laughing robustly energizes and may release boredom or apathy, shifting the previous physiological sensations. Taking a few minutes to meditate or focus oneself on a task while letting go of all other concerns can lead to clarity when stepping back to the previous work. Marge Piercy's (2000) poem *On Six Underrated Pleasures* listed a number of activities that could relieve stress: folding sheets, picking pole beans, taking a hot bath, sleeping with cats, planting bulbs, and canning!

Reaching out to friends and colleagues for support in the form of a phone call, tea break, or sharing a meal rather than consistently isolating oneself, can be very comforting in times of stress, moments of judgment, confusion, or fear. Taking time to deeply listen to another person in a conversation can also decrease frustrations or stresses. Similarly, attending to the needs of something or someone else or working in a garden allows for moments of other-directed care that replenish and revitalize.

Participating in a class that ordinarily is considered trivial could expand one's repertoire of self-care. Scheduling body work, massage, or other forms of physical touch can soothe tight muscles and provide physical relaxation. Choosing foods that support your well being, exercising, and participating in group activities with friends all increase the likelihood of health. And of course limiting work activities, prioritizing time, not overscheduling one's life, and holding commitments to a minimum during stressful times shows kindness and acknowledgment of one's humanness.

Engaging in creativity can be a delightful stress release. In her Jungian story telling series, Estes (1991) likened creativity to the physiological processes associated with nourishment, elimination, and the production of excrement. She alluded to the life sustaining nutrients the body requires and the daily toxicity that builds up if not released. Similarly, creativity moves through, provides nourishment, energy, life-giving properties, and moves onward to liberation or expression. If the eliminatory processes are restricted, the toxicity begins to build up within the body. Once liberated the resulting material may serve as a kind of regenerating fertilizer. Imagine conceptualizing acts of creativity as daily and necessary activities for health, both mental and physical.

Affirmations of creativity can be experienced in peaceful and inspiring moments of artistic self-expression in the form of journal writing, sculpting, drawing, movement, preparing a meal, or sitting down to write a letter. Crafting a novel, short story, or a song for the enjoyment of expression can be exhilarating.

Creating a special place within your imagination, home, office, or outdoors in a park, on a special bench, under a masterful tree, associates one's contemplative time with this special or sacred place. Reframing the way one thinks about certain stressors may also successfully eliminate the perceived burden. Scaling down the importance or severity of some incidents may be more manageable.

MAP to Stress Management

Enlisting the Meridian Assessment Paradigm as a self-assessment "map" of stress management is a systematic way to promote well being, shift one's usual cadence, and attenuate potentially debilitating stress. The following model synthesizes awareness, evaluation, and implementation.

1. Matter. Begin with an assessment of the body or mater. Notice what parts of the body are most in need of attention. Focus on nurturing one's body and opening up the senses through massage, aromatherapy, use essential oils, engage in bodywork, listen to enjoyable sounds and music, obtain relaxing recordings, alter the diet, and

follow-through on physical examinations. Become aware of your sleeping patterns and sleep hygiene, noticing the quality of sleep obtained and whether you are refreshed each morning. Consult with a specialist on sleep disorders if you suspect a problem. Cook a new recipe, exercise in a different style, engage in a sport, or begin a new well-being program incorporating a physical health perspective.

2. Ecological. Span your landscape and assess the elements that contribute or detract from your well-being. Evaluate aspects you have control over and prioritize changing these: perhaps an eventual move to another environment, a job enhancement, an economic investment, consultation with a financial advisor, or packing some possessions for contribution to a charitable organization. Participate in the community in a different way becoming involved in community organization, recycling, or grass roots political efforts. Getting back in touch with nature by spending time strolling, hiking, camping, or allowing quality time with wild animals or companions all address this ecological dimension. Touch back with your child-like self to remember wonder and curiosity. At times simply watching fish swim, listening to songbirds, or sitting among flowers endows well-being. Energizing one's space through redecoration, furniture re-arrangement, or consultation with a feng shui practitioner may create delightful shifts.

3. Relational. Notice the relationships within your life, the level of satisfaction, the amount of extroversion, and quality of nurturance you experience. Assess the ways you can improve and deepen these valuable connections. Examine the relationships with co-workers, family, friends, and acquaintances. Discuss ways of enhancing your intimate relationships, improving sexual expression, and quality of companionship. Perhaps engaging in new adventures, family therapy, or a self-help group would contribute to enhancement. Renew old friendships, nurture new acquaintances, and acknowledge strangers differently within your life.

4. Interiority. Assess the time you allow for introversion and choose to focus on your interior life. Notice the quality of your intrapersonal relationship and whether you permit sufficient time for a rich interior life. Appraise the predominant mood, feelings, and rhythm you regularly experience. Create moments within your schedule for solitude, contemplation, meditation, and journaling. Engage in psychotherapy, experiment with silence, or become involved in a personal growth class. Read a memoir, a science fiction piece, or a thrilling novel. Devote time to a life inventory assessing the aspects of life you are pleased with, noting the developmental phase you are in, thinking through your life mission, and creating future goals, objectives, or direction. Listen to your intuition about these precious aspects of your life.

5. Deportment. Take stock in your overall demeanor and behavior. Imagine what others in your life see. Note the way you carry your body and ways to improve on this. Bring the outward image in line with your interior sense of self. This may include an integration of new movements, participation in personal life coaching

sessions, or acquiring a different wardrobe that is more personally expressive. Involvement in postural improvements, yoga, bodywork, synergy, or integrative body structuring may be rejuvenating.

6. Imaginal. Begin to notice the quality of your imaginal life and how you attend to or neglect it. Begin to tend dreams, notice waking dreams, amplify spontaneous images, review thoughts, and augment your artistic expression. Create time to consciously and intentionally engage the figures and characters of your imagination. Energizing this aspect of existence encompasses interior, relational, and behavioral methods. Partaking of community festivals, art shows, dramatic performances, concerts, and art museum exhibitions magnify imaginal life. Employ active imagination to engage dream figures or images. Create a sand painting, a figure from clay, a mask, drawing, poem, or simply play to enliven your imaginal life. Enlarge the experience by entertaining or involving colleagues and friends.

7. Archetypal. Begin to look at your life as personal mythology. Notice the universal patterns, the recurring symbols, the invisible, the muted, the subtle, and any predominant themes. Who visits in this drama? Notice the other characters within your drama, epic, comedy, tragedy, or lyric. Discover what has been neglected or unseen, as healing comes through the archetype. Perhaps reading more mythology, attending a class, consulting with archetypal psychologists will reveal more.

8. Numinous. Become aware of the level of your spiritual or religious practice. Assess ways to strengthen this facet of your life, perhaps integrating religious observances, praying, reading more literature, or renewing attendance at church, synagogue, or temple. Recall any recent synchronicities or coincidental experiences. Remember the times you experienced epiphanies and what conditions were present in your life. Seek spiritual consultation, participate in oracular divination methods, or engage in an astrological reading. Make a commitment to a practice that is aligned with your beliefs, passions, and interests.

Closing Thoughts

Compassion elicits a sense of interconnectedness among people. The etymological roots of compassion mean *to suffer with, to share solidarity with.* Compassion is knowing pain, entering into it, sharing it and tasting it insofar as that is possible. It transcends an illusion of separateness. The Vietnamese Buddhist monk Thich Nhat Hanh (1999) speaks of this process of compassion in his poem *Call Me By My True Names*, which evokes this connectedness with others. Mary Oliver (1992) the Pulitzer Prize winning poet, writes so eloquently about interconnectedness and interdependence with the earth and its inhabitants in the familiar poems *Wild Geese, The Turtle*, and *Singapore*. Psychologist Ignacio Martin-Baro (1994) wrote passionately about his vision of community and the intimate connection between self and culture. Paulo Freire (1989) speaks to the way out of oppression toward liberation as a mutual process engaged in through action, reflection, and dialogical communication. Martin Buber (1970) acknowledges this most essential ingredient in all relationships with the deeply honoring concept of I-Thou. Theologian and educator Mattew Fox (1990) speaks of the basic law of compassion as interconnectedness among all living creatures.

As I close, my wish is that in all future academic and professional work together, we continue to engage in community life openly, lovingly, and passionately, while remembering to make room for laughter and play as well as silence and solitude. As we move into the world consciously attending to what is seen and hidden with the wisdom that comes from experience, understanding, and suffering, my hope is that we journey with a commitment toward a creative and restorative world. In this way compassion becomes a true celebration and affirmation of life guiding us to the creation of a more peaceful world.

> We shall not cease from exploration.
> And the end of all our exploring
> Will be to arrive where we started
> And know the place for the first time.
>
> (Eliot, 1971, p. 59)

Chartres Labyrinth Mandala

172

Child Abuse and Trauma Resources

Academy of Family Mediators. Non-profit educational membership association. Members provide mediation services to families facing decisions involving separation, marital dissolution, child custody, parenting, visitation, property division, wills and estates, elder care, spousal support, child support, pre-nuptial agreements. Annual conference, mediator referrals, and educational materials. 5 Militia Drive, Lexington, MA 02421. Phone (781) 674-2663. <www.mediators.org>

Adults Molested as Children United (AMAC): Referral source. Groups for all sexual abuse survivors; national referrals. San Jose, CA. <www.movingforward.org>

African Network for the Prevention and Protection against Child Abuse and Neglect, Kenya. Devoted to prevention and child protection efforts. Distributes a quarterly newsletter. PO Box 71420, Nairobi, Kenya. <www.africaonline.co.ke/anppcan/>

Against Child Abuse, Hong Kong. Provides child protection, advocacy, hotline for children and parents, education, training, and networking groups. <www.aca.org.hk>

American Association for Protecting Children, American Humane Assn. National center promotes responsive child protection services in every community through program planning, training, education, and consultation. 63 Inverness Drive East, Englewood, CO 80112-5117. 1(800)227-4645. <www.americanhumane.org>

American Association of Sex Educators, Counselors, and Therapists. A not-for-profit professional organization providing certification. Members include health professionals, clergy, researchers, students, and lawyers. Promotes understanding of human sexuality and healthy sexual behavior. Continuing education and conference. Box 238, Mount Vernon, IA 52314. Fax: (319) 895-6203. <www.aasect.org>

American Human Association. A non-profit organization committed to the well-being of animals and also provides materials on the connection between animal abuse and human violence. Englewood, CO. (800) 277-4645. <www.amerhumane.org>

American Medical Association. Department of Mental Health. Provides referrals related to family violence and child abuse. Brochures on diagnosis, treatment, and medicolegal issues concerning child abuse. 515 State Street, Chicago, IL 60610. (312) 464-5066. <www.ama.org>

American Professional Society on the Abuse of Children (APSAC): Organization for professionals in the field of child abuse treatment and prevention; offers advocacy, information, guidelines, referral services to professionals working in the field. Journal of Child Maltreatment. Headquarters in Oklahoma City, Oklahoma. <www.apsac.org>

American Psychological Association. Professional association for psychologists. Many excellent journals of interest to mental health professionals, e.g., American Psychologist, Professional Psychology: Research and Practice, holds yearly conference, monthly newsletter: The APA Monitor. 750 First St., NE, Washington, DC 20002. Phone: (202) 336-5500. <www.apa.org>

Amnesty International. Amnesty International campaigns to promote human rights worldwide, specifically those addressed within the Universal Declaration of Human Rights. Recent campaign against the torture of children. <www.amnesty.org>

Board of Behavioral Sciences, California. State licensing organization for marriage and family therapists, social workers, nurses, educational psychologists. Responsible for consumer protection through the regulation of licensees, interns, associates, and corporations. 400 R Street, Suite 3150, Sacramento, CA 95814. (916) 445-4933. <www.bbs.ca.gov>

Board of Psychology, California. State licensing organization for psychologists. Committed to protection of health, safety, and welfare of consumers of psychological services. 1422 Howe Avenue, Suite 22, Sacramento, 95825. (916) 263-2699. <www.dca.ca.gov/psych/>

California Association for Marriage and Family Therapists. Professional association for marriage, family, and child therapists, representing over 25,000 members, including students, trainees, and interns. Monthly journal-The California Therapist. 7901 Raytheon Road, San Diego, CA 92111-1606. (619) 292-2638. <www.camft.org>

California Codes. Up to date information on the various California Legal Codes relevant to the practice of psychotherapy may be viewed and downloaded on the website: <www.leginfo.ca.gov>

California Psychological Association. Non-profit professional association for licensed psychologists and others affiliated with the delivery of psychological services. Special low-cost memberships for students. Yearly conference and monthly newsletter. 1022 "G" Street, Sacramento, CA 95814-0817. Phone: 916-325-9786 Fax: 916-325-9790. <www.calpsychlink.org>

Cameroon Society for the Prevention of Child Abuse and Neglect, CAPSCAN, Cameroon. Prevention and treatment, national training seminars, mulitidisciplinary research studies on child maltreatment including infanticide. <www.ipscan.org/resources.htm>

Casa Alianza. Covenant House, Latin America. Programs in Guatemala, Honduras, & Mexico. Provides direct services to street children in Latin America. Protects children against commercial sexual exploitation such as prostitution for the tourism trade and child smuggling. Also focuses on child torture, child labor, and illegal adoptions. <www.casa-allianza.org>

Center for World Indigenous Studies, CWIS. A non-profit research and educational organization committed to the understanding of the ideas and knowledge of indigenous people, and the economic, political, and social realities of indigenous nations. Focus includes health policy, violence, the politics of land and interracial discord, and international law. Serves as a clearinghouse of ideas between nations across the world. CWIS was instrumental in drafting the International Covenant on the Rights of Indigenous Nations, the first modern international law, currently being considered for ratification by nations worldwide. Headquarters in Washington state. <www.cwis.org>

Child Abuse Professional Network, CAPnet. A worldwide internet center devoted to professionals working in the field of Child Abuse in the areas of identification, investigation, treatment, and prevention of familial child abuse and neglect. <http://child-abuse.com/capro/>

Child Rights Information Network. International information network for organizations and individuals working on behalf of children's rights. Disseminates information on activities, research projects, resource collections, and publications produced by member organizations. 17 Grove Lane, London, SE5 8RD, UK. <www.crin.org>

Child Survivor of Traumatic Stress. Electronic version of a newsletter for professionals who work with traumatized children. Articles include specialized assessments and scales for assessing post-traumatic responses. <www.ummed.edu/pub/k/kfletche/kidsurv.html>

Childhelp USA, National Hot Line: (800) 422-4453. Offers 24-hour crisis hot line, information, referral network for support groups and therapists, and reporting suspected abuse. Sponsors Adult Survivors of Child Abuse Anonymous meetings. c/o NSCAAP, PO Box 630, Hollywood, CA 90028. <www.childhelpusa.org>

Childnet International. A non-profit organization invested in promoting and protecting children's interests on the internet in three primary realms: Content, Contact, and Communication. Focus is to enable children to benefit from international communications and be protected from negative influences. Information, education, and research. Headquarters in London, England. <www.childnet-int.org>

Children of Alcoholics Foundation. National non-profit organization that promotes public and professional awareness of issues specific to children of alcoholics. Develops programs and materials to break the cycle of family alcoholism. 555 Madison Avenue, 20th Fl., New York, NY 10163. (212) 754-0656. <www.coaf.org>

Childwatch. Childwatch of North America. National toll free 24 hour information line on missing children. Sponsors a national ID card program for children. 1 888-CHILDWATCH. <www.childwatch.org>

174

Childwatch International. An international network for individuals and institutions conducting research on behalf of children. Special reports on urban childhood, child prostitution, and on-line access to a database on European Research. Headquarters in Oslo, Norway. <www.childwatch.uio.org>

Clearinghouse on Child Abuse and Neglect Information, National. Provides annotated bibliographies of documents on specific aspects of child abuse or neglect, and provides statistics. PO Box 1182, Washington, DC 20012. (703) 385-7565. <www.calib.com/nccanch>

Defense for Children International, DCI. A non-governmental organization founded during the International Year of the Child, 1979, dedicated to the legal and social defense of children internationally. Produces a kit of relevant international legal standards concerning the Rights of the Child. PO Box 88, 1211 Geneva 20, Switzerland. <http://child-abuse.com/childrens-rights/dci-what.htm>

Domestic Abuse Intervention Project (Duluth). A National information center. Provides information on domestic abuse including batterers' treatment information. (218) 722-2781.

Family Violence Prevention Fund. National non-profit organization that focuses on domestic violence education, prevention, and public policy reform. <www.lgc.org/fund>

Family Resource Coalition. Membership organization of social service agencies concerned with strengthening families through preventive services. Maintains a clearinghouse for information on family resource programs, quarterly newsletter. 200 S. Michigan Avenue, 16th Floor, Chicago, IL 60604. (312) 341-0900. <www.frca.org>

Fourth World Documentation Center, Center for World Indigenous Studies, CWIS. The fourth world documentation project offers archived information to tribal governments, researchers, and organizations relating to social, political, economic, and human rights issues faced by Fourth World nations. Many documents related to the rights of children of minority and indigenous peoples. FWDP, PO Box 2574, Olympia, WA 98507-2574. <www.cwis.org>

Global Childnet. On-line child health related information. Access to their on-line database is provided. Headquarters in Vancouver, BC, Canada. <http://edie.cprost.sfa.ca/gcnet/>

Healing Woman. Publishes monthly newsletter for women recovering from childhood sexual abuse. PO Box 3038, Moss Beach, CA 94038-3038. (415) 728-0339. <www.healingwoman.org>

Human Rights Watch. Non-profit organization committed to systematic investigations of human rights abuses internationally. Reports available on-line: detention of children in Jamaica, cruelty and neglect in Russian orphanages, child abuse by paramilitary organizations in Ireland, bonded labor in India, the plight of street children in Bulgaria, and US issues such as capital punishment of children. 485 Fifth Avenue, New York, NY 10017-6104. <www.hrw.org>

Incest Recovery Association. Therapy groups for female & male survivors; education & materials. 6200 N. Central Expressway, Suite 209, Dallas, TX 75206. (214) 373-6607.

Incest Survivor Information Exchange. Newsletter for survivors' writings, art work, & exchange of information. PO Box 3399, New Haven, CT 06515. (203) 389-5166.

Incest Survivors Resource Network International. Information and networking for survivors. PO Box 7375, Las Cruces, NM 88006-7375. (505) 521-4260. <www.zianet.com/ISRNI/>

International Critical Incident Stress Foundation, Inc. Educational organization providing national trainings for professionals. Critical Incident Stress Debriefing Model. 5018 Dorsey Hall Drive, Suite 104, Ellicot, MD 21042. (410) 750-9600. <www.icisf.org>

International Save the Children Alliance. Organizational organization comprised of 30 organizations worldwide in over 100 countries helping to protect children from violence. Publications and training resources for professionals working for children's rights. From their mission statement: "respects and values each child, listens to children and learns, where children have hope and opportunity." Headquarters in the United Kingdom. <www.savechildren.net>

International Society for the Prevention of Child Abuse and Neglect, IPSCAN. Mission is to support individuals and organizations working to protect children from abuse and neglect across the world. Child Abuse and Neglect, the International Journal. Training, educational events, and international conferences. <www.ispcan.org>

International Society for the Study of Dissociative Disorders. Provides professional training and community information. Educational organization; conferences, literature. Journal of Trauma and Dissociation. 60 Revere Drive, Suite 500, Northbrook, IL 60062. (708) 966-4322. <www.issd.org>

International Society for Traumatic Stress Studies. Professional association. Journal of Traumatic Stress, consumer pamphlets on natural disasters and children and trauma, provides a monthly newsletter. 60 Revere Drive, Suite 500, Northbrook, IL 60062 (312) 644-0828. <www.istss.org>

National Association for Prevention of Child Abuse and Neglect, NAPCAN, Australia. Organization with representatives from each state and Territory. Focus on primary prevention, education campaigns, and conferences. <www.napcan.org.au>

National Board for Certified Counselors, Inc. NBCC. Professional certification board which certifies counselors as having met standards for the general and specialty practice of professional counseling established by the Board. 3 Terrace Way, Suite D, Greensboro, NC 27403-3660. <www.nbcc.org>

National Center for Missing and Exploited Children. National clearinghouse and resource center. Funded by U.S. Department of Justice. Provides free single copies of useful publications. 2101 Wilson Blvd., Suite 550, Arlington, VA 22201. (703) 235-3900. 1 (800) THE-LOST. <www.missingkids.org>

National Center for PTSD. Organization founded in 1989. At forefront in research efforts on posttraumatic stress disorder. A Clinical Quarterly focuses on the professional care of trauma survivors. Includes an electronic database, allowing for access to trauma literature. <www.ncptsd.org>

National Center for the Prosecution of Child Abuse. American Prosecutors Research Institute. Legal clearinghouse, literature, research, and professional workshops. 1033 N. Fairfax St., Suite 200, Alexandria, VA 22314. (703) 739-0321. <www.ncjrs.org>

National Center on Child Abuse and Neglect (NCCAN). U.S. Department of Health & Human Services. Established by CAPTA in 1974. Publishes manuals to provide guidance to professionals involved in the child protection system and to nurture community collaboration and quality of service delivery. PO Box 1182, Washington, DC 20013. 1(800)FYI-3366. <www.nccanch.org>

National Clearinghouse for Alcohol and Drug Information. A communications service of the Center for Substance Abuse Prevention. Provides information on research, publications, prevention and education resources, and prevention programs, and a catalog. 11426 Rockville Pike, Suite 200, Rockville, MD 20852. (800) 729-6686. <www.health.org>

National Clearinghouse on Child Abuse and Neglect Information (NCCAN). U.S. Department of Health and Human Services. For professionals seeking information on prevention, identification, and treatment of child abuse, neglect, and related welfare issues. PO Box 1182, Washington, DC 20012. (703) 385-7565. <www.calib.com/nccanch>

National Clearinghouse on Families and Youth. Tailors research to meet the needs of organizations, programs or communities; links people with others facing similar challenges in their work or who have creative ideas about improving youth practice and policy; provides updates on youth initiatives. PO Box 13505, Silver Spring, MD 20911-3505. (301) 608-8098. <www.ncfy.com>

National Coalition Against Domestic Violence. National organization that works to end violence in the lives of families. Information, technical assistance, publications, newsletters, and resource materials. PO Box 18749, Denver, CO 80218. (303) 839-1852. <www.ncadv.org>

National Coalition Against Sexual Assault. Advocacy, education, and public policy information. 125 N. Enola Drive, Enola, PA 17025. (717) 728-9764. <ncasa.org>

National Committee to Prevent Child Abuse. Information and referral. Publishes educational materials that focus on parenting and child abuse prevention. Annual fifty state survey with statistics. Free catalog: (800)835-2671. 206 S. Michigan Ave, 17th Floor, Chicago, IL 60604-4357. (312) 663-3520. <www.childabuse.org>

National Crime Victim Research and Treatment Center. CVC is a division of the Department of Psychiatry and Behavioral Sciences at the Medical University of South Carolina. Research, professional education, direct services, and public policy consultation.

National Organization for the Prevention of Child Abuse, Belize. Founded in 1992 in order to strengthen and preserve the family. Multi-disciplinary organization which sponsors parent empowerment training, school-based prevention activities, and public awareness campaigns.

National Organization for Victim Assistance, NOVA. Wash., DC. Information, Referral, Community Crisis Response Assistance Training. (800) 879-6682. <www.try-nova.org>

National Organization on Male Sexual Victimization. A national organization dedicated to research, education, advocacy, and activism. Focus on the elimination and prevention of sexual abuse of boys and men. Publishes men's issues forum for male survivors and sponsors an annual professional conference. PO Box 380181, Denver, CO 80238-1181. (303) 320-4365. <www.malesurvivor.org>

National Victim Assistance Academy. The National Victim Assistance Academy, created through a Department of Justice grant, provides university based training in victim assistance and victimology. A collaboration among universities and non-profit organizations has resulted in a cutting edge 45 hour course. Sponsors: California State University at Fresno, National Crime Victims Research and Treatment Center at the Medical University of South Carolina, and the Victims' Assistance Legal Organization. <www.ojp.usdoj.gov/ovc/asist/nvaa>

Office for Victims of Crime. Established by the 1984 Victims of Crime Act to oversee programs that serve victims. OVC provides grants for training, contributes funding, and supports compensation programs. Also involved in promoting victims' rights through legislation and public policy. <www.ojp.usdoj.gov/ovc>

PTSD Alliance. Multi-disciplinary professional advocacy organizations providing educational resources. <www.ptsdalliance.org>

Parents United International, Daughters and Sons United. Dedicated to the assistance of children, parents, & adults molested as children, and others concerned with child sexual abuse & related problems. PO Box 952, San Jose, CA 95108-0952. (408) 453-7616; Crisis line: (408) 279-8228. <www.giarretto.org>

People of Color Leadership Institute. Goals are to improve cultural competence in child welfare systems that serve children and families of color. Institute has developed a cultural competence training guide and bibliography of publications about child welfare as it relates to people of color. 714 G St., SE, Washington, DC 20003. (202) 544-3144.

Psychologists for the Ethical Treatment of Animals. A non-profit organization for professionals. PsyETA has two journals, a training manual for counseling with those who abuse animals, and the videotape Beyond Violence: The human-animal connection. P.O. Box 1297, Washington Grove, MD 20880. (301) 963-4751. <www.psyeta.org>

Sidran Traumatic Stress Foundation. A non-profit charitable organization devoted to education, advocacy, and research to benefit individuals suffering from injuries of traumatic stress. Books, articles, and professional education and training materials for therapists. Headquarters in Maryland. <www.sidran.org>

South African Society for the Prevention of Child Abuse and Neglect, South Africa. Founded in 1984 to promote awareness of child abuse and facilitate access to treatment and training. Conferences, seminars, and courses. <www.saspcan.org.za>

Survivors Healing Center. Workshops and groups for female and male survivors. National referrals. PO Box 8491, Santa Cruz, CA 95061. (408) 427-0182.

Survivors of Incest Anonymous. International network of self-help meetings, literature, pen pals, speakers, meeting information, and bi-monthly bulletin. SASE (two stamps) for information about support groups. World Service Office: PO Box 21817, Baltimore, MD 21222-6817. (410) 282-3400. <selfin.org/survivor/survorgs.1.html>

Survivors United Network. National resource center for support groups, therapists. Referrals, community lectures, and support groups in Denver area. (800) 456-HOPE.

UNICEF. United Nations Children's Fund. Unicef Voices of Youth is an electronic forum. Discussions focus on the right of children to live in peace, to have decent shelter, to be healthy and well-nourished, and to be protected from violence, abuse, and exploitation. Web pages contain the downloadable full text version of the Convention on the Rights of the Child, which has been ratified by every country in the world except two. This is the first legally binding international instrument to address the full range of human rights. <www.unicef.org>

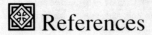 References

Abramson, L., & Martin, D. (1981). Depression and the causal inference process. In J. Harvey, W. Icke, R. Kidd (Eds.), *New directions in attributional research*. Hillsdale, New Jersey: Lawrence Erlbaum.

Abramson, L., Seligman, M., & Teasdale, J. P. (1978). Learned helplessness in humans: Critique and reformulation. *Journal of Abnormal Psychology, 87*, 49-74.

Abreu, J., & Atkinson, D. (2000). Multicultural counseling training: Past, present, and future directions. *Counseling Psychologist, 28*, 641-656.

Ackerman, M., & Ackerman, M. (1997). Custody evaluation practices: A survey of experienced professionals (revisited). *Professional Psychology Research and Practice, 28*(2), 137-145.

Adams, S. (2000). Understanding women who are violent in intimate relationships: Implications for army family advocacy. *Military Medicine, 165* (3), 214-223.

Ageton, S. (1983). *Sexual assault among adolescents*. Lexington, MA: D.C. Heath.

Aguilera, D. (1994). *Crisis intervention: Theory and methodology* (7th ed.). St. Louis, MO: Mosby.

Ainsworth, M. (1989). Attachments beyond infancy. *American Psychologist, 44*, 709-716.

Aizenstat, S. (1995). Jungian psychology and the world unconscious. In T. Roszak, M. Gomes, & A. Kramer (Eds.), *Ecopsychology* (pp.92-100). San Francisco: Sierra Club.

Alexander, P. (1992). Application of attachment theory to the study of sexual abuse. *Journal of Consulting and Clinical Psychology, 60*, 185-195.

Allan, J. (1988). *Inscapes of the child's world: Jungian counseling in schools and clinics*. Dallas: Spring.

Almeida, R., Woods, R., Messeneo, T., & Font, R. (1998). Cultural context model: Revisioning family therapy, race, culture, gender, and sexual orientation in clinical practice. In M. McGoldrick, J. Giordano, & J. Pearce (Eds.), *Ethnicity and family therapy* (2nd ed.), (pp.414-431). New York: Guilldord.

Alpert, J., & Paulson, A. (1990). Graduate level education and training in child sexual abuse. *Professional Psychology: Research and Practice, 21*, 366-371.

Altman, N. (1980). *Ahimsa: Dynamic compassion*. Wheaton, IL: Quest Books.

Ament, A. (1987). Rape and multiple personality disorder. *American Journal of Psychiatry, 144*, 541.

American Psychiatric Association. (2000). *Diagnostic and statistical manual of mental disorders, Text Revision*. Washington, DC: Author.

American Psychiatric Association. (1994). *Diagnostic and statistical manual of mental disorders* (4th ed.). Washington, DC: Author.

American Psychological Association. (1992). Ethical principles of psychologists and code of conduct. *American Psychologist, 47*, 1597-1611.

American Psychological Association. (1994). Guidelines for child custody evaluations in divorce proceedings. *American Psychologist, 49*, 677-680.

American Psychological Association. (1995). *Questions and answers about memories of childhood abuse*. Washington, DC: Author.

American Psychological Association. (1996). *APA presidential task force on violence and the family report*. Washington, DC: Author.

Andrews, A. (1990). Crisis and recovery services for family violence survivors. In A. Roberts (Ed.), *Helping crime victims: Research, policy, and practice*, (pp. 206-230). Newbury Park: Sage Publications.

REFERENCES

Araji, S. & Finkelhor, D. (1994). Abusers: A Research Review. *Sourcebook on Child Sexual Abuse*. Newbury Park: Sage Publications.

Arkow, P. (1996). The relationship between animal abuse and other forms of family violence. *Family Violence & Sexual Assault Bulletin, 12*(1-2). 29-34.

Arkow, P. (1999). The evolution of animal welfare as a human welfare concern. In F. Ascione and P. Arkow (Eds.) *Child abuse, domestic violence, and animal abuse: Linking the circles of compassion for prevention and intervention* (pp.19-37). Lafayette, Indiana: Purdue University Press.

Arons, G., & Spiegel, R. (1995). Unexpected encounters: The wizard of Oz exposed. In M. Sussman (Ed.), *A perilous calling: The hazards of psychotherapy practice* (pp. 125-138). New York: Wiley.

Ascione, F. (1998). Battered women's reports of their partner's and their children's cruelty to animals. *Journal of Emotional Abuse, 1*(1), 119-133.

Ascione, F. (1999). The abuse of animals and human interpersonal violence. In F. Ascione and P. Arkow (Eds.), *Child abuse, domestic violence, and animal abuse: Linking the circles of compassion for prevention and intervention* (pp.50-61). Lafayette, Indiana: Purdue University Press.

Association of Family and Conciliation Courts. (1995). *Model Standards of Practice for Child Custody Evaluations*. Madison, WI: Author.

Atkinson, D., Morten, G., & Sue, D. (1993). *Counseling American minorities* (4th ed.). Madison, WI: Brown and Benchmark.

Auerbach, S. (1989). Stress management and coping research in the health care setting: An overview and methodological commentary. *Journal of Consulting and Clinical Psychology, 57*, 388-395.

Austin, J. (2000). When a child discloses sexual abuse. *Childhood Education, 77*, 2-5.

Azar, S., & Siegel, B. (1990). Behavioral treatment of child abuse: A developmental perspective. *Behavior Modification, 14*, 279-300.

Bachelard, G. (1969). *The poetics of reverie: Childhood, language, and the cosmos* (p.16). Boston: Beacon.

Bachman, R., & Saltzman, L. (1996). *Violence against women: Estimates from the redesigned survey* (Bureau of Justice Statistics special report). Rockville, MD: US Department of Justice. (NCJ No. 154348)

Bagley, C., & Ramsay, R. (1986). Disrupted childhood and vulnerability to sexual assault: Long-term sequels with implications for counseling. *Social Work and Human Sexuality, 4*, 33-48.

Bagley, C., Wood, M., & Young, L. (1994). Victim to abuser: Mental health and behavioral sequels of child sexual abuse in a community survey of young adult males. *Child Abuse and Neglect, 18*, 683-697.

Bard, M., & Sangrey, D. (1985). *The crime victim's book*. New York: Brunner/Mazel.

Barnett, O., & Fagan, R. (1993). Alcohol use in male spouse abusers and their female partners. *Journal of Family Violence, 8*, 1-25.

Barnett, O., Miller-Perrin, C., & Perrin, R. (1997). *Family violence across the life span*. Thousand Oaks, CA: Sage.

Bass, E., & Davis, L. (1988). *The courage to heal: A guide for women survivors of child sexual abuse*. New York: Harper & Row.

Baur, S. (1999). *The intimate hour: Love and sex in psychotherapy*. Boston: Houghton Mifflin.

Bavolek, S., & Henderson, H. (1990). Child maltreatment and alcohol abuse: Comparisons and perspectives for treatment. In R. Potter-Efron and P. Potter-Efron (Eds.), *Aggression, family violence, and chemical dependency*. (pp.165-184). Binghamton: Haworth.

Bean, R., Perry, R., & Bedell, T. (2001). Developing culturally competent marriage and family therapists: Guidelines for working with Hispanic families. *Journal of Marital and Family Therapy, 27*, 43-54.

Beck, A. (1967). *Depression: Causes and treatment*. Philadelphia: University of Pennsylvania Press.

Beck, A. (1976). *Cognitive therapy and the emotional disorders*. New York: International Universities.

Beck, A., & Emery, G. (1985). *Anxiety disorders and phobias: A cognitive perspective*. New York: Basic.

Becker, J., & Kaplan, M. (1993). Cognitive behavioral treatment of the juvenile sexual offender. In H. Barbaree, W. Marshall, & S. Hudson (Eds.), *The juvenile sex offender* (pp.264-277). New York: Guilford.

Becker, J., Skinner, L., Abel, G., & Treacy, E. (1982). Incidence and types of sexual dysfunctions in rape and incest victims. *Journal of Sex and Marital Therapy, 8*, 65-74.

Beckman, L. (1994). Treatment needs of women with alcohol problems. *Alcohol Health and Research World, 18* (3), 206-211.

Beirne, P. (1997). Rethinking bestiality: Towards a concept of interspecies sexual assault. *Theoretical Criminology, 1*(3), 317-340.

Benoit, J., & Kennedy, A. (1992). The abuse history of male adolescent sex offenders. *Journal of Interpersonal Violence*, 7, 543-548.

Berliner, L., & Conte, J. (1990). The process of victimization: The victim's perspective. *Child Abuse and Neglect*, 14, 29-40.

Berliner, L., & Loftus, E. (1992). Sexual abuse accusations: Desperately seeking reconciliation. *Journal of Interpersonal Victimization*, 7, 570-578.

Berliner, L., Murphy, W., & Hardoon, L. (1998). Remarks on Practice parameters for the forensic evaluation of children and adolescents who may have been physically or sexually abused. *Child Maltreatment*, 3(2), 92-97.

Berman, J. (1990). The problems of overlapping relationships in the political community. In H. Lerman & N. Porter (Eds.), *Feminist ethics in psychotherapy* (pp. 106-110). New York: Springer.

Berns, N. (2001). Degendering the problem and gendering the blame: Political discourse on women and violence. *Gender and Society*, 15 (2), 262-281.

Berry, T. (1988). *The dream of the earth*. San Francisco: Sierra Club.

Bettelheim, B. (1976). *The uses of enchantment*. New York: Alfred Knopf.

Biaggio, M., & Greene, B. (1995). Overlapping/dual relationships. In E. Rave & C. Larsen (Eds.), *Ethical decision making in therapy: Feminist perspectives* (pp. 88-123). New York: Guilford.

Blake-White, J. & Kline, C. (1985). Treating the dissociative process in adult victims of childhood incest. *Social Casework: The Journal of Contemporary Social Work*, 394-402.

Boat, B. (1995). The relationship between violence to children and violence to animals: An ignored link? *Journal of Interpersonal Violence*, 10(4), 229-235.

Boat, B. (1999). Abuse of children and abuse of animals. In F. Ascione and P. Arkow (Eds.), *Child abuse, domestic violence, and animal abuse: Linking the circles of compassion for prevention and intervention* (pp.83-100). Lafayette, Indiana: Purdue University Press.

Bograd, M. (1999). Strengthening domestic violence theories: Intersection of race, class, sexual orientation and gender. *Journal of Marital and Family Therapy*, 25, 275-289.

Bohm, D. (1985). *Unfolding meaning: A weekend with David Bohm*. London: Ark Paperbacks.

Bongar, B. (Ed.). (1992). *Suicide: Guidelines for assessment, management, and treatment*. New York: Oxford University.

Bonner, B., Marx, B., Thompson, M., & Michaelson, P. (1998). Assessment of adolescent sexual offenders. *Child Maltreatment*, 3, 374-383.

Borowsky, I., Ireland, M., & Resnick, M. (2001). Adolescent suicide attempts: Risks and protectors. *Pediatrics*, 107(3), 485-493.

Bowlby, J. (1980). *Attachment and loss: Loss* (Vol. 3). London: Hogarth.

Bradbury, T., & Fincham F. (1990). Attributions in marriage: Review and critique. *Psychological Bulletin*, 107, 3-33.

Bradley, A., & Wood, J. (1996). How do children tell? The disclosure process in child sexual abuse. *Child Abuse and Neglect*, 20, 881-891.

Bradway, K. (1990a). Developmental stages in children's sandplay worlds. In *Sandplay studies: Origins, theories, practice* (pp.93-100). San Francisco: Jung Institute.

Bradway, K. (1990b). A woman's individuation through sandplay. In *Sandplay studies: Origins, theories, practice* (pp.133-156). San Francisco: Jung Institute.

Brickman, J., & Briere, J. (1984). Incidence of rape and sexual assault in an urban Canadian population. *International Journal of Women's Studies*, 7(3), 195-206.

Briere, J. (1984, April). *The effects of childhood sexual abuse on later psychological functioning: Defining a post-sexual abuse syndrome*. Paper presented at the Third National Conference on Sexual Victimization of Children, Washington, DC.

Briere, J. (1989). *Therapy for adults molested as children: Beyond survival*. New York: Springer.

Briere, J. (1992). *Child abuse trauma*. Newbury Park: Sage.

Briere, J., & Conte, J. (1993). Self-reported amnesia for abuse in adults molested as children. *Journal of Traumatic Stress*, 6(1), 21-31.

Briere, J., & Runtz, M. (1985). *Symptomatology associated with prior sexual abuse in a nonclinical sample*. Paper presented at the annual meting of the American Psychological Association, Los Angeles.

Briere, J., & Runtz, M. (1986). Suicidal thoughts and behaviours in former sexual abuse victims. *Canadian Journal of Behavioral Science*, 18, 413-423.

REFERENCES

Briere, J., & Runtz, M. (1987). Post sexual abuse trauma: Data and implications for clinical practice. *Journal of Interpersonal Violence, 2,* 367-379.

Briere, J., & Runtz, M. (1988a). Multivariate correlates of childhood psychological and physical maltreatment among university women. *Child Abuse & Neglect, 12,* 331-341.

Briere, J., & Runtz, M. (1988b). Symptomatology associated with childhood sexual victimization in a nonclinical adult sample. *Child Abuse and Neglect, 12,* 51-59.

Briere, J., & Runtz, M. (1989). The Trauma Symptom Checklist (TSC-33): Early data on a new scale. *Journal of Interpersonal Violence, 4,* 151-163.

Briere, J., & Runtz, M. (1991). The long-term effects of sexual abuse: A review and synthesis. In J. Briere (Ed.),*Treating victims of child sexual abuse* (pp. 3-13). San Francisco: Jossey-Bass.

Briere, J., & Zaidi, L. (1989). Sexual abuse histories and sequelae in female psychiatric emergency room patients. *American Journal of Psychiatry, 146,* 1602-1606.

Brodsky, S. (1991). Testifying in court: Guidelines and maxims for the expert witness. Washington, DC: American Psychological Association.

Bronfenbrenner, U. (1986). The ecology of the family as a context for human development. *Developmental Psychology, 22,* 723-742.

Brown, E., & Kolko, D. (1999). Child victims' attributions about being physically abused: An examination of factors associated with symptom severity. *Journal of Abnormal Child Psychology, 27,* 311-322.

Brown, L. (1991). Ethical issues in feminist therapy: Selected topics. *Psychology of Women Quarterly, 15,* 323-336.

Brown, S., & Lent, R. (2000). *Handbook of counseling psychology* (3rd ed.). New York: Wiley.

Browne, A. (1987). When battered women kill. New York: MacMillan.

Browne, A. (1993). Violence against women by male partners. *American Psychologist, 48,* 1077-1087.

Browne, A., & Finkelhor, D. (1986). Impact of child sexual abuse: A review of the research. *Psychological Bulletin, 99,* 66-77.

Browne, A., & Williams, K. (1989). Resource availability for women at risk and partner homicide. *Law and Society Review, 23,* 75-94.

Buber, M. (1970). *I and Thou* (W. Kaufmann, Trans.). New York: Touchstone.

Burgess, A., Hartmann, C., & Baker, T. (1995). Memory representations of childhood sexual abuse. *Journal of Psychosocial Nursing, 33*(9), 9-16.

Burgess, A., & Holmstrom, L. (1974a). *Rape: Victims of crisis.* Bowie, Maryland: Robert J. Brady Company.

Burgess, A., & Holmstrom, L. (1974b). Rape trauma syndrome. *American Journal of Psychiatry, 131,* 981-986.

Burgess, A., & Holmstrom, L. (1978). Recovery from rape and prior life stress. *Research in Nursing and Health, 1,* 165-174.

Burnett, B. (1993). The psychological abuse of latency age children: A survey. *Child Abuse and Neglect, 17,* 441-454.

Burt, M., and Katz, B. (1987). Dimensions of recovery from rape: Focus on growth outcomes. *Journal of Interpersonal Violence, 2,* 57-81.

Calhoun, K., & Townsley, R. (1991). Attributions of responsibility for acquaintance rape. In A. Parrot & L. Beckhofer (Eds.), *Acquaintance rape:* The hidden crime (pp. 57-69). New York: Wiley.

Caliso, J, & Milner, J. (1992). Childhood history of abuse and child abuse screening. *Child Abuse & Neglect, 16,* 647-659.

Campis, L., Hebden-Curtis, J., & DeMaso, D. (1993). Developmental differences in detection and disclosure of sexual abuse. *Journal of the American Academy of Child and Adolescent Psychiatry, 32,* 920-924.

Cantwell, H. (1980). Child neglect. In C. Kempe & R. Helfer (Eds.), *The battered child* (pp.183-197). Chicago: University of Chicago Press.

Caplan, G. (1964). *Principles of preventive psychiatry.* New York: Basic.

Capra, F. (1983). *The turning point: Science, society, and the rising culture.* New York: Bantam.

Carmack, B. (1985). The effects of family members and functioning after the death of a pet. In M. Sussman (Ed.), *Pets and family* (pp.149-162). New York: Haworth.

Carmen, E., Rieker, P., & Mills, T. (1984). Victims of violence and psychiatric illness. *American Journal of Psychiatry, 141*(3), 378-393.

Case, C., & Dalley, T. (1992). *The handbook of art therapy.* New York: Routledge.

Casement, P. (1991). *Learning from the patient.* New York: Guilford.

Caspi, A., Moffitt, T., Newman, D., & Sylvia, P. (1996). Behavioral observations at age three predict adult psychiatric disorder: Longitudinal evidence from a birth cohort. *Archives of General Psychiatry, 53,* 1022-1035.

Caudill, O.B., & Pope, K. (1995). *Law and mental health professionals: California.* Washington, DC: American Psychological Association.

Ceci, S., & Bruck, M. (1995). *Jeopardy in the court room: A scientific analysis of children's memory.* Washington, DC: American Psychological Association.

Celano, M. (1992). A developmental model of victims' internal attributions of responsibility for sexual abuse. *Journal of Interpersonal Violence, 7,* 57-69.

Centers for Disease Control. (1997). Regional variations in suicide risk: United States 1990-1994. *Morbidity and Mortality Weekly Report, 46*(34), 789-79.

Chaffin, M., Bonner, B., Worley, K., & Lawson, L. (1996). Treating abused adolescents. In J. Briere, L. Berliner, J. Bulkley, C. Jenny, & T. Reid (Eds.), *The APSAC handbook on child maltreatment* (pp.119-139). Thousand Oaks, CA: Sage.

Chandy, J., Blum, R., Resnick, M. (1996). Gender specific outcomes for sexually abused adolescents. *Child Abuse and Neglect, 20,* 1219-1231.

Chapple, C. (1993). *Nonviolence to animals, earth, and self in Asian traditions.* New York: State University of New York.

Chemtob, C., Hamada, R., Bauer, G., Torigoe, R., & Kinney, B. (1988). Patient suicide: Frequency and impact on psychologists. *Professional Psychology: Research and Practice, 19,* 416-420.

Children's Defense Fund. (1996).*The state of America's children yearbook.* Washington, DC: Author.

Chopra, D. (1993). Timeless mind, ageless body. *Noetic Sciences Review, 28,* 6-21.

Cicchetti, D., & Toth, S. (1995). A developmental psychopathology perspective on child abuse and neglect. *Journal of the American Academy of Child and Adolescent Psychiatry, 34,* 541-565.

Claman, L. (1993). The squiggle-drawing game. In C. Schaefer & D. Cangelosi (Eds.), *Play therapy techniques* (pp.177-189). Northvale, NJ: Jason Aronson.

Cohen, J., & Mannarino, A. (1993). A treatment model for sexually abused preschoolers. *Journal of Interpersonal Violence, 8,* 115-131.

Cohen, J., & Mannarino, A. (1996). A treatment outcome study for sexually abused preschool children: Initial findings. *Journal of the American Academy of Child and Adolescent Psyciatry, 35,* 42-50.

Cohen, J., Mannarino, A., Berliner, L., & Deblinger, E. (2000). Trauma-focused cognitive behavioral therapy for children and adolescents: An empirical update. *Journal of Interpersonal Violence, 15,* 1202-1223.

Collings, S. (1995). The long-term effects of contact and noncontact forms of child sexual abuse in a sample of university men. *Child Abuse and Neglect, 19,* 1-6.

Conn, S. (1995). When the earth hurts, who responds? In T. Roszak, M. Gomes, & A. Kramer (Eds.), *Ecopsychology* (pp.156-171). San Francisco: Sierra Club.

Connors, R. (1996). Self-injury in trauma survivors: 2. Levels of clinical response. *American Journal of Orthopsychiatry, 66*(2), 207-216.

Conte, J. (1985). Clinical dimensions of adult sexual abuse of children analysis. *Behavioral Sciences and the Law, 3,* 341-354.

Conte, J., & Berliner, L. (1981). Sexual abuse of children: Implications for practice. *Social Casework: The Journal of Contemporary Social Work,* 601-606.

Conte, J., Briere, J., & Sexton. (1989, April). *Moderators of longterm symptomatology in women molested as children.* Paper presented at the meeting of the American Psychological Association, New Orleans, LA.

Conte, J., & Schuerman, J. (1987). Factors associated with an increased impact of child sexual abuse. *Child Abuse & Neglect, 11,* 201-211.

Coons, P., & Milstein, V. (1984). Rape and post-traumatic stress in multiple personality. *Psychological Reports, 55,* 839-845.

Corbett, L. (1996). The religious function of the psyche. New York: Routledge.

Courtois, C. (1979). The incest experience and its aftermath. *Victimology: An International Journal, 4,* 337-347.

Courtois, C. (1988). *Healing the incest wound: Adult survivors in therapy.* New York: Norton.

Courtois, C. (1997). Healing the incest wound: A treatment update with attention to recovered memory issues. *American Journal of Psychotherapy, 51*(4), 464-496.

Covitz, J. (1986). *Emotional child abuse: The family curse.* Boston: Sigo Press.

Crenshaw, K. (1992). Race, gender, and sexual harassment. *Southern California Law Review, 65*, 1467-1476.

Crime and Violence Prevention Center. (2000). *Child abuse prevention handbook*. Sacramento, CA: California Attorney General.

Crittenden, P., & Ainsworth, M. (1989). Child maltreatment and attachment theory. In D. Cicchetti & V. Carlson (Eds.), *Child maltreatment: Theory and research on the causes and consequences of child abuse and neglect* (pp. 432-463). New York: Cambridge University Press.

Csikszentmihaly, M. (1990). *Flow: The psychology of optimal experience*. New York: HarperCollins.

Cusack, O. (1988). *Pets and mental health*. Binghamton, NY: Haworth Press.

Cushman, P. (1995). *Constructing the self, constructing America*. Reading, MA: Addison-Wesley.

Dalenberg, C., & Jacobs, D. (1994). Attributional analyses of child sexual abuse episodes: Empirical and clinical issues. *Journal of Interpersonal Violence, 7*, 57-69.

Dawson, S. (1994). *The mythos of Munchause by proxy syndrome*. Unpublished master's thesis, Pacifica Graduate Institue. Santa Barbara, CA.

Deblinger, E., & Heflin, A. (1996). *Cognitive behavioral interventions for treating sexually abused children*. Thousand Oaks, CA: Sage.

DeJong, A., Emmett, G., & Hervada, A. (1982). Epidemiologic factors in sexual abuse of boys. *American Journal of the Diseases of Children, 136*, 990-993.

Derogatis, L., Lipman, R., Rickels, K., Ulenhuth, E., & Covi, L. (1974). The Hopkins Symptom Checklist (HSCL): A self-report symptom inventory. *Behavioral Science, 19*, 1-15.

DeViney, E., Dickert, J., & Lockwood, R. (1983). The care of pets within child abusing families. *International Journal for the Study of Animal Problems, 4*, 321-329.

DeVoe, E., & Faller, K. (1999). The characteristics of disclosure among children who may have been sexually abused. *Child Maltreatment, 4*, 217-227.

DeVries, M. (1996). Trauma in cultural perspective. In B. van der Kolk, A. McFarlane, & L. Weisaeth (Eds.), *Traumatic stress: The effects of overwhelming experience on mind, body, and society* (pp.398-413). New York: Guilford.

Dillman, D. (1999). Kids and critters: An intervention to violence. In F. Ascione & P. Arkow (Eds.), *Child abuse, domestic violence, and animal abuse: Linking the circles of compassion for prevention and intervention* (pp.424-432). West Lafayette, IN: Purdue University.

Dinsmore, C. (1991). *From survivor to thriver: Incest, feminism, and recovery*. Albany, NY: State University of New York Press.

Dobash, R., & Dobash, R. (1977-1978). Wives: The "appropriate" victims of marital violence. *Victimology: An International Journal, 2*, 426-442.

Dobash, R., & Dobash, R. (1979). *Violence against wives: A case against the patriarchy*. New York: Free Press.

Dobash, R., Dobash, R., Wilson, M., & Daly, M. (1992). The myth of sexual symmetry in marital violence. *Social Problems, 39*, 71-91.

Doherty, W. (1995). *Soul searching: Why psychotherapy must promote moral responsibility*. New York: Basic.

Downing, C. (1992). Unpublished lecture presented at Pacifica Graduate Institute, Carpinteria, CA.

Downing, C. (1996). Revisiting the myth of Demeter and Persephone. In J. Young (Ed.), *Saga: Best new writings on mythology* (pp.30-48). Ashland, OR: White Cloud Press.

Dundas, E. (1990). *Symbols come alive in the sand*. Boston: Coventure.

Dutton, D. (1995). *The batterer: A psychological profile*. New York: Basic Books.

Edinger, E. (1985). *Anatomy of the psyche*. La Salle, IL: Open Court.

Edinger, E. (1994). *The eternal drama: The inner of meaning of Greeek mythology*. Boston, MA: Shambhala.

Edinger, E. (1997). The vocation of depth psychotherapy. *Psychological Perspectives, 35*, 8-22.

Egendorf, A. (1985). *Healing from the war: Trauma and transformation after Vietnam*. Boston, MA: Shambhala.

Einstein, A. (1972, November 28). *New York Post*.

Eliot, T.S. (1971). Little gidding. *Four quartets* (p.59). New York: Harcourt Brace.

Ellinor, L., & Gerard, G. (1998). *Dialogue: Rediscover the transforming power of conversation*. New York: John Wiley.

Elliot, D., & Guy, J. (1993). Mental health professionals versus non-mental health professionals: Childhood trauma and adult functioning. *Professional Psychology: Research and Practice, 24*, 83-90.

Elliott, D., & Briere, J. (1990). *Predicting molestation history in professional women with the trauma symptom checklist.* Paper presented at the meeting of the Western Psychological Association, Los Angeles.

Elliott, D., & Briere, J. (1994). Forensic sexual abuse evaluations of older children: Disclosures and symptomatology. *Behavioral Sciences and the Law, 12*, 261-277.

Ellis, E., Atkeson, B., & Calhoun, K. (1981). An assessment of long-term reaction to rape. *Journal of Abnormal Psychology, 90*, 263-266.

Ellis, D., Zucker, R., & Fitzgerald, H. (1997). The role of family influences in development and risk. *Alcohol Health and Research World, 21*(3), 218-225.

Enns, C. (1996). Counselors and the backlash: "Rape hype" and "false-memory syndrome." *Journal of Counseling and Development, 74*(4), 358-375.

Enns, C., McNeilly, C., Corkery, J., & Gilbert, M. (1995). The debate about delayed memories of child sexual: A feminist perspective. *The Counseling Psychologist, 23*(2), 181-279.

Estes, C.P. (Speaker). (1990).*Warming the stone child.* Boulder, CO: Sounds True Recordings.

Estes, C.P. (Speaker). (1991). *The creative fire.* Boulder, CO: Sounds True Recordings.

Estes, C.P. (1992).*Women who run with the wolves: Myths and stories of the wild woman archetype.* New York: Ballantine.

Everson, M., Hunter, W., Runyan, D., Edelsohn, G., & Coulter, M. (1989). Maternal support following disclosure of incest. *American Journal of Orthopsychiatry, 59*, 197-207.

Factor, D., & Wolfe, D. (1990). Parental psychopathology and high-risk children. In R. Ammerman & M. Hersen (Eds.), *Children at risk: An evaluation of factors contributing to child abuse and neglect* (pp.171-198). New York: Plenum.

Faller, K. (Ed.). (1981). *Social work with abused and neglected chilren.* New York: Free Press.

Faller, K. (1989). The role relationship between victim and perpetrator as a predictor of characteristics of intrafamilial sexual abuse. *Child and Adolescent Social Work, 6*, 217-229.

Faller, K., & DeVoe, E. (1996). Allegations of sexual abuse in divorce. *Journal of Child Sexual Abuse, 4*(4), 1-25.

Famularo, R., Stone, K., Barnum, R., & Wharton, R. (1986). Alcoholism and severe child maltreatment. *American Journal of Orthopsychiatry, 56*, 481-485.

Felthous, A. (1980). Aggression against cats, dogs, and people. *Child Psychiatry and Human Development, 10*, 169-177.

Feminist Therapy Institute. (1987). *Feminist therapy code of ethics.* Denver, CO: Author.

Field, T., Seligman, S., Scafedi, F., & Schanberg, S. (1996). Alleviating posttraumatic stress in children following Hurrican Andrew. *Journal of Applied and Developmental Psychology, 17*, 37-50.

Figley, C. (Ed.). (1985). *Trauma and its wake: The study and treatment of post-traumatic stress disorder.* New York: Brunner/Mazel.

Figley, C. (1995). *Compassion fatigue: Coping with secondary traumatic stress disorder in those who treat the traumatized.* Bristol, PA: Brunner/Mazel.

Finkelhor, D. (1979). *Sexually victimized children.* New York: The Free Press.

Finkelhor, D. (1984). *Child sexual abuse: New theory and research.* New York: Free Press.

Finkelhor, D. (1990). Early and long-term effects of child sexual abuse: An update. *Professional Psychology: Research and Practice, 21*(5), 325-330.

Finkelhor, D. (1995). The victimization of children: A developmental perspective. *American Journal of Orthopsychiatry, 65*(2), 177-193.

Finkelhor, D., & Browne, A. (1985). The traumatic impact of childhood sexual abuse: A conceptualization. *American Journal of Orthopsychiatry, 55*, 530-541.

Finkelhor, D., & Browne, A. (1988). Assessing the long-term impact of child sexual abuse: A review and conceptualization. In L. Walker (Ed.), *Handbook on sexual abuse of children* (pp. 55-71). New York: Springer.

Finkelhor, D., Hotaling, G., Lewis, I., & Smith, C. (1989). Sexual abuse and its relationship to later sexual satisfaction, marital status, religion, and attitudes. *Journal of Interpersonal Violence, 4*, 379-399.

Finkelhor, D., Hotaling, G., Lewis, I., & Smith, C. (1990). Sexual abuse in a national survey of adult men and women: Prevalence, characteristics, and risk factors. *Child Abuse and Neglect, 14*, 19-28.

Finkelhor, D., & Russell, D. (1984). Women as perpetrators. In D. Finkelhor (Ed.), *Child sexual abuse: New theory and research.* New York: Free Press.

Finkelstein, N. (1995). Treatment issues for alcohol and drug dependent pregnant and parenting women. *Health and Social Work, 19*(1), 7-15.

Folkman, S., & Lazarus, R. (1980). An analysis of coping in a middle-aged community sample. *Journal of Health and Social Behavior, 21*, 219-239.

Folkman, S., Lazarus, R., Gruen, R., & DeLongis, A. (1986). Appraisal, coping, health status, and psychological symptoms. *Journal of Personality and Social Psychology, 50*, 571-579.

Fox, M. (1990). *A spirituality named compassion.* San Francisco: Harper.

Fox, M.W. (1996). *The boundless circle: Caring for creatures and creation.* Wheaton, IL: Quest.

Frank, E., Turner, S., & Stewart, B. (1980). Initial response to rape: The impact of factors within the rape situation. *Journal of Behavioral Assessment, 2*, 39-53.

Frankel, R. (1998). *The adolescent psyche: Jungian and Winnicottian perspectives.* London: Routledge.

Frankl, V. (1984). *Man's search for meaning: An introduction to logotherapy.* New York: Simon & Schuster.

Freire, P. (1989). *Pedagogy of the oppressed.* New York: Continuum.

Freud, S. (1962). The aetiology of hysteria. In J. Strachey (Trans.), *The complete psychological works of Sigmund Freud,* (Vol. 3, pp.191-221). London: Hogarth Press. (Original work published 1896)

Freud, S. (1966). *The complete introductory letters of psychoanalysis.* New York: Norton.

Freudenberger, H. (1974). Staff burnout. *Journal of Social Issues, 30*, 159-165.

Friedrich, W. (1990). *Psychotherapy of sexually abused and their families.* New York: Norton.

Friedrich, W. (1996). An integrated model of psychotherapy for abused children. In J. Briere, L. Berliner, J. Bulkley, C. Jenny, & T. Reid (Eds.), *APSAC handbook on child maltreatment* (pp.104-118). Thousand Oaks, CA: Sage.

Friedrich, W., Fisher, J., Dittner, C., Acton, R., Berliner, L., Butler, J., Damon, L., Davies, W., Gray, A., & Wright, J. (2001). Child sexual abuse inventory: Normative, psychiatric, and sexual abuse comparisons. *Child Maltreatment, 6*, 37-49.

Friedrich, W., Grambsch, P., Broughton, D., Kuiper, J., & Beilke, R. (1991). Normative sexual behavior in children. *Pediatrics, 88*, 456-464.

Friedrich, W., Grambsch, P., Damon, L., Hewitt, S., Koverola, C., Lang, R., & Wolfe, V. (1992). Child sexual behavior inventory: Normative and clinical comparisons. *Psychological Assessment, 4*, 303-311.

Frieze, I. (1983). Investigating the causes and consequences of marital rape. *Signs: Journal of Women in Culture and Society, 8*, 532-553.

Fritz, G., Stoll, K., & Wagner, N. (1981). A comparison of males and females who were sexually abused as children. *Journal of Sex and Marital Therapy, 7*, 4-59.

Fromuth, M. (1986). The relationship of childhood sexual abuse with later psychological and sexual adjustment in a sample of college women. *Child Abuse and Neglect, 10*, 5-15.

Fromuth, M., & Burkhart, B. (1987). Childhood sexual victimization among college men: Definitional and methodological issues. *Victims and Violence, 2*, 241-153.

Fulton, D. (2000). Early recognition of Munchausen Syndrome by proxy. *Critical Care Nursing Quarterly, 23*(2), 35-42.

Gabrielli, W., & Mednic, S. (1983). Intellectual performance in children of alcoholics. *Journal of Nervous and Mental Disease, 171*, 444-447.

Gadon, E. (1989). *The once and future goddess.* San Francisco: Harper Row.

Garbarino, J. (1978). The elusive crime of emotional abuse. *Child Abuse and Neglect, 2*, 89-99..

Garbarino, J., Guttman, E., & Seeley, J. (1986). *The psychologically battered child: Strategies for identification, assessment and intervention.* San Francisco: Jossey-Bass.

Gardner, R. (1987). *The parental alienation syndrome and the differentiation between fabricated and genuine sexual abuse.* Cresskill, NJ: Creative Therapeutics.

Gardner, R. (1992). *True and false allegations of child sex abuse.* Cresskill, NJ: Creative Therapeutics.

Gates, K., & Speare, K. (1990). Overlapping relationships in rural communities. In H. Lerman & N. Porter (Eds.), *Feminist ethics in psychotherapy* (pp. 97-101). New York: Springer.

Gelinas, D. (1983). The persisting negative effects of incest. *Psychiatry, 46*, 312-322.

Gelles, R. (1997). *Intimate violence in families.* Newbury Park, CA: Sage Publications.

Gelles, R., & Straus, M. (1979). Determinants of violence in the family: Toward a theoretical integration. In W. Burr, R. Hill, F. Nye, & I. Reiss (Eds.), *Contemporary theories about the family* (pp.549-581). New York: Free Press.

Giarretto, H., Giarretto, A., & Sgroi, S. (1978). Coordinated community treatment of incest. In A. Burgess, A. Groth, L. Holmstrom, & L. Sgroi (Eds.), *Sexual assault of children and adolescents*. Lexington, MA: Lexington Books.

Gibbs, J., & Huang, L. (1989). *Children of color: Psychological intervention with minority youth*. San Francisco: Jossey-Bass.

Gil, E. (1991). *The healing power of play: Working with abused children*. New York: Guilford.

Gil, E., & Johnson, T. (1993). *Sexualized children: Assessment and treatment of sexualized children and children who molest*. Rockville, MD: Launch.

Gilfus, M. (1999). The price of the ticket: A survivor-centered appraisal of trauma theory. *Violence Against Women*, 5(11), 1238-1257.

Gilligan C. (1982). *In a different voice: Psychological theory and women's development*. Cambridge, MA: Harvard.

Gold, E. (1986). Long term effects of sexual victimization in childhood: An attributional approach. *Journal of Consulting and Clinical Psychology*, 54, 471-475.

Goldner, V. (1992). Making room for both/and. *Family Therapy Networker*, 16, 54-62.

Graves, R., Openshaw, D., Ascione, F., & Ericksen, S. (1996). Demographic and parental characteristics of youthful sexual offenders. *International Journal of Offender Therapy and Comparative Criminology*, 40, 300-317.

Green, A. (1986). True and false allegations of sexual abuse in child custody disputes. *Journal of the American Academy of Child Psychiatry*, 25, 449-455.

Greenberg, S., & Shuman, D. (1997). Irreconcilable conflict between therapeutic and forensic roles. *Professional Psychology: Research and Practice*, 28(1), 50-57.

Groth, A. (1979). *Men who rape*. New York: Plenum Press.

Groth, A., Hobson, W., & Gary, T. (1982). The child molester: Clinical observations. In J. Conte & D. Shore (Eds.), *Social work and child sexual abuse* (p.129-144). New York: Haworth.

Guggenbuhl-Craig, A (1971). *Power in the helping professions*. Dallas: Spring.

Guggenbuhl-Craig, A. (1995). Foreword. In L. Ross & M. Roy (Eds.), *Cast the first stone* (p.viii). Wilmette, IL: Chiron.

Guttheil, T., Gabbard, G. (1998). Misuses and misunderstandings of boundary theory in clinical and regulatory settings. *The American Journal of Psychiatry*, 155(3), 409-414.

Haan, N. (1965). Coping and defense mechanisms related to personality inventories. *Journal of Consulting Psychology*, 4, 373-378.

Hall, E., & Flannery, P. (1984). Prevalence and correlates of sexual assault experiences in adolescents. *Victimology*, 9, 398-406.

Hare-Mustin. R. (1978). A feminist approach to family therapy. *Family Process*, 17, 181-194.

Hart, S. & Brassard, M. (1987). A major threat to children's mental health: Psychological maltreatment. *American Psychologist*, 42, 160-165.

Hart, S., & Brassard, M. (1994). *Draft guidelines for psychosocial evaluation of suspected psychological maltreatment in children and adolescents*. Chicago: American Professional Society on the Abuse of Children.

Harter, S. (1988). Developmental and dynamic changes in the nature of the self-concept. In S. Shirk (Ed.), *Cognitive development and child psychotherapy* (pp.119-160). New York: Plenum.

Harvey, M. (1996). An ecological view of psychological trauma and trauma recovery. *Journal of Traumatic Stress*, 9, 3-23.

Hayden, M. (1996). When a lesbian client is attracted to her therapist: A lesbian therapist responds. *Women and Therapy*, 19, 7-13.

Hayles, K. (1995). Towards a conclusion. In W. Cronon (Ed.), *Uncommon ground*. New York: Norton.

Hedges, L., Hilton, R., Hilton, V., & Caudill, O.B. (1999). *Therapists at risk-Perils of the intimacy of the therapeutic relationship*. Northvale, NJ: Jason Aronson.

Heidegger, M. (1959). *An introduction to metaphysics*. (R. Manheim, Trans.). New Haven, CT: Yale University Press.

Helfer, M., Kempe, R., & Krugman, R. (Eds.). (2000). *The battered child* (5th ed). Chicago: University of Chicago Press.

Herman, J. (1981). *Father daughter incest*. Cambridge: Harvard University Press.

Herman, J. (1986). Histories of violence in an outpatient population. *American Journal of Orthopsychiatry*, 56, 137-141.

Herman, J. (1992). *Trauma and recovery*. New York: Basic Books.

REFERENCES

Herrenkohl, R., & Russo, M. (2001). Abusive early child rearing and early childhood aggression. *Child Maltreatment, 6*, 3-16.

Hibbard, R., Ingersoll, G., & Orr, D. (1990). Behavior risk, emotional risk, and child abuse among adolescents in a nonclincial setting. *Pediatrics, 86*, 896-901.

Higgins, G. (1994). *Resilient adults: Overcoming a cruel past.* San Francisco: Jossey-Bass.

Hillman, J. (1975). *Re-visioning psychology.* New York: Harper and Row.

Hillman, J. (1983). *Healing fiction.* Woodstock, CT: Spring.

Hillman, J, & Ventura, M. (1992). *We've had a hundred years of psychotherapy—and the world;s getting worse.* San Francisco, CA: Harper.

Hirschman, E. (1994). Consumers and their companion animals. *Journal of Consumer Research, 20*(3), 616-632.

Ho, M. (1989). Social work practice with Asian Americans. In A. Morales & B. Sheafor (Eds.), *Social work: A profession of many faces* (pp.521-541). Boston: Allyn & Bacon.

Hobfoll, S., Spielberger, C., Breznitz, S., Figley, C., Folkman, S., Lepper-Green, B., Meichenbaum, D., Milgram, N., Sandler, I., Sarason, I., & van der Kolk, B. (1991). War-related stress: Addressing the stress of war and other traumatic events. *American Psychologist, 46*, 848-855.

Hoffman-Plotkin, D., & Twentyman, C. (1984). A multimodal assessment of behavioral and cognitive deficits in abused and neglected preschoolers. *Child Development, 55*, 794-802.

Holahan, C., & Moos, R. (1987). Personal and contextual determination of coping strategies. *Journal of Personality and Social Psychology, 52*, 946-955.1

Holden, E., & Black, M. (1999). Theory and concepts of prevention as applied to clinical psychology. *Clinical Psychology Review, 19*, 391-401.

Holroyd, J., & Brodsky, A. (1977). Psychologists' attitudes and practices regarding erotic and nonerotic physical contact with patients. *American Psychologist, 32*, 843-849.

Hopkins, B., & Anderson, B. (1985). *The counselor and the law* (2nd ed.). Alexandria, VA: American Association for Counseling and Development.

Hotaling, H., & Sugarman, D. (1990). A risk marker analysis of assaulted wives. *Journal of Family Violence, 5*, 1-13.

Hughes, L., & Corbo-Richert, B. (1999). Munchausen syndrome by proxy: Literature review and implications for critical care nurses. *Critical Care Nurse, 19*(3), 71-84.

Isaacs, W. (1999). *Dialogue and the art of thinking together: A pioneering approach to communicating in business and in life.* New York: Currency.

Island, D., & Letellier, P. (1991). *Men who beat the men who love them.* New York: Harrington.

Jacob, T., & Johnson, S. (1997). Parenting influences on the development of alcohol abuse and dependence. *Alcohol Health and Research World, 21*(3), 204-209.

Jacobson, S. (1997). Assessing the impact of maternal drinking during and after pregnancy. *Alcohol Health and Research World, 21*(3), 199-203.

Janoff-Bulman, R. (1979). Characterological versus behavioral self-blame: Inquiries into depression and rape. *Journal of Personality and Social Psychology, 37*, 1798-1809.

Janoff-Bulman, R. (1985). The aftermath of victimization: Rebuilding shattered assumptions. In C. R. Figley (Ed.), *Trauma and its wake: The study and treatment of post-traumatic stress disorder* (pp. 15-35). New York: Brunner/Mazel.

Janoff-Bulman, R., & Frieze, I. H. (1983). A theoretical perspective for understanding reactions to victimization. *Journal of Social Issues, 39*, 1-17.

Jarof, L. (1993, November 29). Lies of the mind. *Time, 142*(23), 52-56, 59.

Johnson, J., & Rolf, J. (1988). Cognitive functioning in children from alcoholic and non-alcoholic families. *Journal of Addictions, 83*, 849-857.

Johnson, M., & Ferraro, K. (2000). Research on domestic violence in the 1990's: Making distinctions. *Journal of Marriage and the Family, 62*(4), 948-963.

Johnson, R. (1986). *Inner work: Using dreams and active imagination for personal growth* (p.13, 23). San Francisco: Harper & Row.

Johnston, J., & Campbell, L. (1993). Parent-child relationships in domestic violence families disputing custody. *Family and Conciliation Courts Review, 31*, 282-298.

Jung, C.G. (1953). Two essays on analytical psychology. In H. Read (Ed.), The collected works (R.F.C. Hull, Trans.) (Vol. 7). Princeton, NJ: Princeton University Press.

Jung, C.G. (1954). The practice of psychotherapy. In H. Read, M. Fordham, & G. Adler (Eds.), *The collected works* (R.F.C. Hull, Trans.) (Vol. 16). New York: Bollingen.

Jung, C.G. (1960). The structure and dynamics of the psyche. In H. Read (Ed.), *The collected works* (R.F.C. Hull, Trans.) (Vol. 8). Princeton, NJ: Princeton University Press.

Jung, C.G. (1961). *Memories, dreams, and reflections.* (A. Jaffe, Trans.). New York: Knopf.

Jung, C.G. (1963). Mysterium coniunctionis. In H. Read, M. Fordham, & G. Adler (Eds.), *The collected works* (R.F.C. Hull, Trans.) (Vol.10). New York: Bollingen.

Jung, C.G. (1964). Civilization in transition. In H. Read (Ed.), The collected works (R.F.C. Hull, Trans.) (Vol.10). Princeton, NJ: Princeton University Press.

Jung, C.G. (1968). Psychology and alchemy. In H. Read (Ed.), *The collected works* (R.F.C. Hull, Trans.) (Vol. 12). Princeton, NJ: Princeton University Press.

Jung, C.G. (1968). Alchemical studies. In H. Read (Ed.), *The collected works* (R.F.C. Hull, Trans.) (Vol. 13). Princeton, NJ: Princeton University Press.

Jung, C.G. (1969). Archetypes and the collective unconscious. In H. Read (Ed.), *The collected works* (R.F.C. Hull, Trans.) (Vol. 9) (p.160). Princeton, NJ: Princeton University Press.

Jung, C.G. (1973). *Letters, Volume 1, 1906-1950.* G. Adler (Ed.). Princeton, NJ: Princeton University.

Jung, C.G. (1974). *Dreams.* Princeton, NJ: Princeton University Press.

Kalff, D. (1980). *Sandplay: A psychotherapeutic approach to the psyche.* Boston: Sigo Press.

Kalsched, D. (1996). *The inner world of trauma: Archetypal defenses of the personal spirit.* New York: Routledge.

Kane, E. (1989). *Recovering from incest: Imagination and healing process.* Boston: Sigo Press.

Kantor, G., & Straus, M. (1990). The "drunken bum" theory of wife beating. In M. Straus & R. Gelles (Eds.), *Physical violence in American families* (pp.203-224). New Brunswick, NJ: Transaction Books.

Kaptchuk, T. (1989). Healing as a journey together. In (Eds.), *Healers on healing.* New York: Putnam.

Kaslow, N., & Carter, A. (1991). Depressed women in families: The search for power and intimacy. In T. Goodrich (Ed.), *Women and power* (pp. 166-182). New York: W.W. Norton.

Kaslow, N., Rehm, L., Pollack, S., & Siegel, A. (1988). Attributional style and self-control behavior in depressed and nondepressed children and their parents. *Journal of Abnormal Child Psychology, 16,* 163-175.

Katz, L., & Gottman, J. (1991). Marital discord and child outcomes: A social-psychophysiological approach. In J. Garber & K. Dodge (Eds.), *The development of emotion regulation and dysregulation* (pp.129-155). New York: Cambridge University.

Kaufman, J., & Zigler, E. (1987). Do abused children become abusive parents? *American Journal of Orthopsychiatry, 57,* 186-192.

Kavanaugh, K., Youngblade, L., Reid, J., & Fagot, B. (1988). Interactions between children and abusive versus control parents. *Journal of Clinical Child Psychology, 17,* 137-142.

Keary, K., & Fitzpatrick, C. (1994). Children's disclosures of sexual abuse during formal investigations. *Child Abuse and Neglect, 18,* 543-548.

Kellert, S., & Felthous, A. (1985). Childhood cruelty toward animals among criminals and noncriminals. *Human Relations, 38,* 1113-1129.

Kempe, C., Silverman, F., Steele, B., Droegemueller, W., & Silver, H. (1962). The battered-child syndrome. *The Journal of the American Medical Association, 181,* 17-24.

Kendall-Tackett, K., Williams, L., & Finkelhor, D. (1993). The impact of sexual abuse on children: A review and synthesis of recent empirical findings. *Psychological Bulletin, 113,* 164-180.

Kerenyi, C. (1967). *Eleusis: Archetypal image of mother and daughter.* Princeton: Princeton University.

Kerenyi, K. (1979). *Goddesses of sun and moon.* Dallas, TX: Spring.

Kernberg, O. (1975). *Borderline conditions and pathological narcissism.* New York: Aronson.

Kilpatrick, D., Best, C., Veronen, L., Amick, A., Villeponteaux, L., & Ruff, G. (1985). Mental health correlates of criminal victimization: A random community survey. *Journal of Consulting and Clinical Psychology, 53,* 866-873.

Kilpatrick, D., Resick, P., & Veronen, L. (1981). Effects of rape experience: A longitudinal study. *Journal of Social Issues, 37,* 105-122.

Kilpatrick, D., Saunders, B., Veronen, L., Best, C., & Von, J. (1987). Criminal victimization: Lifetime prevalence, reporting to police, and psychological impact. *Crime and Delinquency, 33,* 479-489.

Kleinbaum, D., Kupper, L., & Morgenstern, H. (1982). *Epidemiologic research: Principles and quantitative methods.* Belmont, CA: Lifetime Learning.

REFERENCES

Kleinman, A. (1988). *Rethinking psychiatry: From cultural category to personal experience.* New York: Free Press.

Kline, C. (2000). Racism: A learned disease. *Skipping Stones, 12*(4), 9.

Knight, R.,& Prentky, R. (1990). Classifying sex offenders: The development and corroboration of taxonomic models. In W. Marshall, D. Laws, & H. Barbaree (Eds.), *Handbook of sexual assault: Issues, theories, and treatment of the offender* (pp.23-52). Nw York: Plenum.

Kobasa, S. (1979). Stressful life events, personality, and health: An inquiry into hardiness. *Journal of Personality and Social Psychology, 37,* 1-11.

Kohut. H. (1984). *How does analysis cure?* Chicago: University of Chicago Press.

Koocher, G., & Keith-Spiegel, P. (1998). *Ethics in psychology: Professional standards and cases* (2nd ed.). New York: Oxford University.

Korbin, J., & Spilsbury, J. (1999). Cultural competence and child neglect. In H. Dubowitz (Ed.), *Neglected children: Research, Practice, and Policy* (pp. 69-88).

Koss, M. (1985). The hidden rape victim: Personality, attitudinal, and situational characteristics. *Psychology of Women Quarterly, 9,* 193-212.

Koss, M., & Burkhart, B. (1989). A conceptual analysis of rape victimization: long-term effects and implications for treatment. *Psychology of Women Quarterly, 13,* 27-40.

Koss, M., Gidycz, C., & Wisniewski, N. (1987). The scope of rape: Incidence and prevalence of sexual aggression and victimization in a national sample of higher education students. *Journal of Consulting and Clinical Psychology, 55,* 162-170.

Koss, M., & Harvey, M. (1991). *The rape victim: Clinical and community interventions* (2nd ed.). Newbury Park, CA: Sage Publications.

Koss, M., & Koss, P., & Woodruff, W. (2990). Relation of criminal victimization to health perceptions among women medical patients. *Journal of Consulting and Clinical Psychology, 58,* 147-152.

Koss, M, & Oros, C. (1982). Sexual experiences survey: A research instrument investigating sexual aggression and victimization. *Journal of Consulting and Clinical Psychology, 50,* 455-457.

Kovel, J. (1996). Writings for a liberation psychology. *Monthly Review, 48*(4), 46-48.

Kristeva, J. (1989). *Black sun: Depression and melancholia.* New York: Columbia University Press.

Kurz, D. (1990). Interventions with battered women in health care settings. *Violence and Victims, 5,* 243-256.

Lachkar, J. (1998). *The many faces of abuse: Treating the emotional abuse of high-functioning women.* Northvale, NJ: Jason Aronson.

Lane, S. (1997). Assessment of sexually abusive youth. In G. Ryan & S. Lane (Eds.), *Juvenile sexual offending* (pp.219-263). San Francisco, CA: Jossey-Bass.

Langen, P., & Innes, C. 1986). *Preventing domestic violence against women.* Washington, DC: US Department of Justice.

Lanktree, C., Briere, J., & Zaidi, J. (1991). Incidence and impact of sexual abuse in a child outpatient sample: The role of direct inquiry. *Child Abuse & Neglect, 15,* 447-453.

Larkby, D., & Day, N. (1997). The effects of prenatal alcohol exposure. *Alcohol Health and Research World, 21*(3), 192-197.

Larrington, C. (Ed.). (1997). *The woman's companion to mythology.* London: Pandora.

Lawson, L, & Chaffin, M. (1992). False negatives in sexual abuse interviews. *Journal of Interpersonal Violence, 7,* 532-542.

Lazarus, R., & Averill, J. (1966). Emotion and cognition, with special reference to anxiety. In C. Spielberger (Ed.), *Anxiety: Current trends in theory and research.* Vol. 2, New York: Academic Press.

Lazarus, R., & Folkman, S. (1984). *Stress, appraisal, and coping.* New York: Springer.

Lazarus, R., & Launier, R. (1978). Stress related transactions between person and environment. In L. Pervin & M. Lewis (Eds.), *Perspectives in interactional psychology.* New York: Plenum.

Leeder, E. (1994). *Treating abuse in families: A feminist and community approach.* New York: Springer.

Leonard, L. (1989). *Witness to the fire: Creativity and the veil of addiction.* Boston: Shambhala.

Lerman, H., & Rigby, D. (1990). Boundary violations: Misuse of the power of the therapist. In H. Lerman & N. Porter (Eds.), *Feminist ethics in psychotherapy* (pp. 51-59). New York: Springer.

Levine, S. (1987). *Healing into life and death.* New York: Anchor.

Libow, J. (2000). Child and adolescent illness falsification. *Pediatrics, 105*(2), 336-342.

Linehan, M. (1993). *Cognitive behavioral treatment of borderline personality disorder*. New York: Guilford.

Lipinski, B. (1992).*Psychological correlates of women's childhood sexual abuse and adult criminal victimization*. Doctoral dissertation, University of Southern California, Los Angeles.

Lipinski, B. (2001). *Feng shui wisdom*. San Buenaventura, CA: Pacific Meridian.

Lisak, D., Hopper, J., & Song, P. (1996). Factors in the cycle of violence: Gender rigidity and emotional constriction. *Journal of Traumatic Stress, 9*, 721-743.

Lisak, D., & Luster, L. (1994). Educational, occupational, and relationship histories of men who were sexually and/or physically abused as children. *Journal of Traumatic Stress, 7*, 507-523.

Lockwood, R., & Ascione, F. (Eds.). (1997). *Cruelty to animals and interpersonal violence: Readings in research and application*. W. Lafayette, IN: Purdue University.

Lockwood, R., & Hodge, G. (1986). The tangled web of animal abuse: The links between cruelty to animals and human violence. *Humane Society News*, Summer, 10-15.

Loftus, E., & Ketcham, K. (1994). *The myth of repressed memory: False memories and allegations of sexual abuse*. New York: St. Martin's.

Locke, D. (1992). *Increasing multicultural understanding: A comprehensive model*. Newbury Park: Sage.

Lockhart, R. (1997). Cancer in myth and dream. *Spring: An Annual of Archetypal Psychology and Jungian Thought*, 1-26.

Lorenz, H. (2000). The presence of absence: Mapping postcolonial spaces. In D. Slattery & L. Corbett (Eds.), *Depth psychology: Meditations in the field* (pp.225-243). Einsedeln: Daimon Verlag.

Lorenz, H., & Watkins, M. (2000, September). *Individuation, seeing-through, and liberation: Depth psychology and colonialism*. Paper presented at the International Symposium of Archetypal Psychology, Psychology at the Threshold, Santa Barbara, CA.

Lugones, M. (1990). Playfulness, "world" traveling, and loving perception. In G. Anzaldua (Ed.), *Making face, making soul: Haciendo caras* (pp.390-402). San Francisco: Aunt Lute Press.

Luthars, S., & Ziglar, E. (1991). Vulnerability and competence: A review of research on resilience in childhood. *American Journal of Orthopsychiatry, 61*, 6-22.

Mack, J. (1995). The politics of species arrogance. In T. Roszak, M. Gomes, & A. Kramer (Eds.), *Ecopsychology* (pp.279-287). San Francisco: Sierra Club.

MacKinnon, C. (1989). *Toward a feminist theory of the state* (p.178). Cambridge, MA: Harvard University Press.

Main, M., & George, C. (1985). Responses of abused and disadvantaged toddlers to distress in age mates: A study in the day care setting. *Developmental Psychology, 21*, 407-412.

Maltz, W., & Holman, B. (1987). *Incest and sexuality: A guide to understanding and healing*. Lexington, MA: Heath.

Marmor, J. (1977). Designated discussion of the ethics of sex therapy. In W. Masters, V. Johnson, & R. Kolodny (Eds.), *Ethical issues in sex therapy and research* (pp.157-161). Boston: Little Brown.

Marshall, W., & Barbaree, H. (1988). The long-term evaluation of a behavioral treatment program for child molesters. *Behavior Research and Therapy, 26*, 499-511.

Marshall, W., & Barbaree, H. (1990). An integrated theory of the etiology of sexual offending. In W. Marshall, D. Laws, & H. Barbaree (Eds.), *Handbook of sexual assault: Issues, theories, and treatment of the offender* (pp.257-275). New York: Plenum.

Martin-Baro, I. (1994). *Writings for a liberation psychology*. Cambridge: Harvard University.

Marx, S. (1996). Victim recantation in child sexual abuse cases: The prosecutor's role in prevention. *Child Welfare, 75*(3), 219-229.

Maslach, C. (1982). *The burnout: The cost of caring*. Englewood Cliffs, NJ: Prentice-Hall.

May, E. (2000). Nonmothers as bad mothers: Infertility and the maternal instinct. In M. Plott & L. Umanski (Eds.), *Making sense of women's lives*, (pp.363-378). San Diego, CA: Collegiate Press.

May, R. (1975). *The courage to create*. New York: Bantam.

McCann, I., & Pearlman, L. (1990). Vicarious traumatization: A framework for understanding the psychological effects of working with victims. *Journal of Traumatic Stress, 3* (1), 131-149.

McCann, I., Sakheim, D., & Abrahamson, D. (1988). Trauma and victimization: A model of psychological adaptation. *The Counseling Psychologist, 16*, 531-594.

McClelland, D. (1973). Testing for competence rather than intelligence. *American Psychologist, 28*, 1-14.

McCord, J. (1985). Long-term adjustment in female survivors of incest: An exploratory study. *Dissertation Abstracts International, 46*, 650B.

190

McFarlane, A. (1996). Resilience, vulnerability, and the course of posttraumatic reactions. In B. van der Kolk, A. McFarlane, & L. Weisaeth (Eds.) *Traumatic stress: The effects of overwhelming experience on mind, body, and society* (pp.155-181). New York: Guilford.

McFarlane, A., Norman, G., Streiner, D., & Roy, R. (1983). The process of social stress: Stable, reciprocal, and mediating relationships. *Journal of Health and Social Behavior, 24,* 160-173.

McGuire, L., & Wagner, N. (1978). Sexual dysfunction in women who were molested as children: One response pattern and suggestions for treatment. *Journal of Sex and Marital Therapy, 4,* 11-15.

McKay, M. (1994). The link between domestic violence and child abuse: Assessment and treatment considerations. *Child Welfare, 73,* 29.

McLeod, M. (1984). Women against men: An examination of domestic violence based on an analysis of official data and national victimization data. Justice Quarterly, 1, 171-193.

McLeod, J., & Shanahan, M. (1993). Poverty, parenting, and children's mental health. *American Sociological Review, 58,* 351-366.

McLoyd, V. (1998). Socioeconomic disadvantage and child development. *American Psychologist, 53,* 185-204.

McLoyd, V. (1990). The impact of economic hardship on Black families and children: Psychological distress, parenting, and socio-emotional development. *Child Development, 61,* 311-346.

Meier, C.A. (1959). *Asklepios: Archetypal image of the physician's existence.* (R. Manheim, Trans.). New York: Pantheon Books.

Meiselman, K. (1978). *Incest.* San Francisco: Jossey-Bass.

Meiselman, K. (1990). *Resolving the trauma of incest: Reintegration therapy with survivors.* San Francisco: Jossey-Bass.

Melton, G., & Limber, S. (1989). Psychologists' involvement in cases of child maltreatment: Limits of role and expertise. *American Psychologist, 44*(9), 1225-1233.

Merton, T. (1961). *Seeds of destruction.* New York: Farrar, Straus, & Giroux.

Metcalfe, M., Oppenheimer, R., Dignon, A., & Palmer, R. (1990). Childhood sexual experiences reported by male psychiatric patients. *Psychological Medicine, 20,* 925-929.

Meyer, C., & Taylor, S. (1986). Adjustment to rape. *Journal of Personality and Social Psychology, 50,* 126-1234.

Miller, A. (1981). *The drama of the gifted child: The search for the true self.* New York: Basic.

Milner, J. (1991). Physical child abuse perpetrator screening and evaluation. *Criminal Justice and Behavior, 18,* 47-63.

Milner, J. (1994). Assessing physical child abuse risk: The Child Abuse Potential Inventory. *Clinical Psychology Review, 14* (6), 547-583.

Milner, J., & Chilamkurti, C. (1991). Physical child abuse perpetrator characteristics: A review of the literature. *Journal of Interpersonal Violence, 6,* 345-366.

Milosz, C. (1996). *A book of luminous things.* New York: Harcourt Brace.

Mitchell, J., & Everly, G. (1996). *Critical incident stress debriefing.* Ellicott City, Maryland: Chevron.

Moore, T. (1992). *Care of the soul: A guide for cultivating depth and sacredness in everyday life.* New York: Harper Collins.

Moos, R., & Billings, A. (1982). Conceptualizing and measuring coping resources and processes. In L. Goldberger & S. Breznitz (Eds.), *Handbook of stress* (pp. 212-230). New York: Free Press.

Morgan, S. (1984). Counseling with teachers on the sexual acting out of disturbed children. *Psychology in the Schools, 21,* 234-243.

Morse, B. (1995). Beyond the conflict tactics scale: Assessing gender differences in partner violence. *Violence and Victims, 10,* 251-272.

Moustakas, C. (1990). *Heuristic research: Design, methodology, and applications.* Newbury Park: Sage.

Mowaljarlai, D., & Malnic, J. (1993). *Yorro Yorro: Aboriginal creation and the renewal of fire.* Broome, Western Australia: Magabala Books.

Murdock, M. (1987). *Spinning inward: Using guided imagery with children for learning, creativity, and relaxation.* Boston: Shambhala.

Murphy, W., & Smith, T. (1996). Sex offenders against children: Empirical and clinical issues. In J. Briere, L. Berliner, J. Bulkley, C. Jenny, & T. Reid (Eds.), *APSAC handbook on child maltreatment* (pp.175-191). Thousand Oaks, CA: Sage.

Myers, J. (1989). Expert testimony in child sexual abuse litigation. *Nebraska Law Review, 68,* 32-34.

Myers, J. (1992). *Legal issues in child abuse and neglect.* Thousand Oaks, CA: Sage.

National Child Abuse and Neglect Data Systems. (1998). *Fact sheet*. Washington, DC: United States Department of Health and Human Services.

Newlon, B., & Arciniega, M. (1983). Counseling minority families: An Adlerian perspective. *Counseling and Human Development*, *70*, 136-141.

Nisonoff, L, & Bitman, L. (1979). Spouse abuse: Incidence and relationship to selected demographic variables. *Victimology*, *4*, 131-140.

Oaklander, V. (1978). *Windows to our children: A gestalt therapy approach to children and adolescents*. Moab, Utah: Real People Press.

O'Hagan, K. (1993). *Emotional and psychological abuse of children*. Toronto: University of Toronto.

Ochberg, F. (Ed.). (1988). *Post-traumatic therapy and victims of violence*. New York: Brunner/Mazel.

Olin, J., & Keatinge, C. (1998). *Rapid psychological assessment*. New York: John Wiley.

Oliver, M. (1992). *New and selected poems* (p.110). Boston: Beacon.

O'Neill, P. (1998). *Negotiating consent in psychotherapy*. New York: New York University Press.

Otto, R. (1958). *The idea of the holy*. New York: Oxford University.

Oxford Dictionary of English Etymology. (1966). New York: Oxford University Press.

Palmer, S., Brown, R., Rae-Grant, N., & Loughlin, M. (1999). Responding to children's disclosure of familial abuse: What survivors tell us. *Child Welfare*, *78*, 259-282.

Paniagua, F. (1998). *Assessing and treating culturally diverse clients: A practical guide*. Thousand Oaks, CA: Sage.

Patterson, G., Reid, J., & Dishion, T. (1992). *Antisocial boys: A social interaction approach*. Eugene, OR: Castalia.

Pearlin, L., & Schooler, C. (1978). The structure of coping. *Journal of Health and Social Behavior*, *19*, 2-21.

Pearlman, L., & Saakvitne, K. (1995). *Trauma and the therapist: Countertransference and vicarious traumatization in psychotherapy with incest survivors*. New York: W.W. Norton.

Pedersen, P. (1994). *A handbook for developing cultural awareness* (2nd ed.). Alexandria, VA: American Counseling Association.

Pelchat, Z. (2001). Psychotherapist-patient privilege. *California Therapist*, *13*, 14-16.

Perera, S. (1981). *Descent to the goddess: A way of initiation for women*. Toronto: Inner City Books.

Perlman, M. (1995). *The power of trees: he reforesting of the soul*. Woodstock, CT: Spring Publications.

Peters, S. (1988). Children who are victims of sexual assault and the psychology of offenders. In G. Wyatt & G. Powell (Eds.), *Lasting effects of child sexual abuse* (pp. 135-154). Newbury Park, CA: Sage Publications.

Peterson, C., & Seligman, M. (1983). Learned helplessness and victimization. *Journal of Social Issues*, *39*, 103-116.

Peterson, C., Semmel, A., von Baeyer, C., Abramson, L., Metalsky, G., & Seligman, M. (1982). The attributional style questionnaire. *Cognitive Therapy and Research*, *6*, 287-300.

Piercy, M. (2000). *My mother's body*. New York: Alred Knopf.

Pines, A., & Aronson, E. (1988). *Career burnout: Causes and cures*. New York: Free Press.

Polansky, N., Chalmers, M., Buttenwieser, E., & Williams, D. (1991). *Damaged parents: An anatomy of child neglect*. Chicago: University of Chicago Press.

Pope, K. (1991). Dual relationships in psychotherapy. *Ethics and Behavior*, *1*, 21-34.

Pope, K. (1996). Scientific research, recovered memory, and context: Seven surprising findings. *Women and Therapy*, *19*, 123-140.

Pope, K., & Bouhoutsos, J. (1986). *Sexual intimacy between therapists and patients*. New York: Praeger.

Pope, K., & Brown, L. (1996). *Recovered memories of abuse: Assessment, therapy, forensics*. Washington, DC: American Psychological Association.

Pope, K., & Caudill, O.B. (2000). The impact of recovered memories. In F. Kaslow (Ed.), *Handbook of couple and family forensics: A sourcebook for mental health and legal professionals* (pp.375-399). New York: John Wiley.

Pope, K., & Feldman-Summers, S. (1992). National survey of psychologists: Sexual and physical abuse history and their evaluation of training and competence in these areas. *Professional Psychology: Research and Practice*, *23*, 353-361.

Pope, K., Keith-Speigel, P., & Tabachnick, B. (1986). Sexual attraction to clients: The human therapist and the (sometimes) inhuman training system. *American Psychologist*, *41*, 147-158.

Pope, K., Levenson, H., & Schover, L. (1979). Sexual intimacy in psychology training: Results and implications of a national survey. *American Psychologist*, *34*, 682-689.

REFERENCES

Pope, K., & Vasquez, M. (1991). *Ethics in psychotherapy and counseling: A practical guide for psychologists.* San Francisco: Jossey-Bass.

Pope, K., & Vasquez, M. (1998). *Ethics in psychotherapy and counseling: A practical guide.* San Francisco: Jossey-Bass.

Porter, N. (1995). Therapist self-care: A proactive ethical approach. In H. Lerman & N. Porter (Eds.), *Feminist ethics in psychotherapy* (pp. 247-266). New York: Springer.

Porter, F., Blick, L., & Sgroi, S. (1982). Treatment of the sexually abused child. *Handbook of clinical intervention in child sexual* abuse (pp.109-146). Lexington, MA: D.C. Heath.

Putnam, F. (1988). *Diagnosis and treatment of multiple personality disorder.* New York: Guilford.

Putnam, F., Guroff, J., Silberman, E., Barban, L., & Post, R. (1986). The clinical phenomenology of multiple personality disorder: A review of 100 recent cases. *Journal of Clinical Psychiatry, 47,* 285-293.

Quinlisk, J. (1999). Animal abuse and family violence. In F. Ascione & P. Arkow (Eds.), *Child abuse, domestic, violence, and animal abuse: Linking the circles of compassion for prevention and intervention* (pp.168-175). West Lafayette, IN: Purdue University.

Rand, M. (1997). *Violence related injuries treated in hospital emergency departments* (No. NCJ-156921). Washington, DC: US Department of Justice.

Raupp, C., Barlow, M., & Oliver, J. (1998). Perceptions of family violence: Are companion animals in the picture? *Society and Animals: Journal of Human-Animal Relations, 5,* 3.

Raymond, C. (1987). Munchausen's may occur in younger persons. *Journal of the American Medical Association, 257,*(24), 3332.

Renzetti, C. (1992). *Violent betrayal: Partner abuse in lesbian relationships.* Thousand Oaks, CA: Sage.

Rich, A. (1973). *Diving into the wreck* (p.23). New York: W.W. Norton.

Rieser, M. (1991). Recantation in child sexual abuse cases. *Child Welfare, 70,* 611-621.

Rilke, R.M. (2000). *Letters to a young poet.* (J. Burnham, Trans.). Novato, CA: New World Library.

Rilke, R.M. (1984). *Letters to a young poet.* (S. Mitchell, Trans.). New York: Random House.

Risin, L, & Koss, M. (1987). The sexual abuse of boys: Prevalence and descriptive characteristics of childhood victimization. *Journal of Interpersonal Violence, 2,* 309-323.

Roberts, A., Jackson, M., & Carlton-Laney, I. (2000). Revisiting the need for feminism and afrocentric theory when treating African-American female substance abusers. *Journal of Drug Issues, 30*(4), 901-918.

Rohner, R., & Rohner, E. (1980). Antecedents and consequences of parental rejection: A theory of emotional abuse. *Child Abuse & Neglect, 4,* 189-198.

Romano, J., & Hage, S. (2000). Prevention and counseling psychology: Revitalizing commitments for the 21st century. *Counseling Psychologist, 28,* 733-763.

Roscoe, B., Haney, S., & Peterson, K. (1986). Child/pet maltreatment: Adolescents' ratings of parent and owner behaviors. *Adolescence, 21,* 807-814.

Rosenberg, J. (1999). Suicide prevention: An integrated training model using affective and action-based interventions. *Professional Psychology: Research and Practice, 30*(1), 83-87.

Ross, C. (1990). More on multiple personality. *British Journal of Psychiatry, 156,* 449.

Rowan, A. (1999). Cruelty and abuse to animals. In F. Ascione and P. Arkow (Eds.), *Child abuse, domestic violence, and animal abuse: Linking the circles of compassion for prevention and intervention* (pp.328-334). Lafayette, Indiana: Purdue University Press.

Rumi, J. (1995). *The essential Rumi.* (C. Barks, Trans.). San Francisco: Harper Collins.

Runtz, M. (1987). *The psychosocial adjustment of women who were sexually and physically abused during childhood and early adulthood: A focus on revictimization.* Unpublished master's thesis, University of Manitoba, Winnepeg, Manitoba.

Russell, D. (1982). The prevalence and incidence of forcible rape and attempted rape of females. *Victimology: An International Journal, 7,* 81-93.

Russell, D. (1983). The incidence and prevalence of intrafamilial and extrafamilial sexual abuse of female children. *Child Abuse and Neglect, 7,* 133-146.

Russell, D. (1984). *Sexual exploitation: Rape, child sexual abuse, and workplace harassment.* Beverly Hills: Sage Publications.

Russell, D. (1986). *The secret trauma: Incest in the lives of girls and women.* New York: Basic Books.

Russell, M., Henderson, C., & Blume, S. (1985). *Children of alcoholics: A review of the literature.* New York: Children of Alcoholics Foundation, Inc.

Saakvitne, K., Gamble, S., Pearlman, L., & Lev, B. (2000). *Risking connection: A training curriculum for working with survivors of childhood abuse.* Lutherville, MD: The Sidran Foundation Press.

Sabde, N., & Craft, A. (1999). Covert video surveillance: An important investigative tool or breach of trust? *Archives of Disease in Childhood, 81*(4), 291-295.

Safran, C. (1993). Dangerous obsession: The truth about repressed memories. *McCall's*, pp.98, 102, 105, 106, 108, 109, & 155.

Saigh, P., Yule, W., & Inander, S. (1996). Imaginal flooding of traumatized children and adolescents. *Journal of School Psychology, 34*, 163-183.

Samuels, A. (1989). *The plural psyche.* London: Routledge.

Sardello, R. (1988). The illusion of infection: A cultural psychology of AIDS. *Spring*, 15-26.

Sardello, R. (1999). *Freeing the soul from fear.* New York: Putnam.

Saunders, B., Villeponteaux, L., Lipovsky, J., Kilpatrick, D., & Veronen, L. (1992). Child sexual assault as a risk factor for mental disorders among women: A community survey. *Journal of Interpersonal Violence, 7*, 189-204.

Saunders, D. (1986). When battered women use violence: Husband abuse or self defense? *Victims and Violence, 1*, 47-60.

Sauzier, M. (1989). Disclosure of sexual abuse. *Pediatric Clinics of North America, 12*, 445-471.

Schamess, G. (1999). Therapeutic love and its permutations. *Clinical Social Work Journal, 27*, 9-26.

Schechter, S. (1982). *Women and marital violence: The visions and struggles of the battered women's movement.* Boston: South End Press.

Scheppele, K., & Bart, P. (1983). Through women's eyes: Defining danger in the wake of sexual assault. *Journal of Social Issues, 39*, 63-81.

Schinke, S. (1994). Prevention science and practice: An agenda for action. *Journal of Primary Prevention*, 15, 45-57.

Schmolling, R., Youkeles, M., & Burger, W. (1997). *Human services in contemporary America* (4th ed.). Pacific Grove, CA: Brooks/Cole.

Schneidman, E. (1975). *Suicidology: Contemporary developments.* New York: Grune & Stratton.

Schreier, H., & Libow, J. (1993). *Hurting for love: Munchausen by proxy syndrome.* New York: Guilford.

Schwarz, S. (1999). Teens and Tikkum Olam. *Moment, 24*(6), 42-43.

Schwartz-Salant, N. (1984). Archetypal factors underlying sexual acting-out in the transference/countertransference process. In N. Schwartz & M. Stein (Eds.), *Transference countertransference* (pp.1-30). Wilmette, IL: Chiron.

Sears, V. (1990). On being an "only" one. In H. Lerman & N. Porter (Eds.), *Feminist ethics in psychotherapy* (pp. 102-105). New York: Springer.

Sedney, M., & Brooks, B. (1984). Factors associated with a history of childhood sexual experience in a nonclinical female population. *Journal of the American Academy of Child Psychiatry, 23*, 215-218.

Seligman, M. (1975). *Helplessness: On depression, development, and death.* San Francisco: W.H. Freeman.

Sgroi, S. (1982). *Handbook of clinical intervention in child sexual abuse.* Lexington, MA: Lexington.

Shapiro, F. (1995). *Eye movement desensitization and reprocessing: Basic principles, protocols, and procedures.* New York: Guilford.

Shengold, L. (1989). *Soul murder: The effects of childhood abuse and deprivation.* New York: Fawcett Columbine.

Shulman, H. (1997). *Living at the edge of chaos: Complex systems in culture and psyche.* Einsiedeln: Daimon Verlag.

Sigler, R. (1989). *Domestic violence in context: An assessment of community attitudes.* New York: Lexington Books.

Singer, M., Petchers, M., & Hussey, D. (1989). The relationship between sexual abuse and substance abuse among psychiatrically hospitalized adolescents. *Child Abuse & Neglect, 13*, 319-325.

Slattery, D. (2000). *The wounded body: Remembering the markings of flesh.* Albany, NY: State University of New York.

Smith, A. (1990). Working within the lesbian community: The dilemma of overlapping relationships. In H. Lerman & N. Porter (Eds.), *Feminist ethics in psychotherapy* (pp. 92-96). New York: pringer.

Sommers-Flanagan, J., & Sommers-Flanagan, R. (1995). Intake interviewing with suicidal patients: A systematic approach. *Professional Psychology: Research and Practice, 26*(1), 41-47.

Sorensen, S., Stein, J., Siegel, J., Golding, J., & Burnam, M. (1987). Prevalence of adult sexual assault: The Los Angeles Epidemiologic Catchment Area Study. *American Journal of Epidemiology, 126,* 1154-1164.

Sorenson, T., & Snow, B. (1991). How children tell: The process of disclosure in child sexual abuse. *Child Welfare, 70,* 3-15.

Stark, E., & Flitcraft, A. (1988). Personal power and institutional victimization: Treating the dual trauma of woman battering. In F. Ochberg (Ed.), *Post-traumatic therapy and victims of violence.* New York: Brunner/Mazel.

Stebnicki, M. (2000). Stress and grief reactions among rehabilitation professionals: Dealing effectively with empathy fatigue. *Journal of Rehabilitation, 66*(1), 23-29.

Stein, R. (1973). *Incest and human love.* Dallas: Spring.

Stets, J., & Straus, M. (1990). Gender differences in reporting marital violence and its medical and psychological consequences. In M. Straus & R. Gelles (Eds.), *Physical violence in American families* (pp.151-166). New Brunswick, NJ: Transaction.

Stewart, C. (1990). The developmental psychology of sandplay. In *Sandplay studies: Origins, theories, practice* (pp.39-92). San Francisco: Jung Institute.

Straus, M. (1993). Physical assaults by wives: A major social problem. In R. Gelles & D. Loseke (Eds.), *Current controversies on family violence* (pp.67-87). Newbury Park, CA: Sage.

Straus, M., & Gelles, R. (1990). *Physical violence in American families.* New Brunswick, NJ: Transaction.

Straus, M., & Gelles, R. (1986). Societal change and change in family violence from 1975 to 1985 as revealed by two national surveys. *Journal of Marriage and the Family, 48,* 465-479.

Sue, D. (1995). Toward a theory of multicultural counseling and therapy. In J. Banks & C. Banks (Eds.), Handbook of research on multicultural education (pp.647-659). New York: Macmillan.

Sue, D., Bingham, R., Porche-Burke, L, & Vasquez, M. (1999). The diversification of psychology: A multicultural revolution. *American Psychologist, 54* (12), 1061-1069.

Sue, D., Ivey, A., & Pedersen, P. (Eds.). (1996). *A theory of multicultural counseling and therapy.* Pacific Grove, CA: Brooks/Cole.

Sue, D., & Sue, D. (1999). *Counseling the culturally different: Theory and practice.* New York: John Wiley.

Sullivan, B.S. (1989). *Psychotherapy grounded in the feminine principle.* Wilmette, IL: Chiron.

Summit, R. (1983). The child sexual abuse accommodation syndrome. *Child Abuse and Neglect, 7,* 177-193.

Surgeon General's Report on Mental Health. (2000). *Children's mental health.* Washington, DC: Department of Health and Human Services.

Swenson, C., Henggeler, S., Schoenwald, S., Kaufman, K., & Randall, J. (1998). Changing the social ecologies of adolescent sexual offenders: Implications of the success of multisystemic theapy in treating serious antisocial behavior in adolescents. *Child Maltreatment, 3,* 330-338.

Symonds, M. (1975). Victims of violence: Psychological effects and aftereffects. *The American Journal of Psychoanalysis, 35,* 19-26.

Taylor, D. (1997). *Disappearing acts.* Durham: Duke University.

Taylor, S. (1983). Adjustment to threatening events: A theory of cognitive adaptation. *American Psychologist, 38,* 1161-1173.

Terr, L. (1991). Childhood traumas: An outline and overview. *American Journal of Psychiatry, 148,* 10-20.

Thich Nhat Hanh. (1993). *For a future to be possible.* Berkeley, CA: Parallax Press.

Thich Nhat Hanh. (1999). *Call Me By My True Names: The Collected Poems of Thich Nhat Hanh.* Berkeley, CA: Parallax Press.

Thoennes, N., & Tjaden, P. (1990). The extent, nature, and validity of sexual abuse allegations in custody/visitation disptures. *Chld Abuse and Neglect, 14,* 151-163.

Tierney, K. (1982). The battered women movement and the creation of the wife beating problem. *Social Problems, 29,* 207-220.

Tjaden, P., & Thoennes, N. (2000). Prevalence and consequences of male-to-female and female-to-male intimate partner violence as measured by the national violence against women survey. *Violence Against Women, 6* (2), 142-161.

Trickett, P., & Kuczynski, L. (1986). Children's misbehaviors and parental discipline strategies in abusive and nonabusive families. *Developmental Psychology, 27,* 148-158.

Tsai, M., Feldman-Summers, S., & Edgar, M. (1979). Childhood molestation:Variables related to differential impacts on psychosexual functioning in adult women. *Journal for Specialists in Group Work, 8*, 39-46.

Tsai, M., & Wagner, N. (1978). Therapy groups for women sexually molested as children. *Archives of Sexual Behavior, 7*, 417-427.

Tulku, T. (1977). *A gesture of balance.* Emeryville, CA: Dharma Publishing.

United Nations Children's Fund, UNICEF. (2000). *Convention on the rights of the child.* Washington, DC: Author.

US Department of Health and Human Services. (2000). *Healthy people 2010.* Washington, DC: Author.

Urquiza, A., & Keating, L. (1990). The prevalence of sexual abuse of males. In M. Hunter (Ed.), *The sexually abused male, Vol. 1: Prevalence, impact, and treatment* (pp.90-103). Lexington, MA: Lexington Books.

van der Kolk, B. (1989). The compulsion to repeat the trauma: Re-enactment, revictimization, and masochism. *Psychiatric Clinics of North America, 12*, 389-411.

van der Kolk, B. (1994). The body keeps the socre: Memory and the evolving psychobiology of posttraumatic stress. *Harvard Review of Psychiatry, 1*(5), 253-265.

van der Kolk, B. (1996). The body keeps the score: Approaches to the psychobiology of posttraumatic stress disorder. In B. van der Kolk, A. McFarlane, & L. Weisaeth (Eds.) *Traumatic stress: The effects of overwhelming experience on mind, body, and society* (pp.214-241). New York: Guilford.

van der Kolk, B., Blitz, R., Burr, W., & Hartmann, E. (1984). Nightmares and trauma: Lifelong and traumatic nightmares in Veterans. *American Journal of Psychiatry, 141*, 187-190.

van der Kolk, B., Perry, J., & Herman, J. (1991). Childhood origins of self-destructive behavior. *American Journal of Psychiatry, 148*, 1665-1671.

Veronen, L., & Kilpatrick, D. (1983). Stress management for rape victims. In D. Meichenbaum & E. Jaremko (Eds.), *Stress reduction and prevention* (pp.341-374). New York: Plenum.

von Franz, M.L. (1980). *Alchemy: An introduction to the symbolism and the psychology.* Toronto, Canada: Inner City Books.

Walker, A. (2000). In search of our mother's gardens. In M. Plott & L. Umanski (Eds.), *Making sense of women's lives* (pp.226-232). San Diego, CA: Collegiate Press.

Walker, L. (1983). The battered woman syndrome study. In D. Finkelhor, R. Gelles, G. Hotaling, & M. Straus (Eds.), *The dark side of families: Current family violence research.* Beverly Hills: Sage Publications.

Walker, L. (1984). *The battered woman syndrome.* New York: Springer.

Walker, L. (1987). Interventions with victim/survivors of interpersonal violence. In I. Weiner & A. Hess (Eds.), *Handbook of forensic psychology* (pp. 630-649). New York: Wiley.

Walker, L. (1989a). Psychology and violence against women. *American Psychologist, 44*(4), 695-702.

Walker, L. (1989b). *Terrifying love: Why battered women kill and how society responds.* New York: Harper Collins.

Walker, L. (1990). Psychological assessment of sexually abused children for legal evaluation and expert witness testimony. *Professional Psychology: Research and Practice, 21*, 344-353.

Walker, L., & Meloy, R. (1998). Stalking and domestic violence. In J.R. Meloy (Ed.), *The psychology of stalking: Clinical and forensic perspectives* (pp.139-162). San Diego: Academic Press.

Ward, T., & Hudson, S. (1998). A model of the relapse process in sexual offenders. *Journal of Interpersonal Violence, 13*, 700-725.

Ward, T., Louden, K., Hudson, & Marshall, W. (1995). A descriptive model of the offense chain for child molesters. *Journal of Interpersonal Violence, 10*, 453-473.

Watkins, B., & Bentovim, A. (1992). The sexual abuse of male children and adolescents: A review of current research. *Journal of Child Psychology and Psychiatry and Allied Disciplines, 33*(1), 197-248.

Watkins, M. (1984). *Waking dreams.* Woodstock, CT: Spring.

Watkins, M. (1992). From individualism to the interdependent self: Changing the paradigm of the self in psychotherapy. *Psychological Perspectives, 27*, 52-69.

Watkins, M. (2000). Seeding liberation: A dialogue between depth psychology and liberation psychology. In D. Slattery & L. Corbett (Eds.), *Depth psychology: Meditations in the field* (pp.204-224). Einsedeln: Daimon Verlag.

Webster's II New Riverside Dictionary. (1984). Boston, MA: Houghton Mifflin.

Weissbourd, R. (1996). *The vulnerable child.* Reading, MA: Addison-Wesley.

REFERENCES

Werner, E. (1984). Resilient children. *Young Children, 40*, 68-72.

Werner, E. (1989). High risk in children in young adulthood: A longitudinal study from birth to 32 years. *American Orthopsychiatric Association, 59*, 72—81.

Westen, D., Ludolph, P., Misle, B., Ruffins, S., & Block, J. (1990). Physical and sexual abuse in adolescent girls with borderline personality disorder. *American Journal of Orthopsychiatry, 60*, 55-66.

Widom, C. (1989). Does violence beget violence? A critical examination of the literature. *Psychological Bulletin, 106*, 3-28.

Williams, L. (1994). Adult memories of childhood abuse. *Journal of Consulting and Clinical Psychology, 62*(6), 1167-1176.

Wilson, M., & Daly, M. (1992). Who kills whom in spouse killings: On the exceptional sex ratio of spousal homicides in the United States. *Criminology, 30*, 189-215.

Wilson, S., Tinker, R., & Becker, L (1995). Eye movement desensitization and reprocessing (EMDR) treatment for psychologically traumatized individuals. *Journal of Clinical and Consulting Psychology, 63*, 928-937.

Winnicott, D. (1965). *Maturational processes and the facilitating environment: Studies in the theory of emotional development.* New York: International University.

Winnicott, D. (1971a). *Playing and reality.* New York: Routledge.

Winnicott, D. (1971b). *Therapeutic consultations in child psychiatry.* New York: Basic Books.

Winter, N. (1978). *Interview with the muse: Remarkable women speak on creativity and power.* Berkeley: Moon Books.

Wolin, S., & Wolin, S. (1993). *The resilient self.* New York: Villard.

Wolpe, J. (1990). *The practice of behavior therapy* (4th ed.). New York: Pergamon.

Wood, B., Orsak, C., Murphy, M., & Cross, H. (1996). Semistructured child sexual abuse interviews: Interview and child characteristics related to credibility of disclosure. *Child Abuse and Neglect, 20*, 81-92.

Woodman, M. (1982). *Addiction to perfection: The still unravished bride.* Toronto: Inner City.

Woodman, M. (1992). *Leaving my father's house.* Boston, MA: Shambhala.

Wren, G. (1962). *The counselor in a changing world.* Washington, DC: American Personnel and Guidance Association.

Wyatt, G. (1985). The sexual abuse of Afro-American and white American women in childhood. *Child Sexual Abuse and Neglect, 9*, 507-519.

Wyatt, G. (1994). Sociocultural and epidemiological issues in the assessment of domestic violence. *Journal of Social Distress and the Homeless, 3*, 7-21.

Wyatt, G., & Newcomb, M. (1990). Internal and external mediators of women's sexual abuse in childhood. *Journal of Consulting and Clinical Psychology, 58*, 758-767.

Wyatt, G., & Notgrass, C., & Newcomb, M. (1990). Internal and external mediators of women's rape experiences. *Psychology of Women Quarterly, 14*, 153-176.

Wylie, M. (1993). Trauma and memory. *The Family Therapy Networker, 17*(5), 42-43.

Young-Eisendrath, P. (1996). *The resilient spirit: Transforming suffering into insight and renewal* (p.48). Reading, MA: Addison-Wesley.

Zambrana, R., & Dorrington, C. (1998). Economic and social vulnerabilty of Latino children and familes by subgroup: Implications for child welfare. *Child Welfare, 77*(1), 5-27.

Zimmerman, J., & Coyle, V. (1996). *The way of council.* Las Vegas, NV: Bramble Books.

Zlotnick, C., Kohn, R., Peterson, D., & Pearlstein, T. (1998). Partner physical victimization in a national sample of American families: Relationships to psychological functioning, psychosocial factors, and gender. *Journal of Interpersonal Violence, 13*, 156-166.

Zwillich, T. (1998). Risk factors for suicide in children. *Clinical Psychiatry News, 26*(6):18.

◈ Index

◈ Biographical Sketch

Barbara Lipinski, PhD, is a licensed psychologist and family and child therapist in Southern California. Prior to her work as a police psychologist with the Los Angeles Police Department in 2000, she was a member of the core faculty at Pacifica Graduate Institute for ten years. She held positions as the Clinical Coordinator of the Counseling Psychology Program, the Research Coordinator of the Overseas Program, and Chair of the Counseling Psychology Program-Ladera campus. She has devoted her practice to working with psychotherapists, victims of violent crime, and law enforcement professionals.

She received her doctorate at the University of Southern California, her masters at the University of California, and bachelors degree at the University of Illinois at the Jane Addams School of Social Work in Chicago. She holds clinical membership with the American Psychological Association, California Association of Marriage and Family Therapists, California Psychological Association, American Professional Society on the Abuse of Children, Psychologists for the Ethical Treatment of Animals, and is an Associate Member of the International Association of Chiefs of Police. Her lifetime community college instructor credential is in psychology, public services, and administration.

She serves as a forensic witness for the California Board of Behavioral Sciences and is a Diplomate of the American Board of Forensic Examiners, Life Fellow of the American College of Forensic Examiners. She recently served on the Board of the Ventura County Psychological Association as the Chairperson of the Disaster Response Committee and the Executive Advisory Board of the American Psychotherapy Association. She is currently the co-chair of the Ethics Committee for the Ventura County Psychological Association.